The Political Economy
of Tanzania

The Political Economy of Tanzania

Decline and Recovery

Michael F. Lofchie

PENN

UNIVERSITY OF PENNSYLVANIA PRESS

PHILADELPHIA

Published by
University of Pennsylvania Press
Philadelphia, Pennsylvania 19104-4112
www.upenn.edu/pennpress

Printed in the United States of America on acid-free paper
10 9 8 7 6 5 4 3 2 1

Library of Congress Cataloging-in-Publication Data
Lofchie, Michael F.
    The political economy of Tanzania : decline and recovery / Michael F. Lofchie.
— 1st ed.
        p.   cm.
    Includes bibliographical references and index.
    ISBN 978-0-8122-4590-5 (hardcover : alk. paper)
    1. Economic development—Political aspects—Tanzania. 2. Tanzania—Economic
policy. 3. Tanzania—Economic conditions—1964– 4. Tanzania—Politics and
government—1964– I. Title.
HC885.L6374   2014
338.9678—dc23   2013031254

Between what matters and what seems to matter, how should the world we know judge wisely?

—E. C. Bentley, *Trent's Last Case*, Chapter 1

For Kelly and Hudson

C o n t e n t s

Abbreviations

ANC	African National Congress
BAE	British Aerospace Engineering
CCM	Chama Cha Mapinduzi
Chadema	Party of Freedom and Democracy
COSATA	Cooperative Society of Tanzania
CPP	Convention People's Party
CUF	Civic Union Front
DP	Democratic Party
DRC	Democratic Republic of Congo
EAC	East African Community
EPA	External Payments Account
ESRF	Economic and Social Research Foundation
FACEIT	Front Against Corrupt Elements in Tanzania
GDP	Gross Domestic Product
GNI	Gross National Income
HDI	Human Development Index
ILI	International Lending Institutions
IMF	International Monetary Fund
IMoLIN	International Money Laundering Information Network
ISI	Import-Substituting Industrialization
JUWATA	Union of Tanzanian Workers
LART	Loans and Assets Realization Trust
NBC	National Bank of Commerce
NESP	National Economic Survival Programme
NGO	Nongovernmental Organization
NMC	National Milling Corporation
NPART	Non-Performing Assets Realization Trust

NSGRP	National Strategy for Growth and Reduction of Poverty
NUTA	National Union of Tanganyika Workers
OGL	Open General License
OTTU	Organization of Tanzania Trade Unions
PCCB	Prevention and Combating of Corruption Bureau
POLiS	Parliamentary On-Line Legal Information System
PPG	Public and Publicly Guaranteed
PSRC	Parastatal Sector Reform Commission
RDA	Ruvuma Development Association
RER	Real Exchange Rate
SAFLII	South African Legislation Information Institute
SAP	Structural Adjustment Programme
SFO	Serious Fraud Office
SOE	State-Owned Enterprise
TAG	Tanzania Advisory Group
TANU	Tanganyika African National Union
TFL	Tanganyika Federation of Labor
TFTU	Tanzanian Federation of Free Trade Unions
TGWU	Transport and General Workers Union
TPDF	Tanzanian People's Defense Force
UNDP	United Nations Development Programme
UNU-WIDER	United Nations University-World Institute for Development Economics Research
USAID	United States Agency for International Development

Introduction: A Tanzanian Overview

Tanzania has undergone two transformations in the last thirty years. It has transformed its economy from one of state ownership and control to a market-based system. In addition, it has transformed its political system from a constitutionally entrenched single-party system to an openly competitive multiparty system. It has accomplished these transformations peacefully and without major incidents of ethnic violence or civil disruption. Tanzania is conspicuous for what has not taken place there. In a region of the world that has experienced more than its share of political turbulence, including failed states, military coups, local warlords, ethnic cleansing, regional secessions, civil war, severe famine, and dictatorial rule, Tanzania is special because of its sheer normalcy. It has a stable and functioning political system that works: children attend school; civil servants pursue their careers, receive promotions, and retire; the universities admit, teach, and graduate their students; hospitals and clinics provide medical services; bus systems carry workers to and from their jobs; roads are repaired and upgraded; the country's public utilities, such as telecommunications, water, electricity, and trash disposal operate, though sometimes intermittently; and government ministries carry out their assigned functions on a day-to-day basis. To supplement the services it has difficulty providing, the government offers a hospitable atmosphere for innumerable nongovernmental organizations (NGOs), whose activities supplement the public sector in such differing policy areas as environmental matters, gender equity, human rights, poverty alleviation, housing, and education and health services.

Tanzania has a strong claim to academic attention for its history of civil peace during the first five decades of independence. The Chama Cha

Mapinduzi (CCM) or Revolutionary Party, which began life as the Tanganyika African National Union (TANU) in 1954 and which has now been in power since 1961, has compiled an unbroken record of peaceful governance. With the exception of a brief and unsuccessful army mutiny in January 1964, it has never had a military challenge or any other serious challenge to its leadership. The CCM can make a compelling claim to popular legitimation as the heir of the country's nationalist movement and as a political party that enjoys widespread popular support across the country's social and ethnic spectrum. Its record of civil peace has fostered a distinctive climate of public opinion. Tanzanians are aware that their country has managed to avoid the tendencies toward civil strife and failed government that have arisen elsewhere in Africa, and this has created a special sense of pride in being Tanzanian.

Another achievement is Tanzania's principled role in international affairs. During the 1960s, Tanzania provided sanctuary, support, and diplomatic status for a number of southern African nationalist organizations, committing scarce economic resources to their liberation struggles. Following on its commitment to the principle of self-determination, Tanzania was almost alone in recognizing and assisting Biafra's struggle for independence from Nigeria. Tanzania also provided a place of sanctuary for a number of African Americans seeking refuge from the racial atmosphere of mid-century United States. In its determined pursuit of the principle of nonalignment in world affairs, Tanzania was prepared to strain the patience of both sides in the global cold war. A Muslim majority country with a Muslim president, Tanzania aligns itself with the United States in the war against terrorism and is a voice of moderation in international affairs.

Tanzania has distinguished itself from numerous African countries in other important respects as well. One important difference has to do with the persistence of the democratic idea. In common with many African countries, Tanzania underwent a change from the multiparty system of the immediate post-independence period toward a more autocratic pattern of authority in the years following. However, there was an important difference. In Tanzania's case, the changeover took place in a constitutional manner. Tanzanian political leaders sought to validate the change by propounding a democratic theory of single-party rule.[1] They then sought to translate this theory into political reality by creating an elaborate electoral framework whose purpose was to nurture popular participation and candidate competitiveness within the penumbra of single-party government.

The duration, magnitude, and visibility of an electoral process in which voters could choose between two CCM candidates imparted enduring cred-ibility to the democratic idea. Democratic theorists could find much to fault about the way Tanzania practiced single-party democracy. The governing party regulated the country's election procedures with utmost care. It screened its candidates for their loyalty to the party's core principles and then imposed tight controls on their campaigns. These required candidates to appear to-gether so that they could be carefully monitored. The party's electoral rules also forbade candidates from discussing nonsocialist development alterna-tives and proscribed appeals to ethnicity, religion or race. Party authorities disqualified candidates who violated these rules.

Although Tanzania's electoral system imposed these limitations on free-dom, it would be a mistake to dismiss its early elections as simply a demo-cratic subterfuge. Tanzania held six single-party elections between 1965 and 1990, and the debates between CCM candidates were heavily attended and widely discussed. Voters at the district level were presented with a choice of candidates and took this choice with utmost seriousness. Indeed, to make voting possible for voters who could not read the candidates' names, each candidate was assigned a distinct symbol, either a hoe or a house. Throughout the period of single-party rule, the Tanzanian government maintained the premise that legitimate authority was based on the rule of law and not the personal rule of an individual or small elite group. Although the major policy decisions were made first within the higher councils of the governing party, often by the president himself, Tanzania upheld the democratic principle by insisting that each decision then had to be drafted into legislation and passed by a parliamentary majority. These practices meant that Tanzanians have al-ways expected their government to obey the rule of law and they have always believed they could legitimately participate in their country's political process and exert an influence over its legislative branch. In all these ways, the single-party electoral framework kept the democratic idea alive just as it obscured the extent to which it had circumscribed Tanzanians' actual political rights and freedoms. This fact is the essential starting point for any understanding of how the CCM has been able to remain in power for so long: whatever other mechanisms of control it has employed, its status as a popularly elected gov-ernment is not in question.

Tanzania shared with other African countries the experience of severe economic decline during the two decades from the mid-1960s to the mid-1980s. But it differed from other countries in that the governing party sought to explain the country's economic misfortunes with a theory of development that emphasized the overriding value of social equality. Tanzania's economic difficulties included a severe agricultural decline that manifested itself, during the mid-1970s, as acute shortages of basic food staples. However, Tanzania averted widespread starvation by importing and distributing hundreds of thousands of tons of food grains. In addition, when the problem of rural impoverishment began to manifest itself in Dar es Salaam, in the presence of growing numbers of homeless refugees from the countryside, the country's political elite began to explore and then implement alternative economic policies. As conditions began to improve, Tanzanians naturally credited their leaders with the improvement as well as with their flexibility to change.

Tanzania also suffered from sharpening political-economic inequalities as members of the political elite used their positions to assure themselves access to material resources that were unavailable to ordinary citizens. Here, too, there was a critical difference: Tanzania's effort to have a society of social equals, however porous owing to corruption and malfeasance, represented a constraint on the acquisition and display of wealth by public officials. Tanzania did not experience the blatant forms of conspicuous consumption that have destabilized the political elites of many other African countries.

The severity of Tanzania's economic difficulties also caused the Tanzanian state to suffer from what has been commonly called "the shrinking writ of governance," the diminished ability of the central government to extend its authority to more distant regions and districts. But even during Tanzania's period of deepest economic hardship, when the country's transportation and communications infrastructures were barely functional, the central government maintained a rural presence. In the most remote districts and localities, tangible symbols of government remained operational: there was usually a district commissioner's office, a post office, and a primary school. Their physical presence was a signal that the central government continued to function. This helped to prevent the sort of regional lawlessness that has arisen in countries where legitimate forms of authority have all but disappeared from the rural areas.

The Nyerere Factor

Academic discussions of Tanzania inevitably begin—and often end—with an emphasis on the role and impact of the country's founder-president Julius K. Nyerere, who governed the country for twenty-five years, from independence in December 1961 until the end of 1985. His personal reputation as a humanitarian socialist has given the world its enduring image of Tanzania. Nyerere's commitment to the formation of a classless society where development would occur based on collective self-reliance, where rural areas would have a primary claim on the government's resources, and where social equality would prevail over class formation continues to provide the subject matter for countless courses on African politics and presentations at academic conferences. In his writings and speeches, he elaborated a vision of a social order in which public ownership of the society's productive and financial assets would eliminate the exploitation of one class by another and where participatory decision-making would result in greater attention to the needs of small farmers.[2] Although Nyerere stepped down from the presidency nearly thirty years ago, and died fifteen years ago in October 1999, his social idealism continues to be a factor in Tanzanian politics: it provides a counter-culture to the market system that currently prevails.

Scholars of Tanzania who might otherwise agree on very little are practically unanimous in their conviction that Nyerere had a towering influence on Tanzania's political and economic affairs for a period of almost forty years. Acceptance of this premise is, therefore, the essential starting point for any effort to understand the political-economic trajectory of modern Tanzania. Nyerere's personal influence was the major force behind practically all the major policy decisions that defined Tanzania's post-independence political trajectory. The most consequential of these were the decision to adopt a single-party system, which Nyerere announced publicly in 1963, and the decision to adopt a socialist economic framework, which he announced in early 1967. When he formed the Presidential Commission on the formation of a single-party state in 1965, Nyerere made it clear that he had made the basic decision to adopt a one-party system and that the responsibility of the Commission was only to decide what form the single-party state would assume.[3] Nyerere's other personal decisions included the decision to unify Tanganyika and Zanzibar, creating the United Republic of Tanzania in 1964; the decision to extend the socialist framework into the agricultural sector by pursuing collective villagization in 1969; and the decision to relent on that objective and allow resumption of family-based farming in 1975. Close observers fault Nyerere with having caused the rupture in negotiations with the International Monetary Fund in 1979 but credit him with the decision to step down from the presidency in 1985, thereby setting the stage for economic reform. In what may have been his final major contribution, Nyerere used his personal stature to persuade a reluctant people and an even more reluctant governing party to abandon the single-party model he had personally initiated and to allow a resumption of multiparty politics during the early 1990s.[4]

Even this inventory of policy decisions does not fully encompass Nyerere's personal impact on post-independence Tanzania. Despite the presence of a highly bureaucratic party-state, Tanzania had a personal style of decision-making that thrust routine decisions onto the desk of the president for final resolution. Many of Tanzania's major policy initiatives, in fact, began as presidential decisions that the National Assembly then had to formalize with legislation. The policy initiatives that have contributed to Tanzania's distinctively non-ethnic political atmosphere, including the constitutional provisions and electoral regulations that proscribe appeals to ethnicity, race, or religion, also bear the distinctive imprint of a president with a pronounced personal distaste for political organizations or leaders that use these factors as the basis for mobilizing their popular support. It is undoubtedly true, as Daniel Chirot suggests, that "Nyerere would have been less successful if the existing situation had made a few groups think they could gain power by appealing to ethnic identities."[5] However, to the extent that it is possible for a single person to be assigned credit for having an impact on a country's political culture, Nyerere would have the highest possible claim.

Some of the most puzzling questions concerning post-independence Tanzania are unanswerable without reference to the importance of presidential leadership. One has to do with why the Tanzanian government chose a set of economic policies that had such harmful effects on the economic life of the country and why it then continued to pursue those policies long after these effects had become apparent. A complete answer to these questions involves a complex mix of factors including the vested economic interests of the country's rent-seeking elite.[6] However, the search for answers begins with a powerful president so committed to a socialist economic framework that he was unwilling to allow the implementation of market-based policy initiatives that might compromise it.

Tanzania's most puzzling political question has to do with the political-economic evolution of its governing party. How did it come about that a socialist party, which had used a variety of authoritarian measures to implement a tightly regimented statist economy, transformed itself, within a remarkably brief period, into the chief sponsor of a market-based economy and a multiparty democracy? A complete answer to this question also requires a mix of factors, including international diplomatic and economic pressures and the

growing influence of a Tanzanian intelligentsia with reformist views. However, the necessary point of departure in answering this question was that by
the mid-1980s Nyerere had reluctantly concluded that the policy framework
he had so painstakingly put in place over a twenty-year period was no longer
sustainable.

Nyerere's influence on Tanzanian politics has long survived him. That this
would be so became immediately apparent as his funeral cortege passed
through the streets of Dar es Salaam in early November 1999. Firsthand de-
scriptions of the procession, which estimate that nearly a million people lined
the streets, convey a powerful image of a nation of Tanzanians joined in their
outpouring of grief and respect for the man who was the single most important political figure in their country for more than forty years. That Nyerere's
passing was mourned by Tanzanians of all social strata, regions, ethnicities,
and religions seemed to represent the fulfillment of one of his deepest hopes;
namely, that Tanzania would become a nation-state in which the idea of national citizenship would take pride of place over other forms of group
identification.

In certain respects, Nyerere's continuing popularity among Tanzanians is
surprising. Anyone present that day would have been aware that Nyerere's
successors and most of his fellow citizens had long since repudiated his economic views. Anyone present would also have been aware that in a futile effort to translate his social vision into economic reality, Nyerere had
accepted—and indeed initiated—levels of political repression that contradicted his global image as a gentle, humanistic figure. Many of those attending were convinced that Nyerere's economic views had directly caused the
country's economic decline and, by most accounts, the majority of Tanzanians had long since accepted the need for the liberal economic reforms that
the government put in place after he left the presidency. Remarkably, many of
those in attendance were supporters of one or another of Tanzania's new opposition parties.

Why, then, does Nyerere's persona continue to have such a powerful effect
on Tanzanian political affairs? One reason has to do with Tanzanians' discontent about the extent of corruption on the part of the current governing elite.
Many Tanzanians believe although Nyerere was surrounded by political leaders he knew to be corrupt, he was personally incorruptible. There is an element of invented memory about the way some Tanzanians describe Nyerere,
portraying him in almost saintly terms, as a martyr to social ideals that were
ultimately shared by very few of those who surrounded him and that, at the

end, were opposed by entrenched and powerful members of his own political elite. Many also insist that although Nyerere may have engaged in political repression, he acted out of benign impulses and not as a means of acquiring personal wealth or protecting a corrupt oligarchy. The crowds that gathered along the funeral route were giving silent expression to their disappointment in a generation of political leaders they perceive as lacking in Nyerere's personal qualities.

Many Tanzanians insist that there were important differences between the ways Nyerere used his presidential powers and the ways his successors and other African heads of state have abused them. Although he held the reins of power for forty years, he did not accumulate vast personal wealth. Nor did he create a family dynasty that sought to convert the presidency into a family possession by passing the mantle of power from one generation to the next. Indeed, Nyerere's family members and descendants have been singularly unsuccessful in translating the family name into successful pursuit of higher office. By mourning Nyerere, Tanzanians were also affirming their commitment to his belief in a multicultural, multi-ethnic, multireligious Tanzania.

Respect for Nyerere's memory is a part of the answer to another of the political puzzles of modern Tanzania, namely, how has the CCM been able to maintain high levels of popular support despite high levels of official corruption and despite the fact that a rich and powerful oligarchy dominates the political system? As with each of Tanzania's political puzzles, a full answer to this question is complex. A complete inventory of explanations must include such factors as the CCM's extraordinary organizational and fund-raising advantages, which give it a prominent physical presence throughout the country. The CCM also derives popularity from its status as the lineal descendant of the nationalist movement. Owing to its control of the government, the CCM benefits from its ability to provide jobs and other patronage opportunities to countless supporters and their families. But among the many factors that account for the CCM's popularity has been its ability to identify itself publicly as the party of Nyerere. The party's branch offices in even the most remote outposts of Tanzania often display two presidential photographs: one, of current Tanzanian president Jakaya Kikwete; the other, closely alongside, of Nyerere. His image continues to provide a vital element of credibility for a governing party that has become better known for the corruption and cynicism of its top leaders.

There are traces of a generational divide in the way many Tanzanians view

Nyerere. Members of the younger generation, who did not suffer the economic hardships of the socialist period and are seeking an alternative to the acquisitive individualism of the market-based economy Tanzania has pursued since the 1980s, often express admiration for Nyerere's ideas. His emphasis on the need to succeed or fail as a nation provides a basis for criticizing the conspicuous consumption and growing inequality unleashed by the transition to a market economy. Nyerere's philosophy also provides a basis for condemning the affluent lifestyle of the country's political-economic oligarchy, which shows little restraint in its willingness to use political power for material gain. Older Tanzanians, on the other hand, have personal memories of the hardships and scarcities of the post-independence decades, and some remember the oppressive measures that accompanied implementation of the socialist economy. They also recall the way the Nyerere administration virtually eliminated civil society organizations they valued, such as the autonomous trade unions, the primary agricultural cooperatives and the rich array of ethnically or religiously organized welfare organizations. As a result, older Tanzanians tend to offer a mixed appraisal of their first president, citing his economic failures and an unfortunate tendency toward obstinate self-righteousness alongside his idealistic vision and personal incorruptibility.

Finally, however, personality-based explanations of complex political and economic phenomena are inadequate. In the lexicon of social science theories, those that emphasize the influence of individual actors take a distant place in explanatory power to those that emphasize such factors as social class, economic interests, or cultural norms. Nyerere's personal influence is only the starting point but not the end point of an explanation for the key political and economic features of post-independence Tanzania.

Civil Peace in Tanzania

Much of the scholarship on modern Africa takes ethnicity as its point of departure, using ethnic identity as the major variable in explanations of social cleavage and political conflict. Whatever the merits of this approach in viewing other African countries, its applicability to Tanzania is limited. Ethnic theories of African politics do not apply in Tanzania simply because ethnicity plays such a limited role in the political process. In a continent where ethnic identity often provides an important point of entry for understanding a country's political patterns, Tanzania presents a different reality: much of its stability derives from the low political salience of this factor. Although it is arguably as multi-ethnic and multicultural as any country on the African continent, Tanzania, with approximately 120 distinct ethnic groups, has enjoyed a tradition of ethnic peace that is the envy of many sister nations and an object of global admiration.

This is not to say that Tanzanians are unaware of their ethnic differences or that ethnic differences have not begun to assume a larger place in the country's political life. It is to say that Tanzania differs from many other African countries in that ethnicity does not provide the principal wedge between the major parties. It does not describe the differences between the supporters of the major political parties, nor does it provide the principal basis of party identification. Furthermore, ethnic appeals do not provide the candidates who use them with an assured political following. Göran Hydén, widely regarded as the most authoritative political scientist writing on contemporary Tanzania, states:

> Tanzania is especially intriguing as a case study of democratization because it is one of the few countries in sub-Saharan Africa that have erased tribalism and ethnicity as a factor in politics. Of course, people often elect representatives from their own communities, but appeals to tribal or ethnic values do not work in Tanzanian politics. Candidates have to use other grounds to demonstrate why voters should prefer them to their opponents.[7]

Tanzanians do not organize their political parties based on ethnically defined pools of supporters; they do not form their party preferences based on their perceived grievances with members of other ethnic groups. Many recoil against political leaders or political organizations that do so. Most importantly, Tanzanians do not perceive or describe their political process as one in which ethnic communities are pitted in win-lose adversarial relationships against one another.

The CCM is the best example. In Tanzania's four multiparty elections since 1995, the CCM candidate for president has regularly received between 60 and 80 percent of the popular vote, and the CCM candidates for the National Assembly have regularly gained about 65 to 70 percent. The CCM is a genuinely national party with a support base that includes Tanzanians from all regions of the country and all ethnicities and religious groups. Much the same is true for the principal opposition party, the Party for Democracy and Progress

(Chadema), which also enjoys a multi-ethnic support base. Although the CCM is more popular in some regions of the country than in others, a variation that has an obvious ethnic dimension, ethnic differences do not explain the cleavage between the CCM and the major parties that oppose it.

The tradition of ethnic peace has been foundational. It provided the enabling environment for the long and failed experiment with a statist economy and then set the stage for the country's peaceful transition to a liberal one. The low visibility of ethnicity has meant that the political arena has been more open to a politics based on the clash of economic interests and ideas detached from ethnic identification. Tanzania, like every other country, has had winners and losers from the political process. However, Tanzanians do not identify their winners and losers in ethnic terms. Although a politico-economic oligarchy governs the country, this oligarchy is conspicuously multi-ethnic, multireligious, and multiregional in social composition. As a result, Tanzanians do not define or describe their oligarchy by using an ethnic terminology, nor do they describe the opposition parties in ethnic terms. The most basic reason is that Tanzania does not have a hegemonic ethnic group that holds a disproportionate share of the nation's power and wealth.[8]

The atmosphere of ethnic and religious amity that the Tanzanian Government carefully constructed during the period of one-party rule has begun to come under strain during the multiparty era. It would be naïve to suggest that Tanzanian voters are indifferent to ethnicity when casting their votes. The return to multipartyism in the early 1990s brought about a more open political atmosphere and some candidates for public office have sought to take advantage by using religion or ethnicity as a basis for mobilizing electoral support.[9] But fundamental challenges of interpretation arise. Did the emergence of the strident anti-Asian[10] Democratic Party (DP) during the 1990s signal that the culture of ethnic peace had begun to fray? Or was it more significant that this party has never gained the support of more than a tiny fraction of Tanzanian voters and that most Tanzanians found its leader's expressions of racial animosity repugnant? Similarly, is the presence of a party of Muslim identity, the Civic United Front (CUF) evidence of the decline of the cultural norms that stressed religious as well as ethnic inclusiveness?[11] Or is it more revealing that, in a country where Muslims may constitute a majority of the population, and where there have been serious issues of Muslim access to higher education, the higher reaches of the civil service, and the highest levels of business sector, CUF has never gained the support of more than a small fraction of Tanzanian Muslims?

The answer to these difficult questions is that any appraisal of the current state of civil peace in Tanzania requires careful nuance. The founder-leaders of the Tanzanian nation worked assiduously to create a lasting culture of ethnic, racial, and religious inclusiveness. They were largely but not entirely successful in doing so. The emergence of a more liberal economy beginning in the 1980s and the reemergence of a multiparty system in the early 1990s have placed the culture of inclusiveness under strain.[12] However, the vast majority of Tanzanians continue to be uncomfortable with parties and leaders that seek to capitalize on these sources of division, and there is a broad social preference for a political environment in which ethnic, religious, and racial divisions have low salience. As a result, the culture of civil peace remains largely intact; candidates who seek to gain electoral traction by appealing to ethnic or religious animosities do not generally succeed.

The low visibility of ethnicity in Tanzanian political affairs has its mirror image in the limited importance of ethnic identity in everyday life outside the political realm. It would be misleading to suggest that Tanzanians are unaware of one another's ethnic backgrounds. However, it is no exaggeration to note that Tanzanians are comfortable in personal, social, and professional relationships that regularly cross ethnic lines. In their personal friendships, at their workplaces in governmental and business offices, in occupational and recreational organizations, and in the host of casual transactions that form the bulk of everyday life, Tanzanians relate to one another as if differences in ethnic identity were of limited importance. In a wide range of social settings, from the membership of the Dar es Salaam Rotary Club to the drivers in the taxi line at major hotels, the Tanzanians present will be a diverse cross section of their society.

The environment of civil peace provides the indispensable beginning for understanding aspects of contemporary Tanzania that are otherwise puzzling. It provides a compelling explanation, for example, why Tanzanians have reacted peaceably to the two greatest challenges of the post-independence period: twenty years of unremitting economic decline between the mid-1960s and mid-1980s, and the all-pervasive and seemingly intractable problem of official corruption that emerged during that period and continues to exist. The great puzzle of Tanzania's protracted economic decline was that it did not result in serious social fractures such as massive anti-government protests, clashes between supporters and opponents of the ruling party, regime instability, or regional secession. The most important basis of civil peace was that Tanzanians had not come to view their political process as one that involved domination by one ethnic group or a coalition of ethnic groups over all others. Since Tanzania does not have a hegemonic ethnic group, there has never been a sense that the political elite pursues economic policies to favor one group of ethnic supporters over others, or to distribute the positive benefits of political power and the negative effects of disempowerment unevenly across the ethnic spectrum.

Tanzania's atmosphere of civil peace is the product of both a fortuitous inheritance and a set of public policies that the government implemented during the immediate post-independence period. The most important inherited factor has been a common language, Swahili, which is spoken by many Tanzanians as a first language and by practically all Tanzanians as a second language, thus making it possible for Tanzanians to communicate, travel, undertake commerce, and engage in political discourse across ethnic boundaries. Unlike English, which Tanzanians acquire in school as part of the educational curriculum, they acquire Swahili, even in areas where it is not the first language, simply as an aspect of growing up. Tanzania also possesses a national Swahili culture, as evidenced in the countrywide popularity of the Swahili press, Swahili poetry and literature, Swahili humor, and Swahili music.

Geographical factors have also contributed to the atmosphere of civil peace. The most important of these is that throughout the colonial period and during the early post-independence decades, Tanzania was a land-abundant society. With a land area of about 365,000 square miles and a population of just over forty-five million, Tanzania is about one-third the size of India but has only one thirtieth of its population. Vast areas are suitable for intensive agricultural production. The best known of these is the coffee-growing region on the south-facing slopes of the Mt. Kilimanjaro–Mt. Meru region in north-central Tanzania, an area that has also proved well suited to other high value crops. There are other regions of high value agriculture as well. The Shinyanga Region south of Lake Victoria is an area of intensive cotton cultivation; the Sumbawanga area in the southwestern part of the country is an important area of corn cultivation; and the Mtwara Region in the southeastern region of the country is an important area of cashew nut production. The wide distribution of arable lands means that members of many different ethnic groups are able to participate in high value agriculture, thereby preventing the emergence of a sense that high value agriculture is limited to only one or two fortunate communities.

Land abundance has been critically important. With an independence-era population of just over ten million, distributed over an area that contained many regions with good quality agricultural land, there were no land pressures that caused ethnic groups to compete for this resource. As recently as the 1990s, despite a fourfold population increase since independence, from ten million to nearly forty million, developmentally oriented geographers continued to suggest that Tanzania possessed unsettled areas of agriculturally suitable land.[13] Although the quality of this land and therefore its suitability for high versus medium value crops varied from one region to the next, Tanzanians did not experience a land environment in which the land needs of one community could only prevail at the expense of others. Although Tanzania today has begun to experience incidents of competition for land, as when agricultural populations begin to encroach on areas that have been the traditional grazing habitat for migratory pastoralists, such problems are still relatively rare.

The regional distribution of the population also contributed to the atmosphere of civil peace. Most of Tanzania's best land areas are located near the perimeters, along its border with neighboring countries, and not near Dar es Salaam. The dispersed location of quality lands has resulted in a doughnut-shaped population distribution, with significant concentrations near the borders of Kenya, Uganda, the Democratic Republic of Congo, Zambia, and Mozambique and significantly less population density in the center of the country. The ethnic groups that have enjoyed agriculturally based development are at a physical remove from the capital, and this has made it difficult for them to translate their agricultural advantages into commensurate political advantages.

In contrast to numerous African capital cities, Dar es Salaam arose and developed as a multicultural city. It had its earliest beginnings as a commercial center rooted in the Indian Ocean trade in ivory and human beings. Unlike Nairobi, for example, Dar es Salaam is not located in the center of the most fertile agricultural area, and the ethnic group that occupies the region, the Zaramo, has not had the insurmountable double advantage of agrarian prosperity combined with close physical proximity to political power. The slave caravans that fanned out from Dar es Salaam captured their victims from a variety of regions throughout eastern Africa, and some remained behind as a work force in Dar es Salaam and other coastal cities. Over many centuries, Dar es Salaam became a place of residence where Tanzanians of a wide mixture of ethnic groups worked and made their homes. Sociologist Deborah Bryceson has used the term *creolization* to call attention to its rich mixture of the country's many cultures and languages. Individual neighborhoods may have ethnic characteristics but no ethnic group dominates the city's economic, political, or cultural life.[14]

Distinctive aspects of Tanzania's colonial experience further contributed to the low salience of ethnicity. The first thirty years or more of Tanganyika's colonial experience, from 1885 to 1918, took place under German rule. Unlike the British, who emphasized the importance of traditional authorities as the basic administrative units of colonial government, a practice that hardened ethnic identities, German colonial practice emphasized direct forms of administration that suppressed traditional institutions and cultures. German officials tended to disregard indigenous institutions, which they treated with a mixture of indifference and contempt. They preferred instead to govern through a system of centrally recruited administrators called *akidas*, whom they then deployed to localities with which they did not have any cultural commonalities. The akida system diffused Swahili throughout Tanzania, since local communities could only communicate with their appointed akidas through a commonly spoken language. It also perfectly exemplified the German refusal to acknowledge or incorporate local forms of organization.[15]

By the time Britain assumed colonial jurisdiction over Tanganyika in 1918 through the League of Nations Mandate system, local forms of institutional authority had been so thoroughly squelched that it was often necessary to create these anew before implementing indirect methods of colonial administration. Britain's determination to administer Tanzania through the indirect rule system made it necessary to ascribe political identity and impose political organization on language communities that did not have a history of political solidarity. Aili Mari Tripp has shown that a number of Tanzania's largest ethnic groups are of relatively recent colonial creation. Far from having deep historic roots, numerous ethnic groups in Tanzania are the products of Britain's twentieth-century application of the indirect rule system.[16]

Tanzania's status as a ward of the international community from the end of World War I until its independence in 1961 also contributed to ethnic peace. At the end of the war, Tanganyika became a League of Nations Mandate and after World War II it became a United Nations Trusteeship Territory. International supervision caused British colonial rule in Tanganyika to be less severe than that in most other colonial territories. First, it introduced the assumption of an eventual but timely transition toward national independence. The League of Nations did not permit Britain to develop Tanganyika as a permanent settler colony as it had done in Kenya and Rhodesia. Absent a significant settler presence, Tanzania's abundant supply of arable land remained in African hands: land alienation did not foster a problem of land scarcity that pitted one ethnic group against another in a life or death struggle over a scarce resource.[17] International supervision also meant that the British government had to treat emerging African nationalist organizations with greater restraint than it showed elsewhere. Britain was less able to employ ethnically based tactics of divide and rule by creating political alliances with favored groups to maintain better control over others. As nationalism in Tanganyika began to take full shape in the late 1950s, it was not riven by internal strains between ethnic communities that felt differently about how they had been treated by colonial administration.

To preserve and build on this inheritance, Nyerere and the TANU government began to implement a set of policies intended to create a cultural climate in which Tanzanians would not organize their political organizations based on separate ethnic identities. The first step was to ban racially or religiously based schools and hospitals. These had to become public institutions open to Tanzanians of all races and religions. In the effort to create a non-ethnic social culture, the government gave its highest priority to educational policy. It changed most of the country's high schools into boarding schools so that students from diverse regions of the country would live and study together. The government undertook similar efforts with respect to teachers and principals. The goal of educational policy was for each high school to become a microcosm of the nation, where a community of ethnically diverse students would study, play, live, and work together, alongside an equally mixed educational staff.

Following their high school education, Tanzanian students were obliged to participate in a National Service program that continued the process of mingling students of different ethnic groups in common projects in which they worked together building schools, improving roads, and constructing community buildings. Young Tanzanians who joined the military and became members of the Tanzanian People's Defense Force (TPDF) became absorbed in a non-ethnic environment in which military units comprised soldiers from all regions of the country. Countless older Tanzanians remember their high school and National Service experience as a time when they formed friendships across cultural lines, played together on multicultural sports teams, and participated in multicultural musical and dramatic activities.

Many of the factors that initially gave rise to Tanzania's atmosphere of civil peace have long since disappeared. German colonialism in Tanganyika ended almost a century ago. The benign effects of international supervision ended with independence, more than fifty years ago. As Tanzania's economy declined, financial pressures necessarily constrained the scope and scale of the government's efforts to mingle students of various ethnicities together at the secondary school level. Budgetary constraints gradually made it impossible to move students across different regions of the country, much less to support them in a boarding school environment. To the extent that sparse population helped ameliorate the ethnic tensions that might have arisen from competition over scarce land resources that factor, too, is outdated. Tanzania's population has more than quadrupled since independence, from about ten million to more than forty-five million people, and population pressures in some areas have begun to trigger scattered incidents of conflict over land between pastoral and agricultural communities, a division that corresponds to an ethnic cleavage. Although the Tanzanian constitution and electoral laws continue to proscribe ethnically based appeals, the freer political atmosphere that has attended the rebirth of multipartyism has opened a wider political space for ethnic expressions. The new political environment has reduced the government's ability to maintain tight controls over political discourse, including appeals to ethnicity. Perhaps the most consequential change has been the death of Nyerere himself and the loss of the moral force he brought to the idea of a non-ethnic culture for his country.

Why, then, has ethnicity not asserted itself with greater force in Tanzania? A theory of cultural pluralism that emphasizes the importance of inequalities between different ethnic groups provides one answer. Colonial historian John S. Furnivall first developed the idea that ethnicity was a volatile political factor in socioeconomic environments where differing ethnic groups had differing amounts of access to the upper levels of a society, such as the highest positions in government and administration or the business sector.[18] Later cultural pluralists termed this phenomenon "differential incorporation," a concept that called attention to ethnic frictions that arise when a country's patterns of economic, social, and political stratification display distinctively ethnic characteristics. Later cultural pluralists also believed that the volatility of stratification along ethnic lines derived from the tendency for people to perceive this form of inequality as relatively permanent.[19]

Colonial Tanzania exhibited one important element of this phenomenon. Members of Tanzania's Asian community—persons of Indo-Pakistani descent—tended to be concentrated at the middle or upper levels of the Tanzanian social structure. They were prominent in Tanzania's mercantile sector as the owners of the business enterprises that conducted much of the country's retail trade. During the colonial period, Asians were also a conspicuous presence in Tanzania's white-collar professions, in the middle levels of the civil service, and in the clerical and managerial levels of major private sector organizations, such as the country's largest banks, insurance companies, and trading firms. The Asian presence as a predominant middle class seemed to represent a significant barrier to African upward mobility both in the public sector and in the middle levels of these private sector institutions, a goal that was at the heart of the Tanzanian nationalist movement.

At the time of independence, the prominent Asian presence in the middle class gave rise to an intense debate among nationalists over whether their post-independence government should pursue an indigenization policy that would privilege Tanzanians of indigenous descent over those whose family backgrounds traced to different continents.[20] Within TANU, Nyerere favored a nonracial policy. A small number of party members favoring a policy of indigenization, however, split off and formed an opposition called the African National Congress (ANC). Nyerere and the nonracialists won the debate between the two groups, ensuring that the government would not use its powers to create preferred social categories based on ethnicity or race.

The success of this policy is at the heart of modern Tanzanian politics. It helps explain why Tanzanians were prepared to accept the failed economic policies the Nyerere Government implemented along with the conjoined problems of repression and corruption. Tanzanians never perceived the Nyerere government's economic policies as an attempt to confer benefits on favored groups while depriving others. This also explains why Tanzanians have not reacted with greater vehemence to their country's all-pervasive and seemingly intractable problem of official corruption. Although Tanzanians abhor corruption, they do not perceive it as a pattern of economic transfers that moves wealth from ethnic have-nots to ethnic haves.

The limitations of an ethnically based approach to Tanzanian politics call attention to the need for a different way to understand the country's post-independence trajectory. Political economy provides it. Regarding the relationship between ethnicity and politics, Tanzania has little in common with other independent African countries. Regarding its post-independence economic trajectory, however, it has almost everything in common.

Political Economy and Tanzanian Development

In the field of political economy, Tanzania attracts attention because of the extended process of economic decline that began immediately after independence and continued for nearly twenty-five years, until the beginning of economic reforms in the mid-1980s. Tanzania's post-independence policies failed in many respects. The socialist strategy of economic development did not lead to growth; it did not narrow the gap between the country's urban middle class and the vast majority of the rural poor. It did not prevent the emergence of a privileged political-economic elite. The principal reason for Tanzania's economic decline lay in its poor choice of economic policies during the post-independence period. This much is unsurprising: poor policies produce poor results. What remains is the need to answer Robert Bates's enduring question: "Why should reasonable men adopt policies that have harmful consequences for the societies they govern?"[21] The answer is that Tanzania's choice of policies derived from a set of ideas about economic development that prevailed throughout the developing world during the generation following World War II. The ideas that had the greatest influence in Tanzania were those of the sub-field of economics its practitioners termed development economics.

Post-independence Tanzania had two distinct economic philosophies, each important in its own way. The first was the socialist humanism of Julius Nyerere, a set of convictions that grew out of his long interest in the mild socialism of the British Fabian society. Nyerere's ideas attracted global admiration and captured the attention of the Tanzanian people. Because they set forth the normative objectives of Tanzanian development, they attracted the respectful support of his fellow leaders as well as the admiration of students, scholars, and international organizations everywhere. The second set of ideas consisted of the analysis of the development economists. This intellectual framework consisted of a large body of scientific research about how developing countries with agriculturally based economies could best attain rapid economic growth. Although these ideas were less accessible than Nyerere's because of their arcane terminology and daunting mathematics, they had a great influence on the government's day-to-day decisions about development policy.

The core of development economics was simple and compelling. The development economists believed that industry, not agriculture, offered the greatest prospect of rapid economic growth. Governments that wanted to attain economic growth should therefore find ways to launch industrial development. The fundamental challenge was how to go about doing so. Their answer was to create a set of infant industries that, until they could stand on their own, would require protection from competition by global industrial giants. The immediate practical question was how to finance these industries. The development economists' answer was that these industries would require financial support from a variety of sources. One would be foreign public investment, through aid programs that would provide resources for infrastructure and improved public services. The second would be foreign private investment from corporations anxious to do business in a protected environment. The third would be the governments themselves, which would need to impose taxes on the agricultural sector to gain the revenues necessary to provide domestic capital for investment in the new industries. The vast majority of the world's developing countries adopted this strategy, Tanzania among them.

The development economists believed that their strategy for economic growth would enable developing countries such as Tanzania to transform themselves, within a short period from low-performing agricultural economies to higher-performing ones based on an expanding industrial base. The name they assigned to this strategy was *import-substituting industrialization* (ISI), and this approach prevailed in regions of the world as diverse as Latin America and South and Southeast Asia as well as in much of sub-Saharan Africa. Although Tanzania gained global acclaim because of the idealistic approach of the founder-president, its development policies during the decades following independence were closer to the framework prescribed by the development economists. The president's ideas stressed rural development through communal self-help at the local level as a means of improving the socioeconomic conditions of the poorest Tanzanians, the small farmers. In reality, the framework Nyerere's government adopted imposed higher and higher levels of taxation on smallholder farmers to extract the revenues that provided capital and other subsidies for urban industries. Urban Tanzanians, including industrial workers, technocrats, managers, and economic planners, were the winners; small farmers were the losers. There is no great mystery about why the Tanzanian government adopted this strategy: it was acting the same way as countless other governments throughout Africa and other developing regions.

The ISI model derived influence from the scholarly prestige of the development economists as well as from the contagion effect. The development economists' ideas gained additional influence from their prominence in the economics curricula of many of the most prestigious universities in North America and Europe. Students from the developing world were routinely channeled into courses on development economics so that they could better assist with the development of their countries. In addition, the ISI intellectual and strategic framework was operative throughout the major development institutions, such as the World Bank and numerous bilateral aid organizations. The influence of the development economists was so great that very few developing countries sought to give a higher priority to agricultural development than to industry. One of the most powerful sources of attraction was the belief that ISI offered a shortened path to industrial prosperity. Western history had taught that an industrial revolution might take several centuries to accomplish and that it would only come about with a high cost in social misery. The development economists sought to demonstrate that their strategy could shorten the timetable of industrialization to a generation or less, and at a far lower human cost.

The intellectual dominance of development economics explains why Tanzanian leaders adopted the ISI approach, but it does not explain why they kept it in place as long as they did, long after its harmful economic effects had become painfully visible. One reason is the absence of a compelling theoretical alternative. In its approach to developing countries, the economics profession did not begin to undergo a major paradigmatic shift until the mid- to late 1970s, some fifteen to twenty years after ISI had been firmly set in place in countries such as Tanzania. The World Bank did not produce an alternative formula for sub-Saharan Africa until the early 1980s, with the publication of its famous report, *Accelerated Development in Sub-Saharan Africa*.[22] That report combined an analysis of the shortcomings of the ISI strategy as it had been applied in Africa and offered in its place an alternative, market-based strategy that emphasized free trade. Even then, its recommendations required several years to become the basis for specific policy recommendations by on-site donor organizations.

The principal reason for the persistence of economically harmful policies, however, was political. A downward economic spiral does not affect all social strata equally, and the political elites of many developing countries were able to insulate themselves from the environment of economic hardship. The economic interest of a country's political elite is not the same as the social interest of the country as a whole. Tanzania was no exception. Members of the elite were able to enjoy a material lifestyle that contrasted dramatically with the hardships that affected the majority of the population. Through a combination of rent-seeking behavior and legitimate perquisites of power, such as generous fringe benefits and special allowances, members of the Tanzanian elite lived very well. This is the paradox of development first cited by Jonathan Barker in his important early article on Senegal.[23] Barker's paradox points out that reform often depends on the initiative of a class of political leaders whose self-interest lies in a continuation of the existing system, which provides the basis for their wealth and power. This paradox defines the most challenging questions arising from Tanzania's process of economic reform: not why it began so slowly but why it began at all and why, when it did, it resulted in a successful transition to a market-based economic system.

The following chapters attempt to show that Tanzania's program of state-led development fostered the emergence of a powerful and entrenched governing elite. The failure of its economic experiment in socialist development gave rise to the emergence of a larger and larger parallel economy, which grew in the vacuum created by the failures of the official economy. As the state industries and bureaucratic agencies that had responsibility for providing essential goods and services failed in their assigned tasks, the parallel economy began to assume this responsibility. By the time Tanzania began its official reform program, in mid-summer 1986, the parallel sector had attained such large proportions that it was almost as large as the country's official economy and, by some estimates, even larger. Vast numbers of Tanzanians earned a sizable portion of their income in the parallel economy from which they obtained the goods and services they needed.[24] Economic liberalization in Tanzania was not a matter of creating a market economy where none existed. It merely involved setting aside the remnants of an official state economy that most Tanzanians had come to view as an impediment to their most promising economic activities.

The distinctive feature of Tanzania's parallel economy was the involvement of large numbers of public officials. This was Tanzania's answer to Barker's paradox. On the eve of economic reform, many members of the governing elite that presided over a socialist state had become private sector actors in the parallel economy. The economic strategy they adopted is commonly referred to as *straddling*, a term that describes the tendency of families to diversify their portfolio of activities to cope with conditions of stress. Tanzanians in all occupations sought income wherever they could obtain it. For many public officials, this meant finding ways to supplement their increasingly inadequate official salaries by undertaking private economic pursuits. Many civil servants had small gardens or small farms from which they sold foodstuffs. Others raised chickens or goats for sale in the parallel marketplace. Some were more brazen and used their official vehicles as taxis or trucks to provide transportation services. Still others operated small business enterprises producing shoes, furniture, soft drinks, alcoholic beverages, clothing, cooking utensils, farm implements, and a host of other goods increasingly unavailable in the official marketplace. Before long, many public officials derived a larger share of their income from their side businesses than from their government salaries, whose purchasing power had shrunk due to the fall in the value of the Tanzanian shilling.

Economic straddling meant that, on the eve of policy reform, many Tanzanians had a blend of economic identities. Some of Tanzania's most successful entrepreneurs began as public officials, deriving some of their start-up capital and an element of political security from their governmental positions. The parallel economy, however, had important limitations, especially regarding the scale of a family's informal sector activities. It might be possible to operate a small business selling food items, chickens, or goat meat, but it would be impossible to expand those activities to take over an entire brewery, textile mill, or cigarette factory so long as those enterprises were still official state monopolies. Eliminating the state economy with its numerous monopolistic but unproductive firms represented a pathway for greater wealth, not a constraint. This was the great secret to the success of Tanzania's liberal reforms. Much of the social pressure that drove privatization came from state officials whose positions in the government afforded them special advantages in the early privatization process.

Corruption played a major role in all these transformations. It originated in the declining purchasing power of public sector salaries and set down its roots in the countless opportunities for bribes afforded by the country's all-pervasive system of state regulations and controls. Corruption began as an income supplement for hard-pressed public officials seeking to maintain or augment their real incomes. Over time, however, it morphed into something with far greater long-term economic consequences: it became a source of investment capital in the rapidly growing parallel sector, which had arisen in response to the scarcities of goods in official markets. Before long, public officials had become some of the country's most active participants in the informal marketplace. They were active in all aspects of the private economy: as producers; as providers of services, such as transportation; and as sources of capital investment. Public officials had certain special advantages in becoming entrepreneurs. They had the windfall income of funds afforded by corruption and the advantage of de facto immunity from prosecution provided by their official status. There was a sort of income dynamic: government salaries provided a smaller and smaller share of their income, and the income derived from corruption and investments in parallel market businesses became a larger and larger share of what they earned.

Corruption was Tanzania's form of early capital accumulation. Although the decreasing purchasing power of public sector salaries was a major reason government officials turned to corruption, there were other factors as well. These included a governing party leadership code that forbade party members serving the government from earning second incomes and constraints on the banking system that increasingly forced the commercial banks to lend almost exclusively to state-owned enterprises. Corruption became a major source of investible wealth. Almost imperceptibly, vast numbers of Tanzanian officials underwent a socioeconomic transformation from government employee to petty capitalist.

No other factor provides as powerful an explanation of the alacrity with which the Tanzanian elite accepted the country's rapid transition to a market economy during the 1980s. By that time, a sizable proportion of Tanzania's political elite had become actively engaged in the country's market economy. For many, their government positions were a mere adjunct to private sector activity. Some could use state-provided benefits, such as government houses and cars, as assets in their private sector activity. For many, a position in the government provided preferred access to foreign exchange, an especially valuable asset in an environment where hard currency was in extremely short supply. For others, it meant the ability to use state authority to leverage a covert partnership with an established private sector enterprise.

For the more successful members of Tanzania's new class of venture capitalists, the survival of the state economic sector, however encircled by the ubiquitous expansion of gray markets, became a limitation on their entrepreneurial activities. So long as the state was still the official owner of the country's major industrial firms as well as major services, such as hotels and bus companies, Tanzanian entrepreneurs were unable to invest their capital in these areas. This changed dramatically when the World Bank and other donors began to insist that the government of Tanzania divest itself of ownership in its publicly held enterprises. At that point, the newly forming class of private entrepreneurs had a direct stake in timely implementation of the Bank's recommendation. When the divestiture process began in the early 1990s, the highest-ranking officials could position themselves and their family members, through various partnerships, to acquire an ownership share at bargain prices.

Tanzanians have long been aware of the problem of official corruption, and it has been the topic of practically daily reporting in the country's news media as well as the subject of an endless series of government investigations, reports, and studies. It has formed the basis of a widely publicized dialogue between the government of Tanzania and its principal donor organizations. Some of the most prominent agencies of the Tanzanian bureaucracy, such as the Prevention and Combating of Corruption Bureau (PCCB), are devoted to addressing this problem. Perhaps more important, ordinary Tanzanians experience corruption as a fact of daily life in the form of side payments to government officials for practically every bureaucratic transaction.[25] Corruption has been an important cause of the government's willingness to use repression against its political opposition. Since corrupt gains constitute a major source of wealth for members of the political-economic oligarchy, it raises the stakes of losing political office, thereby encouraging the use of repressive measures to remain in power.

The overriding question is why Tanzania has a politico-economic oligarchy. The blunt answer is that twenty years of a state-based economic strategy that depended upon coercive mechanisms of implementation foreclosed the possibility of Tanzanians developing independent bases of wealth or status outside the jurisdiction of the state. Tanzania's oligarchy arose within the state apparatus, which continues to provide it with its major source of investible wealth. Tanzanians who have risen to positions of wealth in Tanzania have done so through their connections to the political process. Much of the wealth of the oligarchy especially that derived from corruption continues to be dependent on their ability to exercise influence within the state apparatus. Wealth and power in Tanzania are so inextricably interconnected that it is impossible to have one without the other.

The politico-economic oligarchy is dependent on the state to suppress opposition leaders and parties. The police and security forces of Tanzania routinely harass the leaders and supporters of opposition parties, sometimes violently. The U.S. Department of State has painted a bleak picture of the human rights environment in Tanzania. In a 2010 report, it listed the following abuses:

use of excessive force by military personnel, police and prison guards as well as societal violence, which resulted in deaths and injuries;

abuses by Sungosungo, traditional citizens anticrime units; harsh and life-threatening prison conditions; lengthy pretrial detention; judicial corruption and inefficiency, particularly in the lower courts; restrictions on freedoms of press and assembly; restrictions on the movement of refugees; official corruption and impunity; societal violence against women and persons with albinism . . . and discrimination based on sexual orientation.[26]

The government's willingness to use its police and security forces to repress opposition activities is a reminder that the Tanzanian oligarchy has a fundamental stake in holding onto public office. It has shown that it is prepared to go to great lengths to do so.

The political alignment that has driven Tanzanian economic policy during most of the past twenty-five years has been a coalition of the political-economic oligarchy acting in concert with donor organizations. The linked processes of economic reform and democratic transition have been accompanied by frustration and misunderstanding on both sides. Much of the frustration misses the point altogether, which is that Tanzania has now become a society in which there are all-too-familiar disparities in wealth between those few Tanzanians who are members of the oligarchy and those who are not.

Chapter 2

Economic Decline and Authoritarian Rule

The economic trajectory of post-independence Tanzania is painfully familiar. A poor choice of economic policies led to economic decline, which manifested itself in growing and acute scarcities of essential goods and services. Pervasive scarcities, in turn, gave rise to the rapid spread of parallel markets, which gradually came to provide a larger and larger proportion of what ordinary Tanzanians consumed on a day-to-day basis. Tanzania developed a binary economic system. The official economy, which was largely state regulated and controlled, delivered fewer and fewer of the goods Tanzanians needed and consumed on a daily basis. The unofficial or parallel economy grew exponentially and provided an increasing proportion. The combination of the two provided fertile opportunity for rent-seeking public officials and politicians.[1] Public sector corruption became blatant, universal, and ineradicable. Using the gains they derived from corruption, many public officials became active in the parallel sector as investors and producers, owning, or co-owning, private enterprises that provided goods and services that the legal marketplace could not.

Tanzania's evolving economic framework never corresponded very closely to President Nyerere's social vision, and the gap between the two only grew greater as the government implemented a policy of protected industrialization. Even the most casual reading of Nyerere's ideas on development suggests that his personal priority had to do with improving the conditions of life for Tanzania's poorest social strata. During Nyerere's presidency as now, this consisted principally of smallholder farmers, who were the overwhelming majority of the Tanzanian population.[2] As it evolved during the twenty-five years of the Nyerere presidency, however, Tanzanian economic policy assigned the highest priority to the creation of large-scale, state-owned industries. These were overwhelmingly urban, and they provided their greatest rewards to the white-collar stratum of managers and technocrats and to the owners of small businesses that provided collateral services, such as transportation and catering. The new industries also offered generous benefits to their industrial workers since, according to economic theory, the industrial wage had to be set at a high enough level to induce farmers to migrate to the industrial sector.

To capitalize those industries and to provide them with a steady flow of machinery, raw materials, and other inputs, the Tanzanian government imposed higher and higher levels of taxation and price regimentation in the agricultural sector. Throughout the Nyerere presidency, Tanzania's rural sector was not treated as the chosen recipient of beneficent transfers from better off segments of the society but, rather, as a source of revenue that could provide capital for the industrial sector. Contrary to much of what Nyerere said and continued to believe, the economic framework that Tanzania implemented during his presidency was perverse with respect to the distribution of wealth. It featured a planned transfer of economic resources away from the poorer elements of the society, the small farmers, to the far better off inhabitants of a new industrial sector, its workers, managers, and civil servants.

If Tanzania has attracted global attention because of the social ideals of its founder-president, it has attracted equal attention for having had one of sub-Saharan Africa's worst performing economies during the decades following independence. During the period between independence in 1961 and the beginning of economic reforms in the mid-1980s, Tanzania's economic record was one of persistent decline. According to World Bank figures, Tanzania's real per capita income stagnated during the forty-year period from 1960 to the turn of this century and actually fell during the 1970s and 1980s.[3] Even these dismal numbers do not provide a complete picture, however. Much of the recorded growth took place in the expanding public sector and reflected the massive growth of the central government's bureaucracy. Most Tanzanians did not benefit from this growth, and many believed that their real standard of living—measured on what they could actually obtain in the way of housing, food, clothing, and other vital amenities—fell during most of that period. The government based its calculations on the official exchange rate, which exaggerated the dollar value of its shilling-based economy. This practice concealed the extent to which living standards had fallen for the ordinary person.

By the early 1970s, it had become painfully apparent that Tanzania was experiencing a broad-gauged and largely self-induced economic decline. The theory that high taxes on agriculture could generate the resources necessary to finance industrial growth always had serious shortcomings. As a few economists had anticipated early on, the burden of heightened taxes on agricultural exports, which steadily reduced the real returns to the farmers of export crops, only resulted in increasingly lower levels of marketed production and, therefore, in a severe deterioration of the country's ability to generate hard currency on world markets.[4] In addition, since hard currency earnings were vitally important to finance the major costs of industrial growth, such as the imported capital goods, spare parts, and raw materials for the new industries, industrial stagnation was a collateral effect of the drop in agricultural earnings.

Shortages of goods caused by lowered earnings of foreign exchange permeated virtually every sector of the country's economy. Scarcities of vital inputs meant that the new industrial framework was at best operating at a small fraction of its installed capacity. This, in turn, meant that the consumer goods these industries produced, ranging from relatively nonessential items, such as beer, soft drinks, and cigarettes, to important goods such as clothing, automobile tires, and construction materials, were perpetually in short supply. As the foreign exchange shortage deepened, the country's public services deteriorated as well. Tanzania was unable to afford the spare parts and fuel supplies required to operate its fleet of publicly operated buses and trash vehicles, the medications and equipment necessary for its public hospitals and rural clinics, the classroom materials necessary for the school and university system, and practically all the inputs necessary to maintain the country's infrastructure. Electricity brownouts and water shortages occurred daily; hospitals were so short of anesthetics, antibiotic medication, anti-diarrheal drugs, saline kits, and even ordinary bandages that patients were frequently required to bring their own. University instructors, lacking paper, wrote their syllabi on the chalkboard; their students took notes on the margins of scrap paper. Tanzanians who commuted to work sometimes had to walk for hours each way when bus service became unavailable. Tanzania in the second half of the 1970s was a country in which practically everything was in short supply: even the most basic consumer goods such as batteries, tools, light bulbs, automobile parts, and kitchen utensils became difficult to obtain.

Scarcities of essential goods gave rise to parallel markets; these spread rapidly throughout the country. The parallel marketplace provided any consumer item that was unavailable in the legal marketplace. The difficulty was that parallel markets were prone to spiraling inflation, which reflected both the scarcity of goods and the element of risk associated with their contraband character. The remarkable feature of the parallel marketplace in Tanzania and in other countries where such markets have assumed a large place is the variety of goods they deliver. Tanzania's parallel markets were brimming not only with core necessities such as clothes, maize meal, cooking oil, and malaria drugs, but with a wide range of luxury goods, including air conditioners, portable generators (popular because of the frequent electricity shortages), and all manner of consumer goods including cameras, watches, music systems, and video players. Tanzania's economic decline became a leading example of a continent-wide story of a seemingly irreversible downward spiral. Falling producer prices for export crops, which lowered farmers' incentives, resulted in a rapid falloff in the country's export earnings, which, in turn, crippled the country's import capability including industrial and agricultural inputs. Decreasing producer prices combined with intensified efforts at social regimentation, such as the collective villages' scheme, also resulted in dramatically lowered levels of marketed food staples. Tanzania was not only suffering from a virtual collapse of industrial production, but also experiencing a series of other critical scarcities, including shortages of food staples such as maize and rice.

By the mid-1970s, the country's leaders found themselves confronted with a painful choice: divert the scarce flow of foreign exchange toward food imports to avert widespread starvation, thereby further hampering the effort to construct an import-substituting industrial sector, or allow foreign exchange earnings to continue to flow to industries, thereby widening the spread of famine. President Nyerere chose the former, allocating several hundred million dollars to food imports between 1974 and 1977. This decision helped to avert a severe famine, but it meant that the government had to withdraw precious financial resources from the industrial and agricultural sectors to finance grain imports. After twenty years of independence, Tanzania's economic state of affairs was a dramatic reversal from the early 1960s, when it had enjoyed robust agricultural growth. Immediately after independence, Tanzania had enjoyed one of the highest rates of growth in food production of any of the newly independent sub-Saharan nations; it was not only self-sufficient in major food staples but was rapidly becoming a significant maize exporter to nearby countries, such as the Democratic Republic of Congo, Zambia, and Malawi. The export sector of Tanzania's agricultural economy was also enjoying some success. At independence, Tanzania had been on track to become a significant coffee exporter as well as an important contributor to international markets in cotton, tea, sisal, and cashew nuts.

Indeed, aside from the epochal failure of the colonial government's attempt to introduce groundnut cultivation, Tanzania's abundant supply of good agricultural land seemed to offer favorable growing conditions for many of the world's major exportable crops.[5]

The immediate post-independence economic success was short-lived. Within less than a decade, Tanzania's production of maize, wheat, and rice fell so far short of self-sufficiency that it was forced to import large volumes of food grains. Imports of various grains during the mid-1970s were averaging more than one hundred thousand metric tons per year, a huge economic cost. During 1974 and 1975 alone, Tanzania imported nearly five hundred thousand metric tons of maize at a cost of almost $100 million. Imports of wheat and rice to supplement the country's maize needs raised the cost of food imports even higher, adding at least an equivalent sum to the burden on the country's meager foreign exchange reserves. These were staggering amounts for a poor agricultural country with a population of only about fifteen million. The collapse of the agricultural sector was so severe that even farmers had to receive food assistance. Although drought conditions in some food-producing districts contributed to agrarian difficulties, the basic fact was that Tanzania had failed to translate the president's vision of agrarian self-sufficiency into economic reality.

The root cause of economic decline was the stagnation of the export sector. Production of virtually every major export crop declined dramatically during that period, diminishing the country's capacity to generate the foreign exchange required to sustain both food imports and the import of inputs necessary for the country's fledgling industries. The World Bank captured the broad parameters of this decline in its classic 1981 study, *Accelerated Development in Sub-Saharan Africa.*

> During the last fifteen years, the volume of exports in Tanzania has declined dramatically. In 1980, the total exports of the country's major commodities (cotton, coffee, cloves, sisal, cashews, tobacco and tea, which account for two-thirds of the country's export earnings) were 28 percent lower than in 1966 and 34 percent lower than in 1973. As a percentage of GDP, export earnings fell from 25 percent in 1966 to only 11 percent in 1979.[6]

Since earnings from agricultural exports were the principal source of funds for food imports, export failure was doubly disastrous. Major contributions of foreign assistance were necessary to avert rural starvation and severe depression in the urban economy.

Evidence of the country's dismal economic performance manifested itself in the deterioration of the roads, schools, and medical facilities and the unreliability of public utilities such as water and electricity. Although members of the political elite managed to live well despite all that was going on, others suffered, especially rural Tanzanians, the designated beneficiaries of the president's vision. Economic decline widened the material gap between urban citizens and rural farmers, already the poorest citizens. By the end of 1975, Nyerere's vision of an agriculturally self-sufficient nation able to support itself and, therefore, free to pursue its own independent course in world affairs had given way to the reality of a nation dependent for its economic survival on the generosity of the donor community.

The decline of the export sector had ripple effects that permeated the entire economy. In addition to making Tanzania dependent on its donors to finance food imports, declining revenues from agricultural exports also resulted in severe constraints on industrial production. Tanzania's industrial sector, largely oriented toward production for domestic needs, was almost entirely dependent on imported inputs. Virtually every requisite of industrial production, including capital goods, spare parts, and raw materials, had to be obtained from international markets, which demanded hard currency. The industrial sector also required a steady flow of hard currency to finance such industrial intangibles as patent rights and royalty fees and pay for costly management contracts with the global companies that provided technical services and skilled personnel. As the earnings from agricultural exports declined, the government had to divert an increased share of what remained toward the cost of food imports. This meant that the import requirements of the industrial sector were accorded second priority. Agricultural export decline manifested itself in scarcities of such consumer items as clothing, medicines, automobile tires, soap, chemical products, plastic goods, and even soft drinks, beer, and cigarettes. The World Bank estimated that, by the mid-1970s, Tanzania's industries were producing these goods at only 20 to 30 percent of installed capacity.[7]

The faltering output of the agricultural export sector also manifested itself in the rapid deterioration of public services. In a largely agricultural country such as Tanzania, education, health, water supply, public transportation, trash collection, and energy provision also require inputs that are only available on international markets. With the supply of hard currency increasingly diminished, schools suffered from the lack of books and other supplies; hospitals, from the scarcity of drugs and medical equipment; public buses and trucks from the lack of replacement parts and fuel; and infrastructure improvement from the lack of virtually everything. Even the most vital urban services became badly degraded: water and electricity supply, trash collection, and public transportation operated intermittently at best and became increasingly unreliable, posing added risks to public health. During the 1970s, Tanzania was struck with a new and more lethal form of malaria, one that required hospitalization and continuous intravenous hydration. The patients with the best chance of survival were those who could bring their own intravenous kits to the country's medical centers. Ordinary Tanzanians found it difficult to afford these kits. Those who could afford them quickly found that the supply in local pharmacies was quickly exhausted, after which, Tanzanians could only purchase the kits in high-priced parallel markets. To make matters worse, the malaria kits had to be stored in refrigerators, also a parallel market commodity.

Daily life for ordinary Tanzanians became painfully difficult. Urban dwellers faced scarcities of virtually every necessity. Dar es Salaam is a sprawling city whose working-class neighborhoods are distant from the city center where most businesses, factories, and government offices are located. For many residents, the daily commute to work became an agony of unavailable or unpredictable bus service. Indeed, many residents simply had to walk, sometimes for several hours each way, between their homes in the residential areas and their jobs in the city center. The deterioration of public and private sector services made it necessary for employees of schools, hospitals, banks, and telecommunications companies to divert much of their time to scouring the marketplace for essential items. There was unremitting uncertainty as to whether such basic household necessities as maize meal, sugar and salt, cooking oil, or natural gas would be available in formal markets—and less uncertainty about their availability in parallel markets, with prices there reflecting the scarcity that prevailed throughout the country.

Life in the rural areas became even more impoverished. Vital consumer goods were even scarcer in the rural areas, where purchasing power was so low that even parallel markets sometimes failed to materialize. Tanzania's rural population consists overwhelmingly of small farmers, and for this major segment of the population, economic life was subject to extreme difficulty. One of the great ironies of food aid programs in contemporary Africa is that they find it necessary to deliver basic foodstuffs to rural populations who, under most conditions, ought to be supplying these for themselves along with a surplus for urban consumption. Throughout much of the Tanzanian countryside, such vitally important production goods as hoes and shovels became scarcer and more costly. Critical inputs such as fertilizers and pesticides became less available at any price. The deterioration of the rural infrastructure made it increasingly difficult to travel from farm to township to market products or obtain inputs. The socioeconomic gap between the countryside and the city grew ever larger.

The economic decline brought latent racism to the surface. In Tanzania in the early 1980s a strain of anti-Asian sentiment began to emerge that had always been present but had remained largely dormant under the influence of the Nyerere government's insistence on multiculturalism and while economic conditions were still relatively tolerable. Anti-Asian sentiment had been a part of the country's political discourse since the nationalist period when the Tanzanian African National Congress (ANC) sought popular traction by criticizing Nyerere and TANU for being insufficiently proactive toward Asian dominance in the mercantile sector. The ANC had also sought political support by asserting that mid-level Asian civil servants tended to stand in the way of upward mobility for Africans. Even Nyerere's government turned to racist measures to deflect attention from economic conditions. The Acquisition of Buildings Act of 1971,[8] though nominally part of the government's socialist agenda, was in reality a legalized confiscation of Asian-owned rental property.

One of the enduring questions in the Tanzanian political economy is why the government delayed so long before implementing reforms that might have reversed the downward spiral. One source of delay was the absence of an alternative economic theory that could explain why the economy was performing so poorly and what steps were necessary to improve things. Although the World Bank had published its transformative report *Accelerated Development* in 1981, and although a small number of Tanzanian economists had begun to envision the need for a more market-based approach to the country's economic management, the political elite continued to be enthralled by the Nyerere ethos of socialism through central planning. Fear of punishment for dissenting views trapped Tanzanian leadership in a perverse game of rescue the failed hypothesis. Anyone who openly challenged the official economic orthodoxy risked harassment, dismissal, imprisonment, or worse.

The economic reasoning that prevailed during this period held that since socialism must be correct, the causes of economic failure must lie elsewhere.

The cloak of infallibility that enveloped the president's approach to development caused Tanzanians to look for traitors in their midst to explain the country's economic decline. A politically popular explanation for the country's economic difficulties was the presence of economic *saboteurs* who were attempting to undermine the economy from within. This, too, was a form of racial scapegoating. Although it was not explicitly racial, everyone understood that the term *saboteur* was code to refer to the Asian merchant class that had historically been a major presence in the Tanzanian retail sector. Under the influence of a highly popular political figure, Edward Sokoine, who became prime minister in February 1983, the Tanzanian government passed an Economic Sabotage Act that gave it broad authority to take action against individuals and businesses suspected of creating and profiting from the scarcities.[9] Under the new law, businesses that sought to maintain an inventory of essential goods could be charged with "economic sabotage," a crime that might be punished with lengthy imprisonment.

To implement the law, the government initiated an anti-economic saboteur campaign, and by April 1983 there were more than four thousand arrests under the law.[10] Although the majority of those arrested were Asian merchants accused of the economic crime of *hoarding*, some were the African managers of state-owned trading companies. Practically all were imprisoned. Most of the private merchants arrested also suffered confiscation of their warehouses and stocks of consumer goods. The anti-saboteur campaign was a dismal failure that only made matters worse. It had a chilling effect on the entire Tanzanian business community; the atmosphere of fear it created only exacerbated scarcities that were already severe because of the degraded economic environment.

Viewed in retrospect, Sokoine's effort to convince the Tanzanian public that the country's economic woes were the result of the self-seeking behavior of a small number of greedy merchants—not the deficiencies of a dubious theory of development—was the last gasp for the Nyerere ethos. Since the Sokoine arrests included a number of successful African business entrepreneurs and managers, his approach to solving the country's economic problems was becoming unpopular before his sudden death in an automobile accident in early April 1984, just over a year after assuming office. The most pronounced effect of Sokoine's anti-saboteur campaign was that it accelerated the growth of the parallel economy. Tanzania's official economy, with its excesses of regimentation and rent seeking, was already a difficult environment in which to operate. The anti-saboteur campaign added an additional element of fear and uncertainty since the government could arrest and imprison a merchant simply for holding a supply of stock in reserve. To evade the anti-saboteur campaign, many entrepreneurs shifted their activities to the parallel sector, where business had long since learned to evade detection, oversight, and intervention by the Tanzanian state.

The Parallel Economy

Scarcities of essential goods generated their own remedies in the form of parallel markets, and a vast parallel marketplace arose to supply goods that were otherwise unavailable. The principal economic difficulty with the parallel marketplace was high prices, reflecting not only scarcity but the element of risk inherent in illegal transactions. The growth of these markets had two immediate effects. The first was to discredit the official economic system by calling attention to its failures and shortcomings. A government-sponsored chain of retail stores, Cooperative Societies of Tanzania (COSATA), became an object of ridicule for empty shelves with posted prices for goods that were unavailable. The social effect of the parallel marketplace was to accentuate the inequalities between the society's haves and have-nots.

The social differences between those who could afford to acquire goods in parallel markets and those who could not would generate demoralization even in societies where an ethos of social equality was not present. However, in Tanzania the differences between haves and have-nots became especially burdensome because the president's philosophy attached such great importance to the idea that all Tanzanians would share the burden of socialist development. The fact that those who could obtain goods in the informal marketplace were often high-ranking members of the country's political elite made the social discrepancy even more demoralizing. Over time, many Tanzanians became convinced that the president had to be personally aware of the widening socioeconomic gap in their society. Some even came to believe that his public message of social equality was a disingenuous attempt to provide legitimacy for members of his own coterie even though he knew that they were behaving in a socially predatory manner.

As is inevitable in an environment of acute scarcity, inflation eroded the purchasing power of both public and private sector incomes. Yet Tanzanians with positions in the public sector, especially those at elite levels, were in a far better position to ride out the economic storm than those who were not. The upper strata of state officials became a privileged class relative to the economic hardships suffered by the vast majority of Tanzanians. However, the political elite was able to hide much of its wealth from public view. A large portion of the elite's real income was in the form of benefits that, while not monetary, nevertheless had great monetary value, such as government-provided houses, official cars, expense allowances, and salaries for household staff. National Assembly members received generous per diem payments while attending legislative sessions. Government officials who had to travel—many contrived to do so—also received generous per diem payments, sometimes in hard currency. Since public officials could easily falsify their expense statements, these payments often became an important source of supplemental income.

The more influential members of the political class enjoyed a wide variety of other nonmonetary benefits as well. They could use their positions to obtain government jobs for relatives and friends, business licenses for family members, government contracts for political allies, and special educational opportunities for their own children and those of their political associates. Although these privileges did not count as income, they were an important part of what differentiated membership in the political elite from nonmembership. Many members of the political class also managed to hide their income by sequestering assets overseas, in bank accounts or real property. High-ranking public officials were also able to use their positions to avail themselves of other opportunities not readily available to ordinary Tanzanians, such as overseas travel and education. The highest-ranking members of the elite were able to obtain special medical services overseas and preferred access to other scarce goods and services. These benefits meant that the highest members of Tanzanian officialdom were able to insulate themselves from the scarcities that affected ordinary citizens. The sum total of their privileges helps explain why Tanzanian officials, like those in so many other comparable countries, were among the most reluctant to change the economic policies that they were fully aware were imposing hardships on the majority of the population.

The early pattern of elite inequality in post-independence Tanzania was so well concealed from public view and scholarly scrutiny that it is all but impossible to determine the extent to which inequality may have worsened during the period of economic reform. The country's socialist ethos and a leadership code that forbade second incomes caused members of the political elite to go to great lengths to conceal their real incomes. Their homes were not generally accessible to the public, and they derived much of their cash income from unrecorded activities such as rent seeking. Public officials could also divert part of their income to the businesses and farms of close family members or political supporters. In contrast to today's Tanzania, where luxury homes and luxury goods abound, there were far fewer opportunities for the elite to engage in conspicuous consumption. Tanzania during the 1970s did not feature expensive hotels or restaurants; there were no dealerships well stocked with late model Mercedes-Benz automobiles, and no shopping malls offering a glittering array of expensive goods. Many of the most lucrative benefits members of the governmental elite enjoyed did not appear in official figures on income distribution, which were based on salaries alone.

A significant source of difficulty for Tanzanian research has been the tendency for the government's statistical data to make the country appear closer to the socialist imagery favored by the president than was in fact the case. Critics of the process of structural adjustment sometimes allege that market-based reforms have led to widening social inequality. However, this is difficult to verify since the monetary value of the total package of privileges enjoyed by the governmental elite is not easily quantifiable. Despite Tanzania's culture of social equality, members of its governing class always enjoyed a material lifestyle far more affluent than that available to ordinary Tanzanians. They continue to do so. But whether—or the extent to which—this income disparity may have worsened during the period of economic reform, or whether it has simply become more conspicuous in the more openly permissive atmosphere of a market economy, remains unclear.

The income gap between members of the elite and smallholder farmers was particularly pronounced. There is a strangely persistent imagery of African smallholder farming as a subsistence economic activity insulated from the up and down cycles of the marketplace. This conception has always been profoundly inaccurate. Tanzanian farmers, like African smallholder farmers everywhere, have participated in the cash marketplace to purchase an array of goods, such as bicycles, radios, wearing apparel, and food items they do not produce themselves, as well as more expensive goods, such as concrete for flooring and galvanized material for roofing. They also needed cash to pay for educational and medical fees, pay local taxes and cooperative fees, and make remittances to urban relatives. As Tanzania's rural economy deteriorated, cash for all these items became less and less available. For larger and larger numbers of rural Tanzanians, the direction of economic change was reversed; it was a matter no longer of moving from a subsistence lifestyle toward widening participation in the marketplace but of moving from a mixed economic pattern back toward subsistence cultivation as a strategy for economic survival. Where it did exist, subsistence production was the effect not the cause of broader scarcities, as degraded economic conditions drove small-holder farmers to give up production for the marketplace. As this process unfolded, the income gap between smallholder farmers and urban elites widened.

For most Tanzanians, the high prices in the parallel marketplace made the goods they had to obtain there unaffordable. Since price inflation in these markets was inevitable, the tendency for them to substitute for official markets as the source of many of the goods actually consumed on a daily basis accentuated the economic differences between the country's haves and have-nots. Attempts to gauge the extent of these differences are notoriously difficult because the prices in parallel markets tend to escape official detection and reporting. By their very nature, informal market prices fluctuate greatly over time and by location; because so many involve gray market activities, they do not appear in systematic form in official surveys. The government figures tended to understate price inflation because they used official posted prices rather than parallel market prices for essential goods.

The magnitude and importance of the parallel marketplace imparted an element of unreality to Tanzania's economic life. The prices set and recorded by the National Price Commission reflected an illusory world of affordability in which even poor Tanzanians could obtain food and other necessary goods. However, the reality was that essential goods were rarely available at the prices set by the government. In the legitimate marketplace, consumers often had to wait in line for endless hours for a trickle of basic items and, even then, went away empty-handed. Those who could afford to do so then made their way to the parallel markets that made those goods available at higher prices that went unrecorded. The most visible feature of the economy during this period was that goods scarcities were an omnipresent feature of daily life. The informal marketplace that arose to remedy these scarcities was a constant and painful reminder of the shortcomings of the government's economic policy.

Corruption

The emergence and growth of the parallel marketplace changed the lives of Tanzania's public officials in two ways. The first was that it provided an incentive for corruption. Public officials had a special advantage over ordinary Tanzanians in that they could more easily augment their incomes by becoming corrupt. This provides the best starting point for an understanding of Tanzania's endemic problem of corruption: it arose as a coping mechanism that enabled public officials, in contrast with ordinary Tanzanians, to augment their incomes. Tanzanian political scientist Gelase Mutahaba has shown the extent of Tanzania's public sector wage problem.

> The period 1975–1985 was a period of uninterrupted real wage decline. Although the situation was not very different in most of Sub-Saharan Africa, with most countries experiencing double-digit real wage declines on an annual basis, Tanzania's decline was more drastic than most other countries apart from those experiencing political instability. Average basic salaries in the public service provided only one-fifth of the purchasing power of equivalent salaries in the 1970s.[11]

Civil servants who could find ways to extract rents from the citizens they were expected to serve—and this was practically everyone from primary school teachers and police officers to high ranking customs officials—began to seek bribes for their services.

The more consequential outcome of parallel markets was their tendency to transform public officials from advantaged consumers to parallel market entrepreneurs. It did not take long for the more entrepreneurial officials to realize that they could earn generous profits by participating on the supply side in the parallel marketplace and that their status as public officials afforded special advantages. One was that the gains from corruption provided a source of start-up capital; another was that the mantle of a government position provided a measure of security from official detection and sanction. These advantages made it possible for public officials to leverage their way into a wide variety of business arrangements with the parallel market entrepreneurs who actually bought and sold goods. The mechanisms for their participation in the parallel marketplace ranged from hidden partnerships with business owners who needed official protection to various forms of economic straddling by close family members. Whatever the mechanism for involvement, the outcome was the same: a certain portion of Tanzanian officialdom began to evolve in the direction of becoming a profit-seeking as well as rent-seeking class.

For large numbers of public officials, rent-seeking behavior was only the first step in a longer and more far-reaching process of social mutation. What began to emerge in Tanzania during the 1960s and 1970s was a stratum of public sector officials who not only were able to augment their incomes by engaging in corruption but were becoming parallel market entrepreneurs in their own right. This transformation, at first gradual and then more rapid, is fundamental to understanding the Tanzanian political economy since the 1980s. The country was moving steadily toward a tipping point in its economic history. The first step was rent seeking, in itself the use of official position as a basis for income-maximizing behavior. The next and larger step in the process was for a portion of Tanzanian officialdom to wedge its way into the parallel economy as a full-scale entrepreneurial element.

This metamorphosis is fundamental to understanding Tanzania's peaceful transition to a market economy. Once it became apparent that high-ranking officials could augment their incomes, sometimes greatly, by functioning as entrepreneurs in the parallel economy, Tanzania's scarcity problem and the vast parallel marketplace to which it gave rise underwent a mutation. It is not possible to fix a precise date for this mutation. Its result, however, was that, at a certain point, a growing portion of Tanzanian officialdom had a deeper economic interest in preserving and even expanding the parallel marketplace than in resolving the conditions that caused it. Because of their rent-seeking skills, the most entrepreneurial officials were never much affected by the failings of the statist system. Indeed, so long as an important portion of their income derived from their ability to rent-seek in the statist economy so that they could profiteer in the parallel economy, they had a stake in maintaining both.

Profit seeking changed the cause and effect relationship between economic policy and scarcity. At first, Tanzania's endemic shortages were the product of policy choices that resulted in poor economic performance. Before long, however, scarcities could not be explained as the unanticipated consequence of a well-intentioned but flawed set of economic policies. When it became clear that scarcity in official markets made for large profits in parallel markets, the public officials who participating in parallel markets had no economic interest in resolving the scarcity problem. The country's failed economic policies became a matter of indifference or even a basis for wealth accumulation.

There was an ongoing dynamic of change at work in this process, however. As public officials deepened their involvement in the parallel marketplace, their economic interests underwent a further change. As rent seeking evolved into profit seeking, the presence of the state sector became a limitation on the accumulation of wealth. At a certain point, parallel market entrepreneurs stood to gain a great deal more if they could transform the official economy into a market economy where they could conduct business activities openly and expand them in scale. This change offers an important lesson in the dynamics of Tanzanian development. At first, public sector officials participating in the parallel economy had a stake in the preservation of the official economy because the scarcities it created raised the prices they could charge in their parallel market activities. As this stratum of officials developed into a more and more robust entrepreneurial class, however, the parallel marketplace, which at first had provided an important opportunity, became a constraint on their ability to expand and diversify their economic activities. The state economy now stood in their way.

This explains why so many Tanzanian public officials were at first opposed to economic reform and then began to welcome it. By the mid-1980s, many members of the political-economic oligarchy began to understand that they could accumulate greater wealth by extending their profitable activities to economic areas still dominated by the state, such as large-scale manufacturing, commercial real estate, and retail trade. To take over these areas of the economy, however, the governing elite needed to institute reforms that would legitimize such entrepreneurial activities. The tipping moment arrived when a sufficient number of Tanzanian entrepreneurs, many of whom had their start in the parallel economy, were ready to spread their wings by investing their resources in legitimate retail and productive enterprise. At that point, the presence of large-scale state enterprise was an obstacle in their evolutionary path. Liberal economic reform was the political precondition for illicit entrepreneurs in the parallel marketplace to become legitimate investors in large-scale enterprise.

What had begun as corruption for the purpose of supplemental income had led, in a series of stages, to the mutation of an entire social class. The first step in that transformation was for corruption to become the basis for concealed entrepreneurial participation in the parallel economy. The final step was for corruption to become the source of investible wealth that would make it possible for the highest-ranking members of the oligarchy to assume a dominant place in a legalized and rapidly expanding free economy. This evolutionary sequence explains why corruption has proven so difficult to eradicate. Although official corruption had its economic point of origin in the low purchasing power of public sector salaries, it has long been clear that wage improvements alone do not provide a solution.

Once corruption had begun, it metastasized through the society's economic, social, and cultural systems in a variety of ways. The income that public officials obtained from rent seeking was not only built into their expectations as consumers, it was also built into their need for investible capital. The term that best suggests the full economic ramifications of corruption in Tanzania is *primitive accumulation*. Before long, the public officials who engaged in corruption did not treat their gains from this practice merely as supplemental income; they came to reckon it as an indispensable source of capital for the acquisition of land and other productive assets.

The opportunity for corrupt gains became a powerful motivation to pursue a public sector career. One source of this difficulty was that the heightened visibility of elite affluence during the era of reform gave rise to a completely new set of expectations about the lifestyle to which public officials could feel entitled. In Tanzania, extended family pressures added even further to the challenge of reducing corruption, as those fortunate enough to have lucrative public sector employment were expected to provide for relatives who did not. The result is that even as scarcities and prices eased during the period of reform, and even as public sector salaries have improved, Tanzania's endemic problem of corruption has remained unabated. To the extent that is so, corruption is now functionally independent of the circumstances that first gave it rise.

Transparency International has taken the position that Tanzania's highly centralized and extensively regulated economy was a major source of corruption.

> Centralisation of the economy through nationalisation meant that the few powerful elites had a monopoly on the allocation of resources; in this situation, corruption was inevitable. Second, bureaucratic causes, such as red tape and rigid rules and regulations imposed by central and local government, contribute to increased corruption. Public officials were tempted to subvert these rules or were pressured into subverting them for individual or group gain, despite the fact that such acts were illegal. For example, one could not acquire a plot to build in Dar es Salaam unless one oiled the hands of bureaucrats.[12]

This was true as the initial source of the problem. Corruption, however, has persisted and even increased as Tanzania's economy has become more open. If anything, the capital requirements for participating in the country's expanding private economy have given many officials a greater incentive to engage in rent seeking.

Corruption thrived because it generated its own enabling environment. Ghanaian novelist Ayi Kwei Armah in *The Beautyful Ones Are Not Yet Born* described a perverse cultural universe in which government officials engaging in corruption became contemptuous of those who were not.[13] Armah's book describes a shame culture in which the few remaining honest officials became the objects of peer group derision and social pressure, often from their own families, to conform to the corrupt system. The force of this culture operated as a powerful motivation to accept the norm of corrupt behavior. The culture of corruption in Tanzania closely resembles that described by Armah. Even in the most prestigious organs of government, such as the court system, there are subtle social pressures to engage in corruption and, thereby, become a part of its normative environment. Jennifer Widner has described this phenomenon in the Tanzanian judicial system in her compelling biography of Chief Justice Francis Nyalali.

> Social pressures meant that judges and magistrates who declined to take bribes were at once esteemed for the model they set, and chastised, for their inability to do better by themselves and their communities. . . . Observed Tanzanian judge William Maina, who had experienced the problem himself, "Magistrates were blamed if they did not engage in corruption. People would say, 'He is a foolish person because he has not used his position.'"[14]

Tanzanian lawyer and legal scholar Dr. Edward Hoseah, also director-general of the PCCB in Tanzania, has written an important book on the extent and impact of corruption in his country.[15] His research, which he bases partly on his role as a leading anti-corruption combatant, provides a compelling account of the effects of this problem. Hoseah observes that villagers in remote areas expect public officials from their village to return with gifts. When they do so, they are welcomed as heroes; when they fail to do so, they have shamed the village community.[16]

For the average citizen, the list of transactions with persons in authority is inexhaustible. Individuals seeking to obtain a driver's license, receive medical treatment at a government hospital, enroll their children in school, report a minor crime at a police station, or mail a package at a post office—all encounter officials who expect an added financial inducement. One of the most common forms of corruption in Tanzania is the extortion of bribes by police for imagined offenses. According to a 2006 Commonwealth Human Rights Report, the Tanzanian police routinely arrest or detain people to extort bribes.[17]

Corruption in Tanzania has become so commonplace that it has generated its own vocabulary. The expression *lete chai* (literally, "bring me a cup of tea"), means "may I have a bribe?" and generally elicits the favorable response, *nitakupa chai* ("I will give you tea"). Encounters with the police also have their own phraseology: the common expression *kuingia bure, kutoka kwa pesa* means that there is no cost to go into a police station, but it will require a bribe to leave. The term *takrima*, which means "gift," has two separate meanings, both associated with corruption. The first is the consideration public officials expect to receive in return for their services; the second has to do with electoral corruption, the small payments the CCM gives to people who attend its rallies and vote for its candidates. Corruption in the CCM is a topic of almost daily conversation among Tanzanians who distinguish within the CCM between *mafisadi* (corrupt ones) and political leaders who are *safi* (clean). Most politicians are in the former category; few are in the latter. Average Tanzanians generally feel powerless to do anything about these problems.

The major government study of corruption in Tanzania, published in 1996 and known as the Warioba Commission report because former prime minister Joseph Warioba wrote it, describes the all-pervasiveness of Tanzania's corruption problem.

> There is no doubt that corruption is rampant in all sectors of the economy, public services and politics in the country. There is evidence that even some officers of Government organs vested with the responsibility of administration of justice namely the Department of National Security, the Police, the Judiciary and the Anti-Corruption Bureau are themselves immersed in corruption: Instead of these organs being in the forefront of combating corruption, they have become part of the problem. Consequently, the ordinary citizen who is looking for justice has no one to turn to. He is left helpless and has lost faith in the existing leadership.[18]

No small part of Tanzania's difficulty in dealing with corruption lies in the fact that the government agencies created to deal with the problem have become susceptible to the same set of difficulties, including inadequate wages, as other portions of the government bureaucracy.

The Warioba Commission's inventory of corrupt practices has two broad categories. The first is petty corruption. This form of corruption is everywhere in Tanzania, and the report lists numerous examples. Teachers demanded bribes from parents to enroll their children in school. Hospital personnel, including doctors, demanded bribes for treating patients. Police officers arrested innocent people to demand bribes for their release. Finance Department personnel demanded bribes from fellow workers to release their payments. Judicial personnel demanded bribes from litigants to process their paperwork. There was no transaction with a government official, however small, that did not require a side payment.

The second form of corruption described in the Warioba Report is *grand* corruption, when high-ranking officials find ways to leverage their government positions for vast sums. This can occur when the government signs fraudulent contracts with suppliers, when it issues business licenses at a tiny fraction of their net worth, or when customs officials underestimate the value of imports to lower duties or charge special fees for the timely clearing of shipping containers. Once embedded in the system, corruption becomes entrenched. Transparency International ranks Tanzania as one of the world's most corrupt countries, but despite an outpouring of donor complaints, media attention, and citizen frustration, the problem remains unabated.[19] The government's anti-corruption efforts are widely perceived as pitiably ineffective. Tanzanians point out that their government has not successfully prosecuted a single case of corruption and that even parliamentary resolutions calling for specific actions against corrupt officials are routinely ignored.

A tacit conspiracy of impunity further enables corruption. Although some high-ranking officials have had to resign or been dismissed from their positions, and a few have even been brought to trial, practically no one has been convicted or required to restore funds to the government. Those who engage in corruption form an unspoken agreement that they will not inform on others who do so. This is what makes corruption so difficult to prosecute. In a culture of corruption, it becomes wholly permissible, almost obligatory, to condemn the generic phenomenon and, indeed, to cry out publicly for reforms that will address it. However, there is an understanding that those who do so will not name names or call for the legal prosecution of particular individuals. Because of all these factors, the problem of corruption has continued unabated during the current era of economic liberalization. Despite a vast and continuous outpouring of official studies and public pronouncements, as well as the formation of a series of government anti-corruption bureaus, and despite unremitting efforts to exhort public servants to cease this practice, the problem persists.[20]

Hoseah's research shows that corruption in Tanzania has contributed to economic decline by imparting an element of unpredictability to the court system. Since there was no certainty that judges would uphold legal documents, prospective investors had every reason to feel insecure. Tanzanian courts have offered no certainty that business contracts would remain binding, that business partners would make payments as scheduled, or that contractors would deliver goods and services of agreed-upon quality. Judicial corruption has caused numerous investors to seek more secure alternate investment locations. Tanzania's first economic shock was the failure of direct foreign investment. This is attributable to numerous causes, and even without corruption foreign firms might have found it more profitable to sell or lease their equipment to Tanzanian enterprises rather than invest directly. However, corruption in the court system has been such a significant deterrent to foreign investment that it has had a direct effect on the country's economic performance.

The cause and effect connection between corruption and low growth is both multidimensional and all-pervasive. Corruption represents a transfer of scarce economic resources away from vitally important expenditures on schools, medical facilities, and infrastructure and toward conspicuous consumption on the part of the elite. Corruption also increased the operating costs of practically all forms of business enterprise. By draining funds that might otherwise have gone to improvement of public services, corruption has lowered government ability to improve the country's energy, telecommunications, and transportation systems. The businesses that depend on these services operated less well or found opportunities to go elsewhere. Tanzanian businesses have also had to contend with the rent-seeking demands of bureaucratic officials seeking to increase their income. In an environment in which virtually every business activity involved some sort of transaction with a governmental agency, bribes increased the costs and the risks of everyday business activity.[21] This has lowered economic performance by shifting investment priorities away from productive enterprises, such as factories and farms, which were proving to be vulnerable to official predation, toward economic activities that exposed less capital to political risk, such as small retail kiosks or other forms of petty trading.

Tanzanians with capital to invest withheld their efforts or devised ways to send their capital to other countries where they could invest more safely. Many emigrated for the same reason. It would be speculative to estimate the amount of additional economic activity that might have taken place if prospective investors had found Tanzania's business environment more attractive. Nor is it possible to make an estimate of the amount of Tanzanian capital that found its way to North America or Western Europe. The critical point nevertheless stands: the depth of the country's economic decline was to some degree a product of the sheer reluctance of both Tanzanians and foreign investors to engage in economic activities that might expose them to the extractions of bribe-seeking officials. The long-term costs of diverting investments away from productive activity also included flight of human capital as numerous aspiring entrepreneurs fled Tanzania to create business enterprises elsewhere in the world.

Corruption also created an incentive for families to divert their investible savings away from productive entrepreneurial activities altogether and toward the costs involved in acquiring rent-seeking positions. This could be the cost of a graduate degree or the cost of the bribe for appointment to a public sector post. In her classic article "The Political Economy of the Rent-Seeking Society," Anne O. Krueger theorized that where rents are available from bureaucratic positions, the economically prudent family would find it more lucrative to use its resources to purchase a civil service position than to rehabilitate its farmland or upgrade its factory.[22] Krueger's analysis describes Tanzania perfectly. It did not take Tanzanians long to discover that funds invested in productive businesses were high risk and low return relative to gains from holding public office. Indeed, Tanzania's socialist ethos accentuated this problem since it meant that investment in a profit-making enterprise was at a particularly high level of risk. Government positions, by contrast, were both secure and remunerative. The desirability of rent-seeking opportunities changed the explanations for Tanzania's tendency toward rampant bureaucratic expansion. Tanzania did not expand its bureaucracy in order to manage economic growth, but because there was a clamor for rent-seeking opportunities among members and supporters of the governing party.

In today's climate of improved freedom of the press, corruption scandals attract the attention of the Tanzanian media. The almost daily reports of corruption scandals are socially demoralizing because they call attention to the unjust enrichment of a few well-connected individuals at the expense of the public. The demoralization corruption creates is obvious everywhere. It fosters an atmosphere of cynicism and mistrust and causes ordinary citizens to become indifferent or even hostile toward government programs, which the public perceives as conduits for the transfer of public resources to private individuals. In Tanzania as in other societies where corruption has contaminated the economic atmosphere, citizens begin to doubt the validity all public sector programs, which, they believe, always have an ulterior purpose.

The demoralization caused by corruption, ironically, has also had some benefit in making it easier to introduce economic reforms. When it came time to move away from the state-centered approach that had caused such deep decline, very few Tanzanians objected. The dog that did not bark in Tanzania was citizen protest against economic liberalization and in favor of retaining the socialist economy. Unlike many countries that undertook sweeping economic reforms demanded by the international lending institutions (ILIs), Tanzania did not experience food riots or other forms of public demonstration against the process. Although some Tanzanian political leaders and intellectuals inveighed against the reforms the World Bank and IMF insisted on, their criticisms were tempered by the fact that they had very little resonance among ordinary Tanzanians. Few Tanzanians regret the passing of the difficult conditions they had to live through during the decades following independence.

Estimates of the budget effects of corruption vary. In 2009, President Kikwete estimated that one-third of Tanzania's annual budget of nine trillion (Tanzanian) shillings was being lost to corruption.[23] Transparency International offers a somewhat lower figure, estimating that about 20 percent of the government budget is lost annually to corruption.[24] Whichever is correct, the result is the same. Corruption is an upward transfer of income: the poorer people in the society pay bribes to relatively better off public officials. The schools, hospitals, and public services that are important to the poor and the middle class became starved for resources; corrupt politicians could afford a lavish lifestyle. The sheer magnitude of this loss has given corruption an additional self-reinforcing quality: lowered revenues make it difficult to raise public sector salaries; low salaries are the starting point for corrupt behavior.

The corruption that emerged during the era of decline remains the scourge of the Tanzanian economy. Despite an outpouring of government reports, practically daily media coverage, and the creation of a series of anti-corruption tribunals within the government,[25] it exists everywhere at both the lowest and highest levels of the system. A 2010 Dar es Salaam *Guardian* article describes the extent of Tanzania's corruption in the following terms:

Dishonest traffic police will use their uniforms to finance their homes, some magistrates sell justice to own posh houses, some bankers, too, will steal to finance their mansions and journalists are not spared; they will use their pens to finance their dream homes, and so goes the shameful game! To some of the business communities the shortcut way to own a palatial home is through tax evasion, frauds or dirty business like drugs trafficking. While in a country like South Africa buying a $1 million home without borrowing from the bank or having clear source of funds can land you in jail, in Tanzania, the situation is the opposite.[26]

According to a 2009 survey of corruption, Tanzanians viewed the police force as the most corrupt institution alongside the judiciary and the health sector, followed closely by land tribunals and local governments.[27] An updated survey conducted in 2011 by the independent anti-corruption NGO Front Against Corrupt Elements in Tanzania (FACEIT), funded by the government of Denmark, added the Tanzania Revenue Authority to this list.[28] A fuller list of corrupt institutions would include the Tanzanian military, recently given the grade D– by Transparency International for a variety of corrupt practices, including procurement, promotions, and extractions from local communities.[29] The *Tanzania Corruption Tracker* has cited numerous complaints about the corruption at the Port of Dar es Salaam, including loss of containers, smuggling of banned cargo, and loss of revenue.[30] It has also cited the National Housing Authority, whose officials continue to extract bribes for rental or repair of government-owned apartments.[31] All these reports point toward a single conclusion: corruption enables a stratum of public officials in these institutions to afford a lifestyle beyond the imagination of most ordinary Tanzanians.

During Tanzania's socialist period, public officials hid the wealth they gained through corruption. The CCM's leadership code and the ethos of social equality discouraged conspicuous consumption. This is no longer so. Today, the wealth of Tanzania's politico-economic oligarchy is easy to observe. Almost any Dar es Salaam taxi driver can provide a guided tour of the city's "posh" neighborhoods as well as a detailed narrative of the lifestyles of the rich and famous who reside there. The exclusive residential communities on the northern coastal shores of the capital city provide visual evidence that the members of Tanzania's political-economic oligarchy no longer feel the need for diffidence about the extent of their personal wealth. And since the owners of these homes, many of which belong to high-ranking political leaders and administrative officials, appear to be widely known among Tanzanians, the opulent walled residences of Oyster Bay and Msasani provide an incontrovertible indicator of the interconnectedness of political power and private accumulation. They also provide compelling evidence of the role of corruption as the link between the two.

Using one of the more powerful images in modern political economy, economists Brian Cooksey and Tim Kelsall have depicted corruption as Tanzania's tragedy of the commons.[32] Their metaphor is apt. Just as pastoralists overpopulate their common grazing lands, Tanzania's public officials engage in corruption even though they are well aware that it degrades the overall performance of their nation's economy. The reason is the same: one official's gain from corrupt activity is greater than his or her share of the collective economic loss. The follow-up question posed by the work of Nobel Prize winner Elinor Ostrom is whether a society generates corrective political mechanisms that address the problem.[33] Whereas pastoral and other communities have been able to invent political institutions that enable them to manage common resources for the public good, Tanzania has thus far been unable to do so. The best prospect may lie in the electoral arena where corruption has become the largest single issue. In the 2010 presidential election, the Chadema Party (Party for Democracy and Progress), which campaigned on an anti-corruption platform, gained about 27 percent of the presidential vote. Its popularity suggests that corruption, left unaddressed, may prove to be the weakness that finally loosens the CCM's grasp on power.

In the eternal quest to develop a political economy that differentiates between causes and effects, corruption has a special position: it functions as both. It is an outcome of economic decline because it takes root in falling public sector incomes. However, as corruption transfers income away from government to private consumption, it is also among the causes of poor economic performance, since it helps to perpetuate the budget difficulties that first brought it about.

The Authoritarian Trend

There is less ambiguity about the relationship between corruption and the tendency toward authoritarian rule. By eroding trust in government authority, corruption diminishes the prospects of government legitimacy based on the consent of the governed. In societies such as Tanzania, where corruption affects nearly everyone, it creates an almost adversarial relationship between citizens and the state, forcing government to turn increasingly to coercive mechanisms to maintain itself in power. Its greatest contribution to the authoritarian tendency, however, is to raise the stakes of holding onto political power. Since political office is the key to acquiring wealth, the loss of political power is an assured way of losing it. This anxiety unifies the members of the CCM political oligarchy and, whatever their other differences, fortifies their resolve not to be defeated in general elections.

The statist economic strategy, the spread of corruption, and the emergence and trend toward authoritarian rule went hand-in-hand. The causal connections were painfully apparent. Rural populations who were the overwhelming majority of the society quickly came to resent the imposition of a policy framework that subjected small farmers to deeper and deeper levels of taxation as well as increasing social regimentation. Until the new industries became sufficiently large to employ significant numbers of workers and managers, the social groups in favor of the industrial strategy would be limited and barely organized as a political coalition. The political dilemma of the ISI strategy in countries where the overwhelming majority of the population was smallholder farmers was that the pain of economic loss would be suffered far earlier and by far greater numbers of families than would benefit in the short term from the emerging industrial sector. To resolve this dilemma, governments would need to resort to authoritarian measures to impose the strategy on reluctant majorities.

A steady drift in an authoritarian direction marked Tanzania's post-independence years. The tendency toward greater and greater state control assumed several different forms. In the legislative realm, it consisted of the continuation of a number of colonial-era laws combined with a set of new laws that gave the Tanzanian government a high degree of coercive authority over the lives of individuals and the activities of civil society associations. Taken as a group, these laws are known as the *forty oppressive laws*, identified as such in the report of the Presidential Commission on Single Party or Multi-Party System in Tanzania in 1991. This report is commonly referred to as the Report of the Nyalali Commission, after its chair, Chief Justice Nyalali. In its inventory of oppressive legislation, the Nyalali Commission report included such laws as the Preventive Detention Act (1962), the Regions and Regional Commissioners Act (1962), the Collective Punishment Ordinance (1921), and the Resettlement of Offenders Act (1969).[34] Under the Preventive

Detention Act, anyone suspected of dissident political activity could be imprisoned and held without trial for a specified period. The National Security Act of 1970 gave the Tanzanian police a wide degree of latitude to arrest (without warrant) and to imprison persons suspected of "sabotage."[35]

Large parts of the oppressive legal framework fell with special weight on the country's rural population. The Regions and Regional Commissioners Act, passed the same year, gave Tanzania's regional commissioners, who represented government authority in the rural areas, the power to use that act, thereby empowering them to become virtual autocrats.[36] The Collective Punishment Ordinance, which gave the government the authority to impose collective punishment on the community with which an accused individual was associated, meant that villages and towns could be held hostage to the political behavior of their individual members. Other legal measures further illustrate the Tanzanian government's determination to impose its economic will on the countryside. The Confiscation of Immovable Property Decree of 1964, for example, permitted the government to confiscate land without compensation. Smallholder farmers, lacking in resources and without the ability to defend themselves in court or in the political arena, were powerless to resist the arbitrary use of this legislation.

The government further disempowered rural communities by abolishing the administrative and judicial role of traditional chiefs. During the colonial era, many important functions of local administration, including local law enforcement and taxation, had been carried out by government entities termed *native authorities*. Traditional chiefs, many of them appointed by colonial authorities, presided over these institutions. However, during the late colonial period, traditional chiefs had also begun to act as spokespersons for local communities, communicating rural grievances over agricultural taxes, inadequate educational facilities, discrimination in government employment, and, more generally, the indignities of the colonial experience. After independence, President Nyerere took the position that the native authorities were feudal institutions that had no place in a modernizing democratic society, and the special powers and financial resources assigned to traditional chiefs were eliminated. Whatever the merits of this viewpoint, it is best viewed in its economic context. As the central government began to escalate its levels of taxation and political control over the Tanzanian countryside, traditional chiefs had become active spokespersons for local communities discomfited by the new economic framework.[37] Dissolving the authority and special status of these individuals was one of several mechanisms for minimizing local resistance to central government control and heightened agricultural taxes.

The major step in Tanzania's authoritarian drift was the creation of a constitutionally mandated single-party state in 1965.[38] The political imperatives that set this transition in motion are self-evident. The economic measures that the government was beginning to implement created an adversarial relationship between a small urban minority of civil servants and industrial workers and the overwhelming majority of the population, which consisted of smallholder farmers. An open, multiparty democracy, which would empower the rural majority to oppose this policy, would place the ISI strategy at risk. If the party of the rural majority were actually to gain political power, the economic framework that over-taxed farmers to invest in urban industry would quickly come to a halt. The only alternative, other than to abandon the strategy, was to eliminate any possibility of opposition parties that might gain the support of the rural majority.

The Policy Factor

Reduced to its essentials, the most elemental question about these trends can be stated simply: what caused all this? The best place to begin looking for an answer is in the area of policy choice. Robert Bates's answer to this question centered on the differential influence of urban versus rural interest groups. He theorized that a powerful coalition of urban interests—including industrial workers and civil servants along with businesses attached to the industrial sector—used their political muscle to impose an economic framework that extracted wealth from the rural population to transfer it to the new state-managed urban industries. The concentrated political power of these groups far exceeded that of smallholder farmers, for whom collective action proved especially difficult because they were scattered over vast distances, physically remote from the capital city, and hampered by a scarcity of organizational skills. As a political explanation for the continent-wide pattern of agricultural decline that followed independence, Bates's theory has dominated discussions of African development. It remains the starting point for any political understanding of Tanzania's agricultural decline.

On closer reflection, however, it became apparent that Bates's urban bias thesis had a serious shortcoming. It overstated the influence of urban interest groups relative to their rural counterparts. Bates himself was among the first to point this out. In a 1991 article, published a decade after his book *Markets and States*, he acknowledged the existence of "discordant facts" that contradicted his earlier depiction of a decisive power imbalance between city and countryside.[39] Bates's discovery of discordant facts applied with special force to Tanzania where interest groups connected to the rural sector were very strong. Export-oriented farmers such as coffee, cotton, and tobacco growers had formed well-organized producer cooperatives, with well-funded apex offices that provided an influential lobbying presence in the capital city. Several of the country's most powerful trade unions were closely tied to the prosperity of the agricultural sector rather than urban industry. One was the agricultural workers' union, whose members depended on planting, harvesting, and processing exportable crops. A second was the transportation workers' union, whose members transported the crops from the agricultural regions to the port cities of Dar es Salaam, Tanga, and Mtwara. The third was the dockworkers' union, whose members then loaded the country's agricultural exports onto ships. Taken together, the membership and influence of these unions far outweighed those of workers in the industrial sector. Policies that diminished the well being of export-oriented farmers would inevitably have a similar effect on these workers as well. The farmer-worker coalition, though unusual in that it jointed together employer and employee, constituted a powerful opposition to policies that imposed costs on the agricultural sector.

Bates's urban bias approach reversed cause and effect. As a matter of historical sequence, urban industrial workers and managers did not become a well-organized political force until state-led industrialization was well underway and until some of the larger publicly owned industries, such as wearing apparel, footwear, brewing, and cigarettes, had grown to the point where they employed a large workforce. In other words, the industrial unions that became a powerful force for the policy bias against agriculture only emerged after the industrialization policy had begun and after the factories that employed large numbers of industrial workers had completed their hiring and begun operations. For Tanzania and a host of other African countries, then, the presence of powerful industrial unions does not explain why the policy of taxing agriculture to fund industries first began. However, it does help explain why this policy remained in place so long after its harmful effects had become visible.

The key question, then, suggests itself: why did Africa's leaders adopt a set of policies so harmful to the development of their societies? The most persuasive answer is the influence of prevailing economic ideas. During the roughly two-decade period from the mid-1950s through the mid-1970s, innumerable African governments derived their policy preferences from a subfield of economics known as *development economics*.[40] Tanzania was among these, and its policy choices throughout these two decades reflected the profound influence of this field. The development economists were intellectually joined by their mutual concern with the question of how primarily agricultural societies might best achieve sustained economic growth. They were pessimistic about the growth benefits of free markets as the best economic model for developing countries; they were pessimistic about the possibility that the agricultural sector might provide the basis for broad-gauged growth. In addition, they had doubts about whether free trade would provide sustainable development for countries dependent upon the export of primary commodities. Their economic strategies derived from these views. They believed industry, not agriculture, should have the highest priority; they believed protectionism, not free trade, would help industry to develop; and they believed the best use of the agricultural sector was as a resource base to provide the input needed to create industries.

The most widely discussed basis for the development economists' agricultural pessimism was the notion of falling terms of trade for agricultural products. Many of these economists believed and tried to show that the prices developing countries received for their agricultural exports would tend to fall relative to the prices of the industrial products and consumer goods they needed to import. To the extent that this was true, rising levels of agricultural exports could only sustain a constant level of imports, and this would cause each producing country to seek to increase its export levels.[41] Agricultural exporters would find themselves in a repetitive cycle of diminished well-being because the downward pressure on agricultural prices would cause them to fall relative to the costs of industrial imports. The difficulty in increasing agricultural prices at a pace commensurate with price increases for industrial goods had to do with the ease with which second- and third-party producers could enter global agricultural markets: it was far easier to capitalize and operate a new coffee plantation than a new automobile industry. The validity of this idea continues to be an unresolved topic of discussion among economists.[42] But so long as it held intellectual sway, it discouraged any tendency to view agriculture as a possible source of robust economic growth.

The development economists were convinced that the best use of the agricultural sector was as a source of resources, such as capital and labor that could be invested in industry. To reinforce this viewpoint, they assembled an entire repertoire of concepts that cast doubt on the wisdom of investing in the agricultural sector. Among other ideas, for example, the development economists stressed the low marginal productivity of labor in agriculture; the idea that labor productivity in agriculture would be less, at the margin, than labor productivity in new industries. The ideas of W. Arthur Lewis were especially influential, and his most famous research sought to show that agriculture could provide a labor supply for industry without adverse effects on agricultural production.[43] Benno Ndulu, today governor of the Central Bank of Tanzania, has stated Lewis's idea succinctly: "Lewis' seminal paper on the dual economy provided the rationale for perfectly elastic supply of labor released from agriculture where its marginal product was zero or released at a constant, institutionally set wage below the industrial wage."[44] Those responsible for framing economic policy in Tanzania and elsewhere interpreted Lewis's research to mean that they could siphon labor out of agriculture without adverse effects on the agricultural sector and deploy that labor to industrial production, where its contribution to economic growth would be much greater.

One of the most influential of the development economists' ideas about agriculture was the so-called backward bending supply curve of agricultural production. According to this notion, smallholder farmers in developing countries did not behave as income maximizers in the traditional economic sense, that is, by increasing their marketed production in response to favorable price incentives and then decreasing their production when prices fell. Instead, the development economists portrayed smallholder farmers as target workers whose participation in the marketplace was motivated by the need to have a certain level of cash income for specific purposes, such as to pay school fees for children, to purchase a bicycle or concrete flooring, or to pay local taxes or medical fees. Once farmers acquired that amount of cash, they would stop producing for the market and withdraw into a local economy of subsistence and barter. If this theory was correct, it meant that farmers benefiting from a price increase might well produce less of the good rather than more since their cash needs would be satisfied with a lower marketed volume. Similarly, if the farmers' price for a good were to decline, they would have an incentive to produce more of the good, rather than less, in order to attain the required level of cash income.

This concept provided the theoretical foundation for policies that increased taxes on farmers. What the development economists appeared to be saying was that governments could adopt tax measures that lowered the producers' net return on an agricultural good without risking a falloff in production for the marketplace. This idea became a fundamental conviction among many of the economists and policy advisors involved in the development process and set the stage for the post-independence era of escalating taxes on agricultural producers. Convinced such taxes might actually yield higher levels of production, many African countries began to impose a whole set of additional taxes on agricultural products. In Tanzania, these additional taxes began with agricultural exports but quickly embraced food staples as well.

During the 1950s and 1960s, the development economists' prescriptions exercised a powerful influence over the policy choices of a host of developing countries, not only throughout sub-Saharan Africa but also in Latin America and South and Southeast Asia. In conception, the ISI strategy of development was simple: it reinvents the old idea of the *infant industries* approach that was popular in the early industrial history of the United States. The infant industries would receive an incubator of protection until they had matured into adolescent or even full-grown industries, able to stand on their own in a competitive world. Both the ISI strategy and the infant industries approach emphasize the benefits of substituting domestic industrial production for imports, and both emphasize the need to provide the new industries with trade protection during their formative phase to insulate them from international competition by more mature firms. To political leaders throughout the developing world, both in sub-Saharan Africa and in other developing regions, the key challenge for policy-makers was to find ways to transfer productive resources from agriculture to industry.

The influence of the ISI model derived from several factors. Many of the development economists were among the most prestigious and highly regarded members of the economics profession.[45] Sir Arthur Lewis and Gunnar Myrdal were Nobel Prize winners; Albert Hirschman was a professor at Yale; Hollis Chenery, a former Harvard professor, was a vice president at the World Bank. Many major universities hired development economists to senior faculty positions and treated development economics as a vital subfield, worthy of its own faculty and eligible for its own qualifying examinations. Many economics departments tended to stream students from developing countries into this field on the premise that it would help them to make a practical contribution to their countries. On their return, many of these students took up positions in critically important government ministries where they had a direct effect on policy choice. In Tanzania, one of the most powerful vectors for the dissemination of the development economics approach was the influence of the major lending institutions such as the World Bank, and the principal bilateral donor agencies such as the U.S. Agency for International Development (USAID), which hired economists imbued with the development economics approach.

The primacy of development economics as the basis for policy choice meant that the dominant goal of the Tanzanian government's rural policies was not to improve the well-being of the agricultural sector. Rather, it was always about how to generate the capital necessary to create an industrial base. The answer to that question was that the agricultural sector had to become a source of revenue that could help capitalize new industries. The Tanzanian political scientist John Shao captured this perfectly: "Behind the enormous expropriation of value from the producers by the state is the belief that the capital required for socialist construction of modern productive forces has to be expropriated from the peasants. No leading government official or supporter of the government dares to admit this in public but the facts belie any other belief."[46] Since the new industries could not be expected to compete in world markets until they matured, the process of expropriation might need to go on for an indeterminate period.

Economic theory, however, provided only the conceptual basis for an ISI program. Beyond that, those responsible for the implementation of an ISI economy needed to address a host of operational questions. Which industries should begin the process and which should follow? What form of protection should be provided to the new industries, at what level, and over how long a period? How should funds be provided to industries that might require several years of gestation before they could begin production and start selling their goods? Some questions were even more mundane. Should worker training be provided through the industrial firms or through the public education system? The core premise of the development economists was that market forces would not provide optimal answers to these questions. Since that was so, the next step beyond economic theory was effective central planning, which was the minimal precondition for the success of the industrial strategy.

Chapter 3

The Failure of Central Planning

To succeed, the strategy of import substitution required a massive transfer of economic resources from agriculture to industry. The development economists had specified that the government should treat agriculture as a source of capital and labor for new, state-sponsored industrial firms rather than as an object of development in its own right. Their ideas had vast ramifications for other sectors of the nation's economy and for other policy areas. Governments interested in industrial development would need to reverse the economic priorities of the colonial era, which had prioritized agricultural exports. Budget appropriations for infrastructure, for example, would need to assign a lower priority to rural road systems and agricultural facilities than to roads and public utilities in the urban areas where the new factories would be located. The government would also need to concentrate its funding for medical clinics, primary and secondary schools, and housing developments in the urban centers, where factories would arise, rather than in rural areas, where there would be slower population growth owing to the anticipated exodus of younger Tanzanians seeking industrial employment.

The development economists did not believe market forces would accomplish all this in a timely manner. For all their differences on other matters, Tanzania's two otherwise distinct philosophies converged on one fundamental point. Nyerere's benevolent Fabian vision and the development economists' faith in industrial growth were rooted in a shared skepticism about the benefit of market forces. For both, government intervention had to replace the market as the mechanism for deploying society's economic resources. The only sure way to achieve a timely transition from a low-performing agricultural economy to a better-performing industrial economy was effective central planning, which would replace the operation of the market by providing a detailed blueprint for the phased re-allocation of resources across the two sectors. This posed a special challenge for political scientists interested in development. Since economists had provided the economic blueprint for the transition, it fell to political scientists to devise appropriate institutional mechanisms for carrying out their ideas. Development administration became the political scientists' equivalent of development economics.[1]

Reliance on central planning had profound implications for the democratic process. Political scientists have speculated broadly about the origins of the authoritarian trend in postcolonial Africa. Scholarly research on this topic has cited such varied factors as the carryover of autocratic practices from the colonial era, the exogenous cultural origins of the parliamentary and presidential systems created at independence, the volatility of ethnically based politics, and the imbalance of power between the military and other segments of the new governments. All these explanatory factors have their place. However, the relationship between central planning and authoritarian rule deserves greater emphasis because there is such a strong cause-and-effect relationship between the two. Central planning requires that a society be able to allocate its resources according to a detailed blueprint over an extended period. To implement an economic plan a government must be able to impose economic costs on some groups while conferring benefits on others. If the groups experiencing economic costs are able to deflect the allocation of resources away from the government's priorities, the plan might fail. This could place the entire industrial experiment in jeopardy. To be effective, in other words, a planning process must provide more than a vision: it must have the power to translate that vision into economic reality by imposing a new order on the economic lives of ordinary citizens.

A plan for industrialization requires a government to impose controls over practically every sector of the economy. Before long, the Tanzanian central government had assumed jurisdiction over crop procurement, processing and marketing, retail pricing and sales, rental housing, imports and exports, labor organization, bank lending, and, of course, industrial winners and losers. The planning process begins with the industrial sector: planners determine the exact sequence of industries for which the government must provide protection; they also specify the level and form of protection each must receive. Once a country has chosen the ISI strategy, it must regulate international trade in minute detail. The industries selected for development must have the very highest priority for the import of their capital goods, spare parts, and raw materials; the import requirements of industries that do not have a place in the plan have a lower priority or none at all. The import needs of other sectors of the economy, such as agriculture, public services, and consumer goods, which have a secondary economic status in the plan, have a secondary priority for their import needs. Precise control over the timing, form, and degree of industrial protection is essential because protectionism against imports cannot begin until the production of domestic goods has begun. Effective enforcement is critical: the plan would be a meaningless theoretical exercise if the industries selected for governmental incubation had to compete for their import needs with unregulated firms or if they had to compete with imported goods for a share of the domestic market.

A centrally planned economy requires all-pervasive control of the banking sector. Industries that have a high priority for their import needs must receive a high priority for foreign exchange. They must have special access to the central bank's foreign exchange reserves. The critical challenge in creating large-scale industries is the long time gap between the planners' vision and the moment when production begins. The factory managers must purchase and install equipment; they must hire and train workers; and they must experiment with production methods that will work in a tropical climate. During the protracted interval between planning and production, the factories must have preferred long-term access to commercial bank loans so that they can meet their payroll and other costs. To see to it that industries receive the capital they need, most centrally planned economies impose a system of mandatory sectoral allocations on their banking systems. These specify the percentage of a bank's loans that it must direct toward the industrial sector. Mandatory sectoral allocations are necessary to ensure that the larger part of the loan portfolio of the banks will flow to specified industrial borrowers rather than traditional clients in the agricultural or retail sectors or to private individuals seeking to pay their children's overseas tuition.

To subsidize the capital requirements of the new industries, ISI governments also impose controls on the interest rates that banks can charge industrial borrowers. These are necessary as a means of seeing to it that the new industries receive their loans at interest rates lower than those available to borrowers in the agricultural or mercantile sectors. Tanzania closely followed this pattern, imposing a set of regulations on the banking system. Its purpose was to see to it that only the industries that had priority status would benefit from government-guaranteed, low-interest loans. Control over the banking system had a series of ripple effects, all of them problematic. Since the interest rates provided to the state-owned industrial enterprises were often negative

because of the high inflation rate, the banks found it difficult to mobilize domestic savings. Without a reservoir of private savings with which to help finance the new industries, the government found it necessary to increase the
taxes it was imposing on agricultural producers.[2] To avoid gaps in the lending
pattern, the government had to intensify its capacity for monitoring and regulation. It was only a short distance from dense regulation of the banking
sector to full ownership. In 1967, Tanzania nationalized the private banks, a
step that transformed the banking system into a financial instrument of the
government's industrialization strategy. As with so many other aspects of its
economic policy framework, the lending policy it imposed on the banks,
which effectively froze out borrowers outside the ISI sector, reached extreme
limits and had conspicuously negative effects.

Central planning also required the government to deepen its involvement
in labor policy. Many developing countries, including Tanzania, have found it
necessary to question the inherited model of independent trade unionism
and, instead, begun to impose a more regulated labor union environment.
The economic reason underlying this change is clear. In market economies,
where there is private ownership of industry and industries operate on a
profit-making basis, trade unions must enjoy the freedom to pursue improved wages, benefits, and working conditions. In ISI economies, however,
the state becomes the major industrial employer and the major provider of
investible capital. The state also provides a wide array of other benefits that
impose costs on the public such as protection from foreign competition. The
taxpayer-provided subsidies to industries include lowered food prices and
improved public services in the urban areas where industrial workers reside.
The purpose of industrial investment in ISI economies is also different from
that in market economies: to generate broad-gauged economic growth that
will provide benefits to the broader society. In this environment, industrial
actions such as strikes or work stoppages by trade unions are strikes against
the taxpayers. Governments pursuing planned industrial development must
therefore reckon the costs of these strikes in taxpayer funds and in their potential to lower the welfare of the society as a whole.

Tanzania followed this reasoning to its logical conclusion: namely, that it
was necessary to move away from the model of independent trade unionism.
Tanzania's socialist government concluded that it must curtail the traditional
freedoms that trade unions enjoyed and impose a restrictive regulatory
framework. In the National Union of Tanganyika Workers Act (NUTA Act)
of 1964, the government abolished its independent trade union movement,

the Tanganyika Federation of Labor (TFL), replacing it with a centralized trade union organization, the National Union of Tanganyika Workers (NUTA), that would be wholly under the jurisdiction of the Ministry of Labor.[3] The government aimed this law principally at the powerful existing unions, such as that of agricultural workers, railroad workers, and dockworkers, whose well-being depended on the rural sector, but it had the additional effect of ensuring that the emerging organizations of industrial workers would also be under central government control.

The necessity for bureaucratic control over key sectors of the economy and the lives of ordinary citizens gave rise to the fatal shortcoming of central planning in Tanzania. The greater the power the new bureaucracies acquired, the more rent-seeking opportunities they provided to those fortunate enough to become public officials. The epicenter of Tanzania's economic story is the use and misuse of bureaucratic power. Over time, an imperceptible transvaluation of bureaucratic purpose took place. At first, the government expanded its bureaucratic capabilities according to the planners' economic vision, which carefully specified the pattern and the timing of the bureaucratic controls that were necessary to assure industrial success. Before long, however, bureaucratic expansion acquired a dynamic of its own. The government appeared to be creating bureaucratic controls and regulations as a means of providing rent-seeking opportunities rather than as a means of carrying out the economic blueprint that appeared in the sequence of multiyear economic plans. It is difficult to escape the conclusion that many other African countries went through the same process. As in so many other areas, Tanzania went further than most.

The tendency for rent seeking to take over as the driving force behind bureaucratic expansion explains why Tanzania went so far in creating a managed economic environment. Few African governments, for example, extended price controls from the export sector to the production of food staples. Of those that did intervene in the markets for food staples, none created a bureaucracy remotely resembling Tanzania's National Milling Corporation (NMC) in scale or in the sheer number of crops covered. Only two other African countries, Ethiopia and Mozambique, experimented with agricultural collectivization as a means of imposing greater control over agricultural production. However, their experiments were briefer and less far-reaching. Tanzania also chose to suppress its agricultural cooperatives, which had historically been such a vital part of rural communities. After it ended the collectivization program in 1975, Tanzania banished its village-based crop marketing cooperatives, replacing them with a system of state-managed, multipurpose cooperatives that quickly became a source of confusion and resentment among affected farmers. No other African government nationalized rental housing. Even avowedly socialist governments such as Ethiopia and Mozambique did not nationalize their banking systems.

Tanzania and many other African countries added a series of implicit or hidden taxes to the burden of direct taxation on the agricultural sector. Its implicit taxes, however, were more burdensome. Many African countries overvalued their currencies as a means of taxing export-oriented producers. Tanzania was among very few countries that pursued overvaluation to the point where it made export-oriented agriculture all but impossible. In addition to currency overvaluation, Tanzania also used inflation as a means of taxing the agricultural sector. By forcing farmers to wait a year or more for the payments on their crops, the government was able to pay them in a currency whose value had dropped considerably since the time when they first delivered their crops to the state marketing apparatus. Few other African governments went so far as to transform the fiscal basis of local government as a means of financing an experiment in state-led industrialization. Perhaps most important, the country's tendency toward all-pervasive corruption imposed a huge tax on agriculture in that farmers dealing with the state procurement apparatus had to pay bribes at several stages of the marketing process.

The Bias Against Agriculture

Once it becomes clear that large-scale industry, not agriculture, was the government's highest priority, it becomes easier to understand the discrepancy between the president's philosophy and the economic program Tanzania actually implemented under his leadership. The most glaring feature of this discrepancy has to do with the government's treatment of the rural areas. For those who took the Nyerere philosophy at face value, the most dramatic glimpse of what was to come took place in 1969, when the government decided to ban a rural cooperative organization known as the Ruvuma Development Association (RDA). The RDA, originally named the Songea Development Association, had started in 1960 as a small group of communally organized villages near the town of Songea, which is in the southwestern corner of Tanzania and near the border of Mozambique. It became the

RDA in 1963 because the communal village effort had expanded throughout the Ruvuma region.

To many, the RDA seemed to epitomize Nyerere's ethos of local self-reliance.[4] In addition to an emphasis on communal farming, the RDA had begun to create its own network of schools, community centers, and medical clinics.[5] There were also the beginnings of economic specialization between villages with different villages starting to place special emphasis on particular craft skills, such as wool processing, carpentry, milling, vehicle repair, and masonry. The government's decision to dissolve the RDA has been taken almost universally as tangible evidence of the government's real intentions toward the rural sector: that rural development was to be a state-controlled, top-down project, driven primarily by the need for revenues rather than as a means of improving the well-being of smallholder farmers.

The bias against agriculture had actually become apparent within a short time after independence. Certain institutional pillars of this policy had been in place since colonial times. The most basic of these was the single channel vertical monopoly mechanism for marketing exportable crops, such as coffee and sisal. Colonial governments almost everywhere in Africa had instituted single channel marketing monopolies for the most valuable agricultural exports on the premise that Africa's small-scale farmers needed insulation from the abrupt and unpredictable fluctuations in the world market prices of such important commodities as coffee, tea, cotton, and tobacco. The principal purpose of the marketing board system during the colonial era was price stabilization. The state-based marketing monopolies would hold back some of the world prices during years when the world prices of these commodities were high and subsidize producer prices during years when the world prices dropped. The marketing boards tried to control farmers' prices at an anticipated average between high and low world prices.

Centrally controlled agricultural prices for export crops, in other words, were nothing new in Tanzania or elsewhere in post-independence Africa. However, the purpose of the price controls changed radically after the adoption of the industrial strategy. The changes were at first almost imperceptible and then more far-reaching. The principal change had to do with the utilization of the cash reserves of the export marketing boards, especially the Coffee Marketing Board (CMB). As early as the mid-1960s, the government began to absorb the cash reserves of the export-marketing authorities to help finance the new industrial sector. The development economists furnished the reasoning behind this shift in purpose. They had taught that the productivity of capital invested in industry was greater than that of capital invested in agriculture. Since industries offered a better prospect of rapid and sustained economic growth, they had a higher claim on economic resources. The increase in the share of the world prices absorbed by the marketing board system was a not-so-subtle signal that farmer welfare had become a lower priority than capital accumulation for industry. What ensued was a wholesale transformation of the relationship between government and the agricultural sector. From having been the object of benevolent intentions during the colonial and immediate postcolonial period, Tanzania's farmer population became a source of capital for industrial investment.

Tanzania's commitment to state-led industrialization closely resembled that of many other newly independent African nations. Indeed, the list of new industries seemed to be identical from one African country to the next. Tanzania's list of industries was an ambitious one. It included textiles, soft drinks, clothing, beer, cigarettes, and construction materials, such as concrete and galvanized roofing. Economic planners advocated these industries because they shared an important economic characteristic—low demand elasticity among consumers. The economic planners used this concept to show that even if the new industries produced a poor quality product at a higher price than comparable imports, consumer demand for their products would remain stable. The ISI formula seemed compelling: the state would provide protection from foreign competition and, through adroit central planning, an optimal pattern of industrial selection, careful sequencing of protection from import competition, and access to subsidized capital. The rural areas, where life would become more difficult, would provide capital and a supply of labor. Once the infant industries had grown to maturity, they would provide economic benefits that everyone could share.

The First Economic Shock

Although this growth strategy seemed compelling, its shortcomings were apparent at the very outset. The first has to do with the government's assumptions about its ability to control the economic life of the country down to a fine level of detail. Tanzania's first five-year plan reflected the exuberant optimism of a newly independent nation. It is a remarkable two-volume document notable for its scope and ambition and for an uncritical expectation that the government would be able to impose far-reaching controls on every significant sector of the Tanzanian economy.[6] The breadth of economic man-agement envisaged in this plan would have challenged even the most well institutionalized government, one that had an adequate flow of revenue for bureaucratic expansion and large numbers of skilled managers and technical personnel. Tanzania did not meet any of those criteria: it had been indepen-dent for less than three years, it was still in the midst of a transition from co-lonial personnel to a civil service staffed by Tanzanians, and there were acute shortages of intermediate and managerial level civil servants. Its revenue base consisted principally of smallholder agriculturalists, many of whom were partially engaged in subsistence production.

Tanzania's early planners had also assumed that Kenya and Uganda would cooperate in a regional pattern of industrial allocation so that the three coun-tries would not compete with one another in specific industrial areas. This would make it possible for the new industries in each country to find export markets in the other two countries, thereby adding to the efficiency of their industrial investment.[7] This never occurred, however, and the three countries soon found themselves developing nearly identical sets of industries. Tanza-nia's early development plans also envisioned a process of industrialization in which a large proportion of the investment capital would come from external sources, in the form of foreign aid and foreign direct investment. The first development plan estimated that more than half the capital investment in the newly forming manufacturing sector would come from foreign sources.[8] Part of this would consist of foreign aid, mostly in the form of spending to im-prove the country's physical infrastructure, and part would consist of foreign direct investment to capitalize the new industries. Less than half the total capital investment would need to come from either the central or the local governments. The planners' estimates of foreign participation proved unreal-istic. During the five years of Tanzania's first development plan, less than one-third of Tanzania's funds for industrial investment came from external sources. The shortfall meant that more than two-thirds of the monies ex-pended on capital formation had to come from local sources.[9]

Within two years, Tanzanians had discovered the extent of their mistaken reliance on external support for planned industrialization. By early 1967, the Ministry of Economic Affairs and Economic Planning had conducted an in-ternal study of the country's progress toward the goals articulated in the first plan. The report presented a dismal picture of external financial support dur-ing the first two years of the plan. It acknowledged that the Tanzanian gov-ernment had in fact relied on public and private external support to provide about 80 percent of planned expenditures, with the government providing only about 20 percent. It noted "during the first half of the plan, external sources provided only . . . 40.9 percent of total expenditure, the balance of 59.1 percent came from internal sources."[10] The contrast between the government's mid-term appraisal and the original plan could not have been greater. The Mid-Term Appraisal was less than forty pages in length, as contrasted with the two volumes in the original plan document. Despite its brevity, it was of monumental importance. The government's discovery that foreign private firms were not prepared to invest in Tanzanian industry was the basis of its realization that the public sector would need to provide the capital for the new industrial firms. This understanding informed Tanzanian leaders' growing insistence that state funding required state ownership.

The Tanzanian planners' original dream, that the government and international investors would share the cost of industrialization, was nowhere to be found in Tanzania's second five-year plan. In the received narrative of Tanzania's post-independence economic history, the failure of foreign investment stands out as one of the country's earliest economic "shock" events, and there was much speculation as to its causes. The government's explanation for the failure of the plan's target figures for external funds acknowledged donor skepticism about the realism of the planning process and about the government's technical ability to implement large-scale industrial projects.[11] However, the failure to judge the real economic incentives of multinational investors was also of critical importance. Tanzanians had believed that foreign corporations would find it attractive to produce consumer goods under the cocoon of protection from international competition and with the boost of other large subsidies, such as artificially cheapened hard currency. Instead, the multinational corporations quickly discovered that it was not necessary to place their capital at risk by investing directly; they could earn larger profits by selling developing countries capital goods, raw materials, and patent rights. In addition, they could increase their profits on sales through the practice of over-invoicing. Sales of goods had an important advantage over direct investment: the profits on sales were quicker and risk free.

Donor and investor skepticism about Tanzania's industrial plans may have been the least of its problems. A regionally focused explanation held that other countries offered a more attractive investment climate. Kenya, for example, already had well-developed banking and credit institutions, a better infrastructure, and an existing set of factories that could provide many of the inputs for the proposed ISI industries.[12] Nairobi also offered a more cosmopolitan urban environment, a better physical climate, and a development ethos that placed greater emphasis on the role of the private sector. Whatever the causes of investor reluctance toward Tanzania—and one was undoubtedly the increasingly audible anti-capitalist rhetoric of the country's president—the result was clear. By the late 1960s, Tanzania's leaders understood that industrialization would need to be almost entirely government financed rather than a product of mutual arrangements with private investors.

This fact had profound implications. It meant that virtually the entire burden of financing the new industries would have to be borne by Tanzanian taxpayers. That meant farmers. The government would need to ratchet upward the levels of taxation on the agricultural sector to compensate for the shortfall in external funds. From the mid-1960s, agricultural policy in Tanzania had one purpose: namely, to generate sufficient revenue for the government to absorb the larger share of the cost of the new industries. To implement this policy objective, the Government of Tanzania introduced a set of measures that gave it increasing control over agricultural prices at the producer level. The purpose of those controls was to lower the real prices that farmers were receiving for their goods and, in so doing, to transfer a portion of the nation's wealth from farmers to those associated with the newly emerging industrial sector.

Even the most rudimentary inventory of the ways Tanzania changed the tax system suggests how far the government was prepared to go to finance its new industries. The Tanzanian government began to impose a host of new taxes on rural sector producers. Some were more visible than others were. One of the earliest was the so-called *development tax*, a 10 percent tax on the value of exports to create a special development fund. Henceforth, the government would remit 10 percent less of the value of exports to farmers and divert the tax revenue to the pool of funds for capitalizing the new industries.

Tanzania's first development plan had anticipated that the domestic costs of industrial investment would come from a combination of central government revenues and the taxes collected by local governments. Since this model did not permit the central government to have adequate control over what local governments did with their funds, the planning process had a structural deficiency. Although responsibility for formulating the plan rested with the central government, Tanzania's independent municipalities enjoyed a certain level of autonomy with respect to how they spent their local revenues.

Repairing this flaw would require extensive changes in the method for financing local government. At independence, Tanzania had enjoyed a robust system of decentralized local government modeled somewhat along British lines. The country's towns and municipalities had independent sources of tax revenue, including property taxes and business licenses. Traditionally, the local governments had used these revenues to finance locally provided services, such as education, health, and road maintenance.[13]

Tanzania's development plan, however, called for publicly provided services and amenities to be located in Dar es Salaam and one or two other major cities, where industries would be located, not in rural towns that provided services to the agricultural sector. To bring about the change in service allocation, Tanzania changed the decentralized tax model for local government to a French model called *deconcentration*. Henceforth, the central government would collect these taxes and, in return, assume the responsibility for providing public services at the local level. Although this was officially justified as a means of equalizing the quality and distribution of public services between the country's more prosperous and less prosperous regions, the result was altogether different. What transpired was that the revenue stream formerly collected by local governments now became available to the central government. Instead of using these revenues to equalize services between well-off and poorer municipalities, the central government used them to implement the ISI strategy. Local governments became greatly impoverished, and the replacement value of centrally provided services rarely matched the value of those that had derived their funding from local taxes.

Economist Frank Ellis conducted the definitive research on the effects of agricultural taxes on producer prices during that period. His research showed that between the late 1960s and the mid-1970s, the real value of the producer prices received by the farmers of Tanzania's three major export crops (cashews, cotton, and coffee) declined on average by more than 36 percent. His research also showed that the real value of the producer prices received by the farmers of Tanzania's three principal food crops (maize, rice, and wheat) declined on average by nearly 33 percent. Ellis concluded that export crops suffered a price terms of trade[14] loss of over 40 percent, and that smallholder food farmers suffered a price terms of trade loss of nearly 21 percent.[15] Tanzania's extractive approach to the rural sector, which was the basis of agricultural policy from the mid-1960s through the mid-1970s, was exactly what the development economists had in mind, a tax framework that treated the rural sector as a source of revenues.

By the late 1960s, Tanzania's rural population had begun to suffer from a double tax pincer. The first was the heightened levels of direct taxation on agricultural products. The second was the deterioration in local services caused by the transfer of tax revenues from local governments to the central government. The cumulative effect was that farmers' incomes declined, sometimes precipitously. It became more and more evident that the movement of wealth was not from the urban well to do to the rural poor but from the rural poor to the capital city, where the new industries were taking shape. In the countryside, where approximately 80 percent of Tanzania's population lived and worked, impoverishment became a daily fact. Little has changed since that time: smallholder farmers in remote rural areas remain the poorest Tanzanians.

The combination of tax increases and lowered living standards gave rise to a mood of political disquiet in the countryside and murmurs of rural dissent began to impose a political constraint on the way in which the government was pursuing the ISI approach. At a certain point, the Tanzanian government concluded that it had reached the politically feasible limits of the readily available forms of rural taxation. Tanzanian leaders felt compelled to seek out tax instruments that were less visible and therefore less likely to provoke opposition but that would have the same effect in shifting real income away from agricultural producers and toward urban industries. The government began to prefer implicit or hidden taxes to more transparent methods of taxation. This explains why, in the decade after independence, virtually every independent government in sub-Saharan Africa began to engage in systematic currency overvaluation. Tanzania was no exception. In 1967, Tanzania, like Kenya and Uganda, replaced the East African shilling, which was issued and regulated by an independent currency board, with the Tanzanian shilling, which the government could regulate through its own Central Bank.

Overvaluation acts as a tax on export-oriented agriculture.[16] For countries pursuing the ISI strategy of development, therefore, it is an ideal form of taxation. It imposes a tax on the producers of exportable agricultural commodities who receive far fewer units of local currency per dollar value of exports than would be the case under equilibrium exchange rate conditions. For exactly the same reason, currency overvaluation transfers financial benefits to industrialists who, as the importers of capital goods, receive inexpensive allocations of hard currency. Overvaluation is also a highly efficient tax in that the net economic value of the tax greatly exceeds the cost of collecting it. The Tanzanian shilling quickly became one of the more overvalued currencies in sub-Saharan Africa. Overvaluation increased steadily throughout the 1970s and, by the end of the decade, parallel currency markets were offering several hundred shillings per U.S. dollar, twenty or thirty times its nominal (officially assigned) value. Overvaluation of the currency was the most telling barometer of government willingness to impose confiscatory levels of taxation on the rural sector.

The National Milling Corporation

One of the most glaring and consequential differences between Tanzania and other countries pursuing the ISI strategy had to do with its approach to the food-producing sector. Since this sector was simply too important, too vast, and too complex to lend itself to any form of governmental control, the majority of African countries chose not to interfere in their nations' systems of food production, distribution, and marketing. The idea that a newly formed government might be able to manage a sprawling economic sector that consisted of millions of independent farmers producing an array of commodities purchased by millions of consumers in millions of separate transactions was too unrealistic to contemplate. In most countries, even the most ardent supporters of centrally planned economies acknowledged that their food sectors must indefinitely remain outside the scope and jurisdiction of the central planning process.

With the failure of foreign investment, however, the Tanzanian government found itself searching for additional ways to impose taxes on farmers. This became a matter of such vital importance that Tanzanian leaders decided that they could not allow the largest subsector of the agricultural economy, the production, processing, and marketing of food staples, to remain outside its system of bureaucratic controls. To accomplish this, Tanzania chose to extend the single channel vertical monopoly marketing model, which elsewhere was confined to the export crop sector, to the procurement, processing, and marketing of food staples. In February 1968, the Tanzanian parliament passed legislation creating the NMC, a state entity mandated to assume monopolistic jurisdiction for the purchase, processing, and distribution of approximately a dozen of the country's most important food staples, including corn, wheat, millet, sorghum, and rice.[17]

The administrative challenge inherent in creating a bureaucracy that could manage this sprawling sector was daunting in the extreme. Export crops lend themselves to the single-channel marketing model. Since the exports must exit the country at one or two ports of embarkation, there is a bottleneck effect. It is a simple matter to require that each unit that passes through this bottleneck must make the necessary tax payments before it can be loaded on a ship. Food crops are a different matter altogether. The food crop system of an agricultural society such as Tanzania is hugely complex. The end-consumer of one farmer's maize surplus, for example, could as easily be a schoolteacher in the same village or a bank official in the capital city, hundreds of kilometers distant. The distribution and marketing systems that made this possible were complicated beyond description. Indeed, food distribution and marketing in a predominantly smallholder society provide one of the great examples of the efficiency of Adam Smith's invisible hand of the marketplace.

With the creation of the NMC, however, farmers of the country's major food crops could not market their products to buyers of their choice. They had to sell their marketable surpluses to the NMC at prices the NMC would set and at NMC buying stations scattered throughout the countryside. The NMC had exclusive responsibility to process and package these crops and to market them to Tanzanian consumers. The government forbade the private processing, transportation, and marketing of staple grains. The NMC had two purposes, both related to the fundamental economic goal of industrialization. The first was to cheapen the cost of food for urban consumers, including industrial workers. Since food staples were a wage good, a significant determinant of wage levels, this should have made it possible to lower the labor costs of the new industries. The second was to operate like the export crop marketing boards, that is, to generate a profit from the margin between its acquisition price and its selling price and make this profit, or a part of it, available to the banking system for transfers to the industrial sector.

The NMC did not achieve either of these purposes; in the end, it represented one more planning effort that contributed to the country's economic decline. Far from delivering an economic surplus to industry, the NMC became such an expensive bureaucracy that it regularly incurred large operating deficits that had to be absorbed out of other governmental revenues. The economist Reginald Green, one of the principal architects of the Tanzanian government's economic policies and one of its most eloquent defenders, has acknowledged the disarray in the NMC system: "The net loss on lost, strayed, stolen or deteriorated stocks and on exports of surpluses sold below cost . . . is likely to be on the order of $30 million. The most alarming facts, however, are those in respect to NMC loss of internal physical and financial control and of coherent data flows and of NBC/Bank of Tanzania failure to monitor and investigate the abnormal credit balance movements more promptly."[18] By the end of the 1970s, the cumulative deficit of the NMC amounted to nearly three billion Tanzanian shillings or, at official exchange rates, U.S.$750 million.[19]

The creation of the NMC had a wrenching effect on the lives of countless Tanzanians. Its negative effects only began with smallholder farmers. Almost overnight, thousands of independent transporters, millers, and retailers lost their major source of livelihood. Farmers of the country's major food staples had no voice in the setting of farm-gate prices for their products, and consumers of such basic items as corn and rice could obtain these goods only at retail prices set by the NMC. The NMC became a huge physical and bureaucratic presence throughout the country. In the rural areas, NMC buying stations, where farmers were required to deliver their marketable grain surpluses, seemed to spring up in virtually every town and village of any size; NMC vehicles could be seen everywhere, traversing the roads between the village-level NMC buying stations and the larger towns where NMC storage and processing facilities were located. The NMC bureaucracy quickly became one of the country's largest employers at a staggering cost to the government in wages, benefits, and other emoluments.[20] In Dar es Salaam and other large cities, the NMC's national and regional administrative headquarters were a visible physical presence and an even greater source of social demoralization. Tanzanians complained constantly that even relatively junior level NMC administrators seemed entitled to an NMC car, NMC-provided housing, and a host of other NMC benefits. The ability to administer the procurement, processing, and distribution of essential grains also gave even minor NMC officials a host of rent-seeking opportunities.

The NMC food distribution system rested uneasily on exactly the same economic assumption as the new industries, low demand elasticity among consumers. The Tanzanian government believed that consumers of basic food staples would have no choice but to accept the NMC system even though it delivered fewer goods at higher prices and lower levels of quality than had previously been available through private distribution networks. The NMC system also introduced a greatly heightened level of political coercion into the lives of rural Tanzanians. The need to enforce the NMC system dominated economic life in the rural areas. District and regional administrators as well as regional police officers and customs inspectors specially appointed to monitor inter-district trade were now tasked with criminalizing individuals who sought to evade the NMC's monopolistic control over the acquisition, processing, and marketing of food items. One of the most common experiences in the daily life of rural Tanzanians traveling from one part of the country to the other was to be stopped and searched for contraband food items.

The NMC food delivery system was notoriously unreliable. Having made the near fatal error of creating a bureaucratically centralized system of food distribution in the first place, the government ensured its failure by introducing pricing policies that led to the worst possible outcomes. The NMC grain procurement system was based on pan-territorial (countrywide) and pan-seasonal (year-round) pricing. Both of these had negative effects. Pan-territorial pricing was justified on the egalitarian principle that grain farmers should not have differential incomes based on location. Its effect, however, was to introduce huge and costly distortions in the geographical distribution of food production. It meant that producers located near large population centers would no longer enjoy a price advantage owing to their lower transportation costs. There was no incentive to produce grains close to urban areas where there were concentrations of population and where transportation costs would be low. Nor was there a disincentive to produce grains in areas far removed from consumer populations, where transportation costs would be high. Nearby producers were, in effect, forced to subsidize the greater costs of those located at great distances from the major cities. The average cost of producing and delivering grain began to increase even as the government was seeking to lower food prices to reduce the cost of living for the growing population of urban industrial workers. The government found itself pursuing incompatible goals: there was no way to reconcile the idea of equal grain pricing across the country with the idea of wage cost containment in the urban industrial sector.

Because of the rigidity of the pan-territorial pricing system, areas of surplus seemed to exist alongside areas of deficits. Under more open market conditions, food prices will tend to rise slightly in food-deficit areas, encouraging delivery of grain to those places. Not only did pan-territorial pricing remove any incentive for grain farmers to seek the higher prices available in regions of scarcity, the law that created the NMC and forbade private transporters from entering grain markets made it illegal for individual farmers to respond to the higher prices that would prevail in grain deficit regions. Because the NMC held the farm-gate price and consumer price constant for all parts of the country, the system seemed to lack any flexibility to use the price mechanism to deal with regional variations in the food supply.

Year-round pricing had even worse effects in introducing costly inefficiencies into the country's food distribution system. Under open market conditions, most farmers tend to sell a portion of their grain during the harvest period, when their cash needs are relatively great, but hold back some fraction for the off-season, when supplies become scarce and prices rise. Although the open market pricing system did not operate perfectly, it did help assure that some portion of the nation's annual grain supply would be available year-round. Year-round pricing removed farmers' incentive to hold a portion of the crop back for the off-season, when prices would rise. Without this incentive, most farmers chose to sell their grain immediately after the harvest. The economic inefficiency of year-round pricing was catastrophic: it meant the NMC had to plan its physical capacity based on the procurement, processing, and distribution of grain during the peak period. The NMC installed a network of buying centers, purchased trucks, and constructed processing and storage centers that were fully utilized only during the two months or so of the harvest period and sat idle most of the year. The net result was an over-supply of grain during the harvest season and shortages for the nine or ten months between harvests. With year-round pricing, periods of glut alternated with periods of scarcity.

The NMC system of grain procurement also contributed to the authoritarian tendency in Tanzanian politics. The idea that a monolithic state bureaucracy could substitute itself for an indescribably complex system of private networks was fatally flawed from the outset. The most conspicuous feature of the system was its utter porosity, as parallel markets in grain products sprang up virtually overnight. Opportunities for parallel market entrepreneurs arose in the interstices between bureaucratic controls. Owing to the sheer impossibility of administering the economic life of millions of peasant producers spread across hundreds of thousands of miles of countryside, these were everywhere. The existence of spiraling parallel markets led the government to undertake greater and greater efforts to prevent farmers from evading price controls at the farm level. It also exerted greater efforts to prevent parallel market entrepreneurs from operating outside the system, and to prevent individual consumers from obtaining their grain staples from the parallel marketplace. However, since NMC officials were among those profiteering from the country's spiraling informal grain markets, it added to the atmosphere of disillusionment in the countryside. Rural Tanzanians listening on Radio Tanzania to President Nyerere's speeches about rural self-reliance were paying bribes to the NMC officials enforcing its monopoly over grain purchases.

Tanzanian officials defended the NMC system publicly on the basis that it was essential to protect less well-to-do Tanzanians from economic exploitation by a growing class of successful capitalist farmers. However, the real economic purpose of the system was to subsidize urban industrialization. By the late 1970s, nearly half the grain being purchased by the NMC was being delivered to the city of Dar es Salaam, where the majority of new industries were located.[21] Because of nationwide scarcities that created expensive parallel markets, urban consumers were rarely able to satisfy family needs at the official NMC prices. By the mid-1970s, the NMC came to exemplify all that had gone wrong with the Tanzanian development process. It had become a gargantuan, corrupt, hugely inefficient bureaucracy that conferred significant benefits only to the civil servants who administered it. It lowered prices to farmers, raised them to consumers, and delivered products of poor quality and unreliable availability to those who had to purchase food in the marketplace.

All these costs might have been worthwhile if the NMC had contributed to the country's industrial goals, its intended purpose. That did not occur either. NMC record keeping was so poor that no one has ever provided a definitive assessment of its balance sheet. But given its many inefficiencies, the only reasonable conclusion is that it imposed costs on the agricultural sector without providing any commensurate benefit elsewhere in the economy except to the rent-seeking bureaucrats who administered it. The NMC system also fed the growing levels of public cynicism about the true motives of the country's political elite. The economists' term for a regulatory system such as the NMC is deadweight loss, a concept that describes a bureaucracy that imposes costs on society without providing corresponding benefits.

Even that term does not begin to describe the extent of the economic damage. Since the NMC price controls had to be bureaucratically enforced, it provided vast opportunities for rent seeking. The real beneficiaries of the NMC system were the NMC employees themselves and members of the political elite who had preferred access to the NMC grain outlets. Government officials ranging from junior police officers who set up roadblocks on rural roads to district and regional commissioners could extract bribes from farmers and truckers seeking to evade the system. Bureaucratic rent seeking reached the height of economic absurdity when NMC officials used NMC vehicles to deliver stocks of grain to their associates in the parallel market. The NMC became one of Tanzania's most despised examples of the gap between the government's egalitarian ethos and the reality of an economic

system that transferred wealth upward from the poorest Tanzanians—
smallholder farmers—to corrupt government officials.

The failure of the NMC system was among the most important factors
accounting for the country's spiraling levels of corruption and political cynicism. While few Tanzanians doubted the sincerity of their president's philosophical commitment to social equality, many became cynical about their
country's economic system, viewing it as a kind of game in which the political
elite engineered pervasive scarcities of goods and services in order to benefit
personally from the profit-making opportunities these created. Evasion of the
NMC was systemic and ubiquitous. It is a measure of the magnitude of the
cost of the NMC system that, when the Nyerere government briefly agreed to
entertain a limited and ultimately unsuccessful negotiation with the IMF in
1979, IMF officials chose only two policy matters to negotiate. One was the
exchange rate and the second was the NMC.

The National Price Commission

In a last ditch effort to impose regulatory order on an economy that seemed
to be spiraling downward and out of control at an accelerating rate, the Tanzanian government decided to impose price controls on essential goods. The
logic of this decision was clear, if bizarre: in the Tanzanian political climate of
the early 1970s, the remedy for the shortcomings of central economic planning was an intensification of central economic planning. In early 1973, the
National Assembly passed a Regulation of Prices Act,[22] creating a National
Price Commission (NPC), which had a broad and unchallenged mandate to
set the prices of goods throughout the economy. By May that year, the NPC
had price control over more than 1,100 items. Tanzanian economists Joseph
Sembuja and S. M. H. Rugumisa have shown that practically none of these
items were ever available at the prices set by the price commission.[23]

Although the intention of the Price Control Act was to provide a measure
of protection for Tanzanian consumers, its effects were wholly perverse. It
drove an even larger proportion of day-to-day economic transactions into the
unregulated parallel marketplace where prices were already high due to the
elements of scarcity and risk. As part of a national income policy whose purpose was to foster greater equality among Tanzanians, the NPC's inability to
carry out an impossible mandate only seemed to accentuate the growing socioeconomic differences between Tanzanians who could afford to purchase

goods in informal markets and those who could not.[24] In the end, NPC seemed to represent one more vast bureaucracy that required financial support from the government. The principal beneficiaries were its own administrators, who extracted side payments from merchants who wished to evade the control system. The price controls on consumer goods made no discernible contribution to the economic model the government was pursuing.

Socialist Villagization

By the late 1960s, it had become all too clear that neither Nyerere's personal popularity nor the moral appeal of his social ideas was enough to enlist voluntary citizen compliance with the system. The government's efforts to impose the controls that were required to implement its multiyear economic plans were a conspicuous failure. The disjuncture between policy and reality had become painfully apparent to any Tanzanian who had to purchase a good or enter an interaction with a government official. In the cities and towns, the NPC would routinely post controlled prices for the necessities of daily life. However, its posted prices bore almost no relationship to what Tanzanians had to pay for goods they purchased on a regular basis. In the countryside, the official policy was that the NMC would purchase the most important food staples from farmers and then assume responsibility for retail sales. In the real economy, parallel markets handled much of the country's grain supply. And the real costs of grain transactions were governed less by officially posted prices than by the rent-seeking opportunities conferred by an overbearing bureaucracy.

Throughout this period, Tanzanian planners operated on an economic logic that was even more detached from reality than the pricing system. Many officials behaved as if the remedy for the failure of their economic controls was to heighten the level of economic control. According to this logic, the remedy for the NMC's failure to regiment rural behavior was an additional effort at regimentation. This logic was at the basis of Tanzania's adoption of the social experiment for which it has become best known in the annals of post-independence African history: the effort to collectivize the countryside by moving the rural population into socialist villages. This plan, also known as "ujamaa," called for the wholesale transformation of agricultural production throughout the Tanzanian rural areas. Once ujamaa was fully implemented, rural life would become an environment where collective land would be collectively farmed and the product of the village's socially owned farm would be collectively shared. Socialist villagization was first announced in early 1969 and implementation began almost immediately.

The ujamaa village program has been the subject of an encyclopedic volume of academic and journalistic interpretation.[25] The result is that there is no single aspect of the program, from the motivations of the leaders who called for its implementation to the reasons for its ultimate failure, that is undisputed. Supporters of the Nyerere ideal viewed the ujamaa village program as a reasonable attempt to implement his personal commitment to a classless rural society where the value of social justice would prevail over the values of profit and personal accumulation of wealth. Rural Tanzanians have been more inclined to describe the program as one more mechanism among many for imposing administrative regimentation over their production and marketing of agricultural goods.

By the end of 1969, Tanzania had formed approximately 800 socialist villages with a total population of approximately 250,000. By the end of 1974, there were approximately 5,000 socialist villages with a total village population of about 1.6 million, roughly 10 percent of the country's total population. As an indication of socialist progress, however, these numbers were misleading. The ujamaa village program classified the new villages into three stages of implementation: roughly, those where collective settlement had just begun, those where collective farming was underway but not yet sufficient to provide a majority of village income, and those which were more or less fully operational as socialist communities. Significantly, of the 5,000 villages enumerated during 1974, less than 400, with a total population of only about 120,000, had moved to the third stage, the point at which the villagers obtained the majority of their food and income from collective cultivation as opposed to their continuing involvement in individual or family farming. Although many Tanzanians resided in socialist villages, only a small proportion ever engaged in the socialist lifestyle anticipated by the president's plan.

A large portion of the extensive literature on the Nyerere period is devoted to an academic dialogue over the causes of the program's failure.[26] One was the tendency for the program to alienate a large portion of the Tanzanian peasantry. Many rural Tanzanians grew to fear government confiscation of traditionally held farmlands that had been in their families since time immemorial. The model of collective production to which Nyerere was committed required that rural Tanzanians should detach themselves from a relationship to the land that had deep ancestral origins. It required farmers to disconnect from a way of life that had evolved organically over many generations and abandon methods of cultivation they knew to be suitable for their particular local environment. Collective production required farmers to embrace a method of agricultural production that was unfamiliar, unproven, and singularly apt to fail when it came to the actual crop yields needed for survival. Social anthropologist Graham Thiele has stated the coercive aspect of the program with great persuasiveness.

> The period 1971–75 was for many people one of massive upheaval. They had been forcibly moved to a new site and had had to reorganize patterns of consumption and production in the context of the new location. . . . Of course, many households had experience of strategies for relocation, but the conditions under which these strategies were to be applied were quite exceptional. In the past, when homesteads had moved individually, resources outside the individual homestead could be used to facilitate the move. In this case, everyone was in the same predicament. Homesteads were forced into a kind of independence, which they had never experienced within natural economy, which was based upon kin and neighborly reciprocity.[27]

In the final analysis, the socialist villages program failed because the social model of cultivation favored by the president was at fundamental odds with the family-based pattern of agricultural production with which rural Tanzanians were familiar.[28]

Rural Tanzanians also became resentful of the paternalistic aspect of the collective villagization program, the implication that central government administrators knew best how, where, and under what circumstances they should cultivate their crops. Tanzanian farmers were mistrustful of the officials charged to implement the program, whom they perceived as motivated by their own bureaucratic and career interests. Rural sociologist Louise Fortmann has stated this aspect of the program as follows: "Bureaucrats, faced with people whom they may look down on class and/or tribal grounds and who present technically incomplete or unfeasible proposals, are likely not to be sympathetic. The system rewards responses to orders from above. There is no one whose job it is to listen to and advocate for the peasantry. Bureaucrats, in addition to the national agenda, have their own career agendas to look out for."[29] Sheer administrative blunder also contributed to the failure of the program. In some instances, rural administrators moved families from their farms between planting and harvesting seasons. In others, they moved families from areas suitable for crops with which they were familiar to districts that required a different crop palette and different production techniques.

The cumulative weight of excessive taxation, unrealistic price controls, political regimentation, administrative blunders, and outright corruption was more than Tanzania's rural economy could bear. It declined precipitously. Key export crops stagnated and the production of basic food staples fell further and further behind the country's needs. The contrast with the immediate post-independence period was painful. In the early 1960s, Tanzania had enjoyed one of the highest rates of grain production in all of sub-Saharan Africa and was becoming a major regional exporter of food grains. Only a decade later, it had become heavily dependent on food aid supplied by the international donor community.

This would all be a distant and mostly forgotten historical episode were it not for the fact that memories of the experiment in socialist agriculture continue to inform the relationship between the Tanzanian government and small farmers. The climate of mistrust fostered by that program persists today. Once farmers come to perceive their relationship to the state in adversarial terms, they do not quickly abandon that attitude simply because there is a new president in power or a new set of economic policies in place. To this day, rural Tanzanians cite the ujamaa villages program as an example of the Nyerere government's willingness to use coercive means to bring about the president's social ideas. And although they appreciate the greater degree of political freedom that came about with the restoration of multipartyism in 1992, there remains an element of watchfulness in the way they view the central government. Many rural Tanzanians continue to harbor the view, which originated during the ujamaa experiment, that neither their central government nor its local officials have their best interests at heart. Their long-standing feelings of mistrust toward authority are kept alive and even reinforced by their awareness that present programs of vital interest to them, such as water provision, road repair, or improvement of local schools and clinics, tend to be degraded by bureaucratic corruption.

The Causes of Industrial Failure

The heavy burden of taxes and controls on rural farmers might have been justified if the benefits flowing to the new industries enabled them to develop as the planners had intended—namely, to the point where they could provide economic benefits to the broader society. Tanzania's infant industries, however, never reached adolescence, much less full maturity. They remained a more or less permanent burden on the government. The infant industries never developed to the point where they could survive without subsidies, tax transfers and trade protection. Both major sectors stagnated disastrously: agriculture, because it was subjected to levels of taxation and regimentation that made it all but impossible for farmers to survive, and industries, because the very premise of protected industrialization seemed to lack economic feasibility.

The failure of the ISI model has preoccupied countless economists seeking to explain its generic weaknesses.[30] There are challenging questions that cry out for persuasive answers. Was the infant industry model fatally flawed from the outset? Could the ISI strategy have succeeded if governments implemented it in a more prudent manner? Why did prudent implementation elude all but a tiny number of countries? Why does the ISI appear to have been more successful as a vehicle for industrialization in some regions of the world than in others?[31] A case study of a single country cannot provide final answers to these global questions. However, it can offer a suggestive approach.

Some of the factors that contributed to Tanzania's industrial failure were specific to Tanzania and have little carryover value in explaining other cases of failed industrialization. One was Tanzania's abortive and costly effort to use its emerging industries to engage in urban-based agricultural production. During 1973 and 1974, Tanzanian political leaders interpreted their country's declining agricultural production as a function of rural drought conditions rather than poor policy choices. Other regions of Africa such as the Sahel and Ethiopia were experiencing severe drought during this period and it seemed only natural to conclude that Tanzania's agricultural difficulties were a by-product of the same climate patterns that were producing food shortages elsewhere. The solution was to find ways for urban populations to supply themselves with food crops until the agricultural sector could recover from the effects of drought. The cornerstone of the government effort to do so was a program called the Agriculture Is a Matter of Life or Death Campaign ("Kilimo ni jambo la kufa na kupona"), which began in 1975. The idea was to have government, industrial, and other enterprises engage in agricultural production.

The representatives of donor organizations had told government officials on a number of occasions that the state industrial enterprises had an installed capacity far in excess of the country's demand for their goods. However, this was by way of a warning about the shortcomings in the planning process. Instead, some government officials concluded that the country's industries had unused capacity that they could direct toward other economic activities such as agriculture. Textile factories, breweries, cigarette and soft drink plants, shoe factories, and other parastatal institutions such as TANESCO (the electricity supply company) and the University of Dar es Salaam were assigned plots of land, sometimes amounting to hundreds of acres, and instructed to use these for agricultural purposes. The idea was that, at least one day a week, each of these government entities would allocate its available resources, such as its transportation equipment and labor force, to engage in farming activity. Industrial and utilities workers, civil servants from a range of public agencies, and university professors found themselves spending a portion of their time engaged in farming. Until the drought was over, the city could supply itself, and the rural areas would revert to a subsistence survival strategy.

The Agriculture as Life or Death Campaign was a costly policy failure. It was wholly impractical, in a short time, to reconfigure the state-owned enterprises (SOEs) in such a way that their production capacities could be efficiently divided between industrial and farming activities. Nor was it possible to develop an accounting methodology that allocated costs between industrial and agricultural production. The costs of the urban farms including labor, energy, and equipment were absorbed in the core activities of their parent industrial enterprises. If a truck or other expensive piece of equipment failed, its replacement cost was borne by the parent SOE. SOEs that were already incurring such large deficits that they needed huge budget subsidies simply to operate on a narrow industrial basis now found that they were exhausting their physical inputs and budgeted allocations for wages, capital equipment, energy, and other inputs at an even more rapid rate. The SOEs' labor costs were especially prone to upward pressures as workers who might have been furloughed because there were not enough inputs for industrial purposes now continued on the workforce to be engaged on the farming side of a firm's activities. The industrial enterprises were producing a certain amount of food, but at a price no one could even begin to calculate.

The industrial enterprises also lacked any provision for marketing the agricultural goods they produced on their farms. Officially, the NMC had jurisdiction over procurement, processing, and marketing food staples. But the NMC was basically set up to acquire its supply of grains from small farmers in the countryside. It would have seemed bizarre, even by the NMC's lax bureaucratic standards, to locate grain procurement centers next to the business offices of cigarette and soft drink factories. Nor was the NMC organizationally adapted to procure its supply of agricultural commodities from such large state entities as the electricity company or the Friendship Textile Factory. Similarly, the SOEs had no accounting mechanism that would enable them to receive and record payments from the NMC for such limited amounts of agricultural commodities as they might hand over. Given the improvised nature of the Agriculture as Life or Death Campaign, it is surprising that any of the food these firms produced made its way into the larger marketplace; much either passed into the hands of the individual workers who were growing it or spoiled for lack of an outlet that could distribute it to the broader public. The impact on the industrial sector was decidedly negative: the SOEs tended to exhaust their capital stock and increase their wage bill even more rapidly than if they had been allowed to remain purely industrial enterprises.

The government abandoned the Agriculture as Life or Death Campaign within a year or two, but not before it had worsened the already poor condition of a number of the country's industrial SOEs. Later, some were to argue that the industrial SOEs might have been on a trajectory toward viability had it not been for the government's ill-considered decision to involve them in agricultural production. This is doubtful. Even without the Agriculture as Life or Death Campaign, Tanzania's industrial SOEs had little chance of economic success. Most were already practically bankrupt well before the Life or Death Campaign began, and the campaign ended in a very short time, but not before university professors and industrial managers had the opportunity to discover first-hand how onerous agricultural labor can be.

The ISI industrial strategy has failed in country after country that has attempted it. Even countries where conditions were more auspicious have largely abandoned it.[32] Although country-specific factors are a part of the story of the failure of the Tanzanian implementation of ISI, the most theoretically compelling explanation for Tanzania's industrial failure has to do with the causal factors it shared with all those other countries that sought—and failed—to attain rapid industrialization through the ISI model. Tanzania's industries exhibited three troublesome features that are generically inherent in the ISI approach: (1) failure to solve the problem of moral hazard; (2) overreliance on heavily subsidized capital; and (3) the overcapacity problem.

Taken together, these global factors strongly suggest that the centrally planned ISI industries had very little chance of ever succeeding.

Moral Hazard

An ISI economy is inherently prone to moral hazard and one of the most basic reasons for the failure of Tanzania's ISI firms was the government failure to address this problem. *Moral hazard* is the term economists use to describe an economic environment in which there is decentralized authority to incur expenditures from a pool of funds that is someone else's responsibility to provide. In Tanzania, those who had authority to spend funds were the payroll officers, human resource managers, marketing strategists and contracting officials of the new industries. The central pool of funds was the Tanzanian Treasury, the government's tax revenues. There seemed to be legions of industrial administrators entrusted with the authority to spend taxpayer monies. The list began with the managers of the new industries who were very aware that the deficits that arose from their expenditures on plant, equipment, salaries, and subcontracts with suppliers would have to be absorbed by the central government. The list further included the officials responsible for hiring and training the industrial workers. Since the government was a guarantor of the industrial loans, the loan officers at the banks that advanced the funds were aware that any defaulted loans would become a central government responsibility, to be funded as an expenditure item in the government's annual budget. The owners of business firms that provided services to the new industries also knew that the expenses on the contracts they signed would have to be borne by the Tanzanian taxpayer.

Since the Tanzanian government was the final guarantor of loans, it seemed that no one had the responsibility to behave in a financially prudent manner: spending the government's money had become a culture. This culture was gravely reflected in the amount of money the government had to spend annually to fund SOE indebtedness. By the mid-1980s, the service on public debt, which consisted almost entirely of the debts of the SOEs, was absorbing 25 percent or more of the government's budget. That figure continued to escalate and during the early 1990s, on the eve of divestiture of the SOEs, was well over 30 percent of the government budget.[33] This figure provides a measurement of the extent to which Tanzania's centrally planned industrial strategy had become an exercise in economic failure: deficits of that magnitude suggested that the ISI firms had little prospect of ever operating on a profitable basis.

The challenging question about Tanzania's attempt to implement its economic model was not whether it might ever succeed but why it was allowed to continue accumulating such large deficits for so long. The answer to that question is that the managerial elite that incurred such large costs was not constrained by a system that limited the authority to spend with an element of accountability for the funds that were being spent. Tanzania's industrial managers had an interest in their authority to incur indebtedness and there did not appear to be any institutional locus in the government with a countervailing responsibility to hold them accountable for their expenditures. This was a moral hazard in an extreme form, and, absent any other explanatory variable, it alone provides a powerful explanation for why Tanzania's factories never operated with a sufficient degree of efficiency to recover even a small fraction of their operating costs.

The concept of moral hazard does not depend upon an assumption of rent-seeking behavior to provide it with explanatory power. It arises whenever the responsibility for risk appraisal is removed from the relationship between lender and borrower and when borrowers and lenders alike know that the financial costs of their mistakes will be absorbed by a third party. In Tanzania, however, rent seeking aggravated the moral hazard problem. It pervaded the lending process that required the banks to make large loans to industries that, at best, had little chance of ever being able to repay them. There is no algorithm that makes it possible to quantify the bad loans that arose because of the absence of risk assessment from those that took place because they provided rich opportunities for side payments to the political associates enabling the system. Rent seeking, in other words, existed everywhere in the Tanzanian bureaucracy, both outside and inside the system of financing industries. However, it was not long before the system of bank lending to industrial firms became an important addition to the inventory of rent-seeking possibilities.

Later, during the period of economic reform, the government of Tanzania sought to address the problem of moral hazard by creating a financial entity called the Loans and Assets Realization Trust (LART). The purpose of the LART, which Chapter 6 discusses more fully, was to participate in the divestiture process by recovering as much as possible of the government funds that were lent to the SOEs. The question that arose in the midst of that process was whether it might not be easier for the government to forgive that accumulated debt, since it was debt that one set of state-owned entities, the SOEs, owed to another, the nationalized banks. Instead, the government made a vigorous effort to recover the taxpayer funds it had squandered on the industrial enterprises. The answer to this question is that the LART's purpose was not narrowly economic. Its purpose was to establish the principle that the mistakes that arise from irresponsible arrangements, even well intended ones, have lasting consequences. One of the objectives of an economic reform program is to create a normative environment that makes it less likely for a government to repeat policies prone to moral hazard.

Capital Intensiveness

The second generic explanation for the failure of Tanzania's ISI industries was their tendency toward capital intensiveness. The Tanzanian factory system was perverse from an economic standpoint: whereas the factories should have been designed with systems of production that were intensive in their use of labor, which Tanzania had in abundance, or land, which was also abundant, they were constructed with technology that was minimalist in its use of both factors.[34] The difficulty that arises in the reliance on capital-intensive production is that, once it is in place, it is next-to-impossible to disengage.[35] The challenge in making a transition from capital intensiveness to labor intensiveness is overwhelming. At the very least, it would have required a wholesale structural reconfiguration in the way economic planners designed the factories. It might have required a different set of industries altogether.

The extreme overvaluation of Tanzania's currency was just one mechanism among several that encouraged the use of capital-intensive technologies. The ISI firms also enjoyed the opportunity to borrow operating funds without competition from other sectors and at artificially low, governmentally specified interest rates, and for indefinite periods. Although Tanzania had a shortage of investible capital, its industrial managers were systematically encouraged to behave as if industrial capital were in abundant supply. They did so with alacrity, and in factory after factory they purchased capital-intensive production technology for everything from fabrics and clothing to automobile tires. Tanzania's economic contradiction was that of countless other developing countries during that period: gleaming factories with the most advanced production technologies situated in urban settings that also featured large numbers of unemployed and underemployed persons.

For many African countries, the tendency to rely on capital-intensive technology has remained an unexplained departure from one of the major admonitions of the development economists, many of whom, including W. Arthur Lewis, had insisted that developing countries enjoyed an economic advantage in their abundant supply of low-cost labor.[36] The answer to this puzzling tendency is that at a certain point, the pattern of planned industrialization in countries such as Tanzania was driven less and less by the economic theories of its intellectual pioneers and more and more by the rent-seeking opportunities it conferred. Among the many rent-seeking opportunities available, few exceeded the monetary gains from preferred access to hard currency. The authority to construct, equip, and operate a new factory carried almost unlimited access to a country's foreign exchange reserves. Individuals who sought to use capital sparingly, and thereby lowered their hard currency withdrawals from the Central Bank, would have been forgoing one of the most lucrative side benefits of the ISI system.

This tendency provides an answer to the otherwise puzzling question: why did so many African countries such as Tanzania choose a common set of industries and a common industrial format to launch industrialization? The first part of the answer is that since they all enjoyed capital subsidies, there was no incentive to plan their industrial evolution based on other factors of production. The operative part of the answer, however, is that capital intensiveness conferred far greater rent-seeking opportunities than labor intensiveness would ever have done. As it actually proceeded, Tanzania's pattern of planned industrialization was not only a fundamental departure from Nyerere's Fabian vision; it was also a departure from the ideas of the economists who first devised the strategy.

Overcapacity

The combination of moral hazard and heavily subsidized capital created a systemic tendency to over-invest in capital goods. Each of Tanzania's industrial sectors was prone to an uncontrolled tendency toward over-investment, as each factory manager seemed to install a manufacturing capability without regard to what was being done elsewhere in that sector or others. Some over-investment in capital goods may also have grown out of the economic planners' conviction that as consumer demand began to grow, the machinery they purchased would be used to its installed capacity. However, the tendency to over-invest in capital goods was principally a function of the combination of moral hazard and the opportunity to provide rent-seeking opportunities for oneself and one's political cronies. Owing to this pressure, the installed capacity in the Tanzanian factory system far exceeded any foreseeable trend in consumer demand. Since it was never really a product of consumer purchasing power or consumer needs, most of the country's industrial capacity remained unutilized. Many factories operated at a fraction of their installed capacity. Others closed altogether.

Since the base cost of a piece of industrial machinery is the same whether it is used to its full productive capability or not, the cost per produced unit of that capital good when it is not used to its full capacity is high and irreducible.[37] All too often, the inefficiency of African industries such as those in Tanzania has been blamed on unskilled management or the fact that the labor force has not yet been fully acculturated in the discipline of an industrial lifestyle. These problems, while pertinent, could be remedied with additional experience and training. The problem of inefficiency caused by the high cost of capital per unit of good actually produced was less amenable to managerial intervention.

Under-utilization of installed capacity quickly became the dominant characteristic of Tanzania's import-substituting industries. Dean E. McHenry, Jr., has shown that in the textile industry, which was the first of the new industries and which had been intended as the showcase for Tanzania's industrial future, capacity utilization had fallen to about 25 percent by the early 1980s. The situation in other industries was even worse. In the shoe industry, capacity utilization plummeted, from about 60 percent in 1979/80 to 10 percent in 1986/87. The economic effects were catastrophic. McHenry states the losses as follows: "The underutilization of capacity meant billions of shillings in losses and many consequent problems. Workers could not be paid, resulting in layoffs; electric bills could not be paid, resulting in power cuts; and the government sales tax and excise duty could not be paid, resulting in seized property."[38] The net financial losses seemed to compound one another, as the debts of one parastatal enterprise inevitably became a source of operating deficits in others. This happened, for example, when the unpaid electricity and water bills of the state's textile, shoe, and paper companies became operating losses in the state-owned utility firms. The social effects were even more dismal. Poorer Tanzanians wore threadbare hand-me-down clothing and shoes fashioned from discarded automobile tires even while their government continued to pour billions of shillings into state-owned textile and shoe companies.

In the end, each of these problems contributed to the failure of the state-owned firms. By the mid-1970s, the economy was in a precarious condition. Export agriculture had declined because of price suppression through the marketing board system and the over-valuation tax; the food staples sector of the economy had declined because of the inefficiencies and corruption of the NMC marketing system; and the state industries were suffering from a hard currency scarcity that made it all but impossible to acquire inputs. Industry, like agriculture, had begun to suffer from acute capital starvation. Lacking funds for spare parts, replacement machinery, or vital inputs, factories became derelict. On the eve of divestiture in the early 1990s, many of the ISI factories had become all but abandoned buildings where token staff maintained a physical presence for security purposes. Others were operational but producing low volumes of such poor quality products that Tanzanian consumers largely shunned them. Tanzanian wearing apparel and beer became the equivalent of the East German Trabant, embarrassing objects of street humor and tangible symbols of industrial failure. Tanzania's real economy consisted of parallel markets; the day-to-day operation of the government depended on donor generosity.

Tanzania's period of extreme economic misery began in the summer of 1974 when, for the first time, famine conditions began to appear in several regions. Many rural families, facing famine, managed to make their way into the cities, where they became part of a growing homeless population, a visible human symbol of failed economic policies. The downward spiral seemed only to continue during the remainder of that decade. It is not possible to pinpoint the exact moment at which Tanzania's economy reached its bottom point. By general estimates, however, Tanzania's worst economic moment was the period during and after the Tanzania-Uganda War. This took place between early November 1978, when Idi Amin occupied a 700 square mile portion of Tanzania south of the established boundary, and April 1979, when the Tanzanian army was able to occupy the twin Ugandan cities of Entebbe and Kampala and oust Amin.[39]

Tanzania won a military victory, but at horrific economic cost. Among other burdens imposed by the war, Tanzania had to absorb the costs of expanding its army from about 40,000 to 100,000 soldiers by mobilizing various reserve forces including a citizens' militia. All these soldiers needed to be equipped and transported from the eastern areas of the country where the larger military bases were located to the northwestern region of the country north of the Kagera River where the war was being fought. The war lasted approximately five months; diplomatic observers have estimated its direct financial cost at about $1 million per day, or approximately $150 million. A Tanzanian economist, taking into account the indirect costs of the war, has estimated its total cost as $500 million.[40] The additional costs included lost agricultural production, lasting damage to infrastructure, and further disruption of other parts of the civilian economy. To transport its military units the government commandeered much of the country's transportation system including the central railroad line, which runs from Dar es Salaam through Tabora to Mwanza. The government also confiscated large numbers of private trucks and buses few of which were ever returned to their civilian owners. By the time the war ended, the transportation infrastructure in the northern half of the country, where the most productive sectors of the Tanzania's agricultural economy are located, barely operated.

No portion of the economy was untouched by the war effort: administrative personnel and even office supplies were drawn off to sustain it. A large proportion of the war's cost was in the form of foreign exchange and represented the import of armored vehicles, fuel supplies, weapons, munitions, and the countless items needed to provision an army, make it mobile, and equip it to fight. Since military requirements had to be given absolute priority over all other imports, the war temporarily froze what remained of the country's ability to purchase production inputs for the agricultural and industrial sectors. That the war began during the country's principal harvest season, when many of major crops were awaiting harvest and transportation from growing areas in the north-central and western regions, made matters even worse.

When the war ended, many of the soldiers were quickly de-mobilized. Some took their weapons with them. Returning to an economy that was in tatters and where there was almost no employment opportunity available, some turned to crime. Dar es Salaam began to experience a wave of armed robberies.

Chapter 4

The Path to Economic Reform
I: The Aid Debate

Despite desperate economic conditions, Tanzania did not initiate an economic reform program until summer 1986, nearly seven years after the end of the Ugandan War. If the famine conditions that prevailed during summer and fall 1974 are taken as Tanzania's low point, twelve years elapsed before the 1986 IMF agreement, which most observers view as the beginning of the transition to a market economy.[1] During all that time, Tanzania managed to limp along with only minor changes in its policies: the pattern of poor policy choices leading to poor economic conditions persisted. The seemingly inexplicable delay between low point and economic reform raises an obvious question. How could a country in such dire economic straits possibly have continued so long without changing the economic framework that had brought it to that predicament?

Part of the answer has to do with the assumption that economic reform begins at a specific moment. The idea that Tanzania's economic history can be bifurcated into a pre-reform period ending with Ali Hassan Mwinyi's election in fall 1985 and a reform period beginning after he took office in 1986 does not convey the full picture. Internal voices for economic reform had always been present in Tanzania. Despite President Nyerere's towering stature, the CCM never united behind his socialist approach to development. Indeed, a treason trial that took place during 1969 and 1970 revealed that the party had always harbored a moderate faction that favored a more pragmatic approach to economic management.[2] The 1974 agricultural crisis, which had led to pockets of famine in the countryside, a growing problem of homeless refugees in the city of Dar es Salaam, and the crushing burden of financing food imports at a time when world grain prices were at a peak, provided a brief window of opportunity for early reformers to exert some influence over government policy.

The Dar es Salaam Spring, 1975–1976

The modest changes reformers brought about have become known as the Dar es Salaam Spring. The reason for this terminology, which resonates with the better-known Prague Spring of 1968, is that the window for economic reform opened and closed quickly. Within a year, the government's determination to continue the state-driven economic system overshadowed the reforms that came about in spring and summer 1975. The early reformers' first successes had to do with retail trade. Arguing that even socialist governments do not need to manage small businesses, the reformers persuaded the government to denationalize a number of retail businesses, such as stationery and bookstores, butcher shops, and petrol stations. The immediate result was dramatic. Despite the scarcity of foreign exchange, the partial liberalization of the retail sector resulted in an improved availability of consumer goods. For a brief moment, there was an almost festive atmosphere as Tanzanians found it possible to purchase a range of consumer goods, including gasoline and food items that had been unavailable or obtainable only in expensive parallel markets.

The early reformers focused their principal attention on the agricultural sector. To stimulate agricultural production, they persuaded the government to increase agricultural prices, nearly doubling the NMC producer prices for such critical staples as maize, rice, and wheat. Although there was no change in NMC authority to set prices or act as the sole procurement and distribution mechanism for major crops, the price increases alone yielded positive results. They increased the supply of staple grains and helped reduce the country's dependence on food aid and grain imports.

The improvement in producer prices, however, did very little to alleviate the underlying atmosphere of insecurity and fear caused by the government's decision to collectivize the agricultural sector and its open use of coercion to do so. The use of military force in Operations Dodoma and Kigoma was widely known throughout the Tanzanian countryside, where there was widespread concern that the government might continue to use force to remove rural families from their traditional homes and farms. As one close observer noted, "Anyone who was unwilling to be located [in a socialist village] was 'persuaded' to do so by the army or militia."[3] The reformers believed that it was essential to persuade Tanzanian farmers that the use of force in moving them into villages would end and that the government would allow farmers to resume their customary methods of production.

The early reformers had a partial success on this matter as well. They persuaded the government to pass legislation that redefined the social goal of the ujamaa villages. The new law, the Villages and Ujamaa Villages Act of 1975 (hereafter, Villages Act),[4] formalized publicly what had already begun to take place informally in practice: backing off from the government's insistence that collective production was the goal of the village community. The Villages Act created village assemblies and village councils and allowed these bodies to assume responsibility for social and economic aspects of village life. This empowered village-level authorities, if they so chose, not to push forward with collectivized agricultural production. The ambient conversations surrounding the new law compared the new village environment with the Israeli Moshav settlements, where a communal entity such as a village would own the land but individual family units would engage in production. The government's public terminology for the new approach was *bega kwa bega* (shoulder to shoulder), meaning that the central government would allow family farming even in a village officially designated socialist.

The discussions that preceded the passage of this law took place in the National Executive Committee of the governing party, a relatively closed group with fewer than fifty members. It is, possible, however, to infer their content from conversations with officials close to the process. All the available interpretations point toward the buildup of political pressures for economic reform. No one doubts that the president found it personally difficult to abandon his most cherished ideal, full collectivization of the Tanzanian countryside, and there is no single explanation for his agreement to do so. One possibility was that Nyerere had been embarrassed by the spectacle of famine conditions in a formerly self-sufficient agricultural country and by the need to enter global markets at a time when world prices for grains had reached all-time highs because of soaring demand for imports in Russia and China. In traveling abroad to make appeals for food aid, the president suffered the discomfort of having to entertain critical questions about his country's agricultural policies.

The more plausible explanation for the change is that the president and his advisors had become concerned about rural resistance to the collectivization program. One of his most devoted regional commissioners, Andrew Wilbert Klerruu, was assassinated on Christmas Day 1971, as he was pursuing the process of collectivizing farmland in the Ismani District of Iringa Region. The accused person was a Muslim farmer, Saidi Abdallah Mwamwindi. Klerruu had just used his powers as a regional commissioner to confiscate the larger part of Mwamwindi's farm as part of a newly formed collective village. Mwamwindi's murder trial, which lasted throughout 1972 and was appealed in early 1973, became a highly publicized event with almost daily reporting in the national press and frequent public comments by the highest-ranking members of the governing party. Even in a political context, with the government-controlled media portraying the slain commissioner as a socialist martyr, the government could not conceal Mwamwindi's popularity as a symbol of local resistance to an unpopular program. Some Tanzanians compared Mwamwindi to legendary local resistance leader Chief Mkwawa, who had led an uprising against German colonialism in the late nineteenth century.

Mwamwindi's trial and execution for the murder, which took place in December 1973, was a tipping point: it marked the end of serious efforts at collectivization. Popular support for Mwamwindi, combined with the wave of revulsion against the excesses of Operations Dodoma and Kigoma, seemed to convince government officials that they were facing a groundswell of rural opposition. Some were fearful that the resistance to ujamaa that manifested itself so violently in Ismani District might spread to other rural areas. The image of a socialist government facing a popular resistance movement from the very segment of society its policies claimed to benefit was impossible to contemplate. Rather than risk further damage to Tanzania's image as a benevolent socialist society, Nyerere relented. The Villages Act was an attempt at a face-saving compromise with the early reformers. It enabled the Nyerere group to maintain the nomenclature of socialist villages and gain a measure of legal status for the new villages even while backing away from the collective ideals that had been the core purpose of the program. At the same time, it enabled the reformers to set aside collectivization and reestablish the principle of family farming.

As a law intended to address an immediate crisis, the Villages Act did not resolve the most difficult questions. Under the Act, village authorities had responsibility for year-to-year land allocations. Some used this authority to shift families from one year to the next. This gave rise to concerns about political favoritism and insecurities over land entitlements. Since the Villages

Act did not permit families to return to their traditional farmlands, painful questions were unanswered. Would families that had been "persuaded" to move onto collective farms now be free to return to their traditional homes? Would the previous occupants of a farm area that had been taken for an ujamaa settlement now have permission to return and reclaim their land? Whose rights would take precedence, those of the traditional occupants or the newly settled ujamaa families? These questions continue to create an atmosphere of insecurity about the legal basis of land entitlements in parts of rural Tanzania.

The Dar es Salaam Spring lasted only about a year, and the return to family-based farming was the last of the early reformers' temporary successes. After that, the governing party's anti-reform elements reasserted political control both within the government and over the organization of economic life in the countryside. Political repression in the rural areas intensified. Some members of the Nyerere government had begun to perceive the country's agricultural marketing cooperatives as gathering points for rural resistance. In May 1976, the prime minister, acting on Nyerere's behalf, issued an executive order dissolving and banning these organizations. Professor Sam Maghimbi, one of Tanzania's leading scholars of this subject, has described Nyerere's edict as follows.

> On 14th May 1976 all primary [marketing] cooperatives were abolished by the government. Their crop marketing functions were taken over by communal villages. At the same time cooperative unions were also abolished and their functions were taken over by parastatal crop authorities, which had to buy crops directly from villages. The abolished cooperative unions never bought crops directly from peasants, but through primary cooperatives. The other services which were rendered by the abolished cooperatives, such as wholesale and retail trade, were taken over by state owned companies, such as the Regional Trading Companies and District Development Corporations.[5]

The abolition of the producer cooperative societies, which Nyerere later acknowledged as the worst mistake of his presidency, was an unmistakable signal that the Tanzanian government, though prepared to forgo full collectivization, was not prepared to relax control over the agricultural economy any farther. It also showed that, although there were reform pressures within the government, the regime conservatives were dominant.

For rural Tanzanians, the 1976 decision marked another low point of the Nyerere regime. The irony was that the Villages Act, intended as a piece of reform legislation, had also paved the way for the assertion of central government control of local villages. The stated purpose of the law was to lay out a political format for agricultural villages, including creation of a Village Assembly and election of a Village Council. The existence of these bodies made it possible for the village to register as a legal entity. Once that took place, the village could conduct business on behalf of its members: it could contract loans, make purchases of agricultural inputs, and sell crops. Previously, villages in Tanzania, though they were the residential locus of a majority of the country's population, had not had a legal standing that permitted them to act on behalf of residents. The principal legal entities were the primary producer cooperatives, which had legal standing under cooperative laws that had been in place since colonial times. When the village became a legal entity, the government could argue that the crop-marketing cooperatives were redundant.

The government justification for the new system of village government, which empowered village councils at the expense of the crop-marketing cooperatives, had to do with allegations about organizational difficulties in the cooperatives. The government alleged that the marketing cooperatives were prone to financial misbehavior that was costly to their members. It would be naïve to believe that Tanzania's cooperative societies were perfect organizations: rural cooperatives everywhere are notoriously prone to principal-agent difficulties. Problems of administrative and budgetary mismanagement were as common in Tanzania as elsewhere. Government officials used these problems as the basis for their decision to ban the crop-marketing cooperatives, arguing that the village councils, which would operate under the benevolent oversight of the governing party, would be an improvement. The kindest interpretation of the 1976 decision to ban the cooperative societies is that it was an ill-considered reassertion of the government commitment to a socialist economy. The least kind interpretation is that it amounted to retribution for the peasant farmers' nearly universal rejection of collectivized agriculture.

The dissolution of the marketing cooperatives, however, only deepened the mood of estrangement between the Tanzanian government and its rural population. No matter how many organizational difficulties the cooperatives may have had, they had grown organically out of the needs and interests of smallholder farmers. Local farmers had created and developed the societies by contributing a portion of their earnings to fund the construction and staffing of cooperative facilities. Many cooperative societies had historical roots that dated to early colonial times and several had obtained official registration generations earlier. They were also hugely important as social institutions at which village members gathered for important events, such as weddings, holidays, and village festivals. The members' periodic election of their management boards and the annual meetings at which these officials reported back to their members were an expression of village-level democracy that a remote government in Dar es Salaam could never replicate. Rural Tanzanians considered them infinitely superior to the chaotic and unfamiliar pattern that followed. Like cooperative organizations everywhere, they arose out of the villagers' need to have some sort of organizational protection in their relations with the wider marketplace and especially with the merchants and companies that bought their crops. They represented an invaluable heritage of skills and experience; their records, accounting, and payment systems were a repository of the agricultural history of the families that belonged.

By banning the primary cooperatives, the government accomplished its signal of resolve about the maintenance of statist controls, but at a huge cost. The newly formed state crop authorities referred to by Maghimbi were unable to perform the important functions their predecessors had carried out, whether crop procurement and marketing or provision of inputs and credit. The government officials appointed to administer the cooperative facilities were often neglectful in their treatment of cooperative records, many of which were lost, discarded, or destroyed. When the government assumed control of the cooperative societies, it confiscated their cash reserves and took possession of their physical assets, including vehicles, office equipment, and processing machinery. Several government-appointed trustees absconded with cooperative funds.

As civil servants of the central government, the government's administrators lacked any direct interest in how well the farmers under their jurisdiction performed. In addition, they lacked the skills of the cooperatives' personnel, such as the accountants and equipment managers, many of whom left to take positions elsewhere either in Tanzania or overseas. The loss of cash reserves and the loss of financial accounts meant that many farmers went unpaid for crops they had already delivered to the cooperative societies. Several of the more enterprising regional societies had also developed secondary businesses, such as hotels, restaurants, and transportation companies, to provide employment opportunity and additional income for their members. The government closed those businesses as well and confiscated their assets.

The effects of banning the cooperative societies have been long-lasting.

One was the loss of the vital element of trust between the government and the rural population. To this day, the government's efforts to regain that trust have had only limited success. Despite the passage of a series of laws intended to re-create a favorable legal and political environment for traditional cooperatives,[6] the government has not had the financial resources to indemnify the cooperatives for the losses they suffered when the government took over their facilities. There are unresolved legal issues about land rights. Who has occupancy rights to village land? Do the original villagers, whose lands were taken to make way for the socialist settlements, have priority over the recently settled families and their descendants, most of whom are now second- and third-generation occupants? Some of the most long-lasting effects have been economic: insecurity over land rights combined with the difficulty of reassembling the producer cooperatives slowed efforts to boost crop production. The long-term economic effects have been especially severe in the export crop areas where faltering production levels have continued to deprive the government of badly needed foreign exchange and tax revenue. The international marketplace for primary agricultural commodities is unforgiving: once a country has forfeited its share of an international market, other countries are certain to take advantage.

The economic crisis that began in summer 1974 induced the Tanzanian government to accept the modest reforms of the Dar es Salaam Spring but only insofar as these did not compromise its commitment to state-led industrialization. The reassertion of economic controls that followed the Dar es Salaam Spring revealed the perverse logic that sometimes sets in when an economic strategy is failing. Those with a stake in a program profess to believe that the remedy for its shortcomings is to intensify their efforts, as if the reason for policy failure were an insufficient pursuit of the policy. This is exactly what happened in Tanzania. The academic proponents of the ISI strategy had always seen it as a multistage process. The first stage would consist of building consumer goods industries that could supply the usual items, such as beer, cigarettes, soft drinks, and clothing. A second stage focused on production of industrial goods would follow in due course. As the consumer goods industries became more and more self-sufficient, their workers and managers gained in skills, and the society gained in its overall capacity to build and manage an industrial sector, attention and resources could shift to intermediate and capital goods industries that demanded a greater degree of investment and engineering precision. The development economists were clear in their insistence that a country should not move forward to the second stage until it met these preconditions. Tanzanian leaders held a different view. As if to demonstrate their unflagging commitment to ISI, they decided in 1976 to move on to the second stage, which they called the basic industries strategy.

The purpose of the basic industries strategy was to expand the scope of the industrial sector beyond the production of consumer goods into the manufacturing of intermediate and capital goods such as irrigation pumps, agricultural implements, and transportation equipment. Some planners asserted that Tanzania could fund this augmentation of the ISI approach from the hard currency earnings it was receiving because of the mid-1970s global boom in coffee prices. The chances of this happening were nil. The idea that a temporary increment of foreign exchange earnings could be utilized to finance a whole new set of industries, whose foreign exchange needs would be even greater and of longer duration, made little economic sense. Not only was the 1970s coffee boom a transitory event whose effects had largely disappeared by 1979, but there were acute scarcities of virtually every input needed for the industries that were already in place. The existing factories were already suffering from shortages of the foreign exchange they needed to replenish their capital stock, acquire raw materials, and renew management contracts with foreign firms.

The basic industries policy did not have any accompanying provision to boost foreign exchange earnings over the longer run by, for example, increasing the price incentives for export crop production. Tanzania's method of implementing ISI required it to suppress producer prices for coffee and other exports. The government chose not to pass on the increases in global coffee prices to coffee producers where they might have provided the wherewithal to recapitalize the coffee farms or motivated a long-term increase in coffee production.[7] Tanzanian coffee production continued to stagnate even as the boom in coffee prices resulted in increased production in competitor countries.

The problems with the basic industry strategy were not narrowly economic. At an even deeper level, the basic industries strategy reflected an acceptance of long-term dependence on foreign aid. By the mid-1970s, Tanzania's economic planners were well aware of the extent to which such endemic problems as moral hazard and rent seeking had contributed to economic losses in the existing consumer goods industries. The basic industries were bound to fail for exactly the same set of reasons the consumer goods industries had failed. There was not enough foreign exchange to provide a dependable flow of replenishment capital and necessary inputs. Domestic markets were too small to absorb the production of industries that had far more productive capacity than needed for a small agricultural country, and government officials who had the authority to spend would often do so in an irresponsible manner, finding ways to drain off industrial funds as personal wealth. In the early 1960s, a fair-minded observer might have considered industrialization through import-substitution a plausible economic strategy. By the mid-1970s, that was no longer so.

One difference was that the new industries could not count on capitalization from the central government. Whereas the government had planned the first generation of industries on the expectation that it would share the burden of capital investment with international investors, the 1970s transition to intermediate and capital goods industries had no such expectation. The level of capital investment required was too great and industries producing capital goods were so complex that there would need to be a long-term donor commitment to provide the necessary financial resources. The new industries, in other words, required dependency on foreign assistance.[8] By implementing the basic industry strategy, Tanzania had transformed the ISI approach, taking it from an economic program whose goal was industrial self-sufficiency into a purposeful means of extracting long-term financial support from the donor community.

The 1970 treason trial, which had purged the party of its most prominent moderates and intimidated others, caused the voices of Tanzanian reformers to go temporarily silent. Although there were still some pragmatic officials who spoke out in favor of a change in the country's economic course, they were largely without significant political support in the party or government. The banning of the marketing cooperatives demonstrated how politically impotent the pragmatic element of the party had become. In Tanzanian intellectual circles, dependency theory, which blamed Western capitalism for the poverty of third world countries, became a popular and safe approach: it laid the responsibility for national poverty on the predatory nature of global capitalism and not the shortcomings of domestic policy. The Tanzanian political elite were especially comfortable with dependency theory because its emphasis on global factors appeared to exonerate national leadership from responsibility for the economic decline. The few Tanzanian intellectuals who challenged the economic framework found themselves marginalized. Some were harassed for their dissenting views; others sought academic opportunities outside Tanzania.

Among the reasons for the victory of the old guard over the reformers was Nyerere's presence at the top of the political system. Despite everything that had gone on, his personal ability to control the system was unchallenged and his personal commitment to the socialist idea of an egalitarian society was unflagging. He used his authority to surround himself with like-minded leaders who exhibited an uncritical willingness to continue the state-led approach to development. Nyerere was an invaluable economic asset for Tanzania: he had an uncanny ability to charm the donors into continuing their financial support. The majority of Tanzania's political leaders, whether out of genuine conviction or because it was expedient to do so, continued to blame the country's impoverished circumstances on exogenous factors, such as economic shock events, drought, crop failures, or the unanticipated need for war with Uganda, rather than inappropriate policy.

Rent seeking by members of the political elite became all-pervasive: Tanzanians who managed to occupy a rent-seeking niche in the bureaucracy, especially those who could gain access to foreign exchange, could sustain their lives at a better level than those who could not. The elaborate system of import controls, which had begun as a mechanism for orchestrating the pattern and tempo of industrialization, had now become a vehicle for obtaining foreign exchange allocations. Those Tanzanians who were able to do so—and there were many—often used their allocation of funds to create private foreign exchange accounts overseas, depriving the country of hard currency that might have helped to alleviate the hardship. Some donors began to believe their funds were only making up for revenues the government lost because of corruption.

The answer to the question about Tanzania's long delay before implementing reforms lay primarily in the economic interests of the rent-seeking class: Tanzanians who occupied rent-seeking positions, of whom there were many thousands, had no interest in changing an economic system that provided them with great benefits. Repression and rent seeking became the political equilibriums; scarcity, the economic one. Foreign aid helped to sustain this equilibrium.

Foreign Aid

By the second half of the 1970s, Tanzania had entered an economic state of suspended animation. Fifteen years of poorly chosen and poorly implemented economic policies had degraded the country's output to the point where it was barely adequate to sustain the country even on the most minimal survival basis. The country was able to avoid a collapse only because members of the donor community seemed resigned to the role into which they had been cast, as providers of long-term financial support to avert short-term economic catastrophe. Pervasive corruption degraded the minimal levels of service the government was able to provide even with foreign assistance because it drained government revenues and distorted government ability to allocate its meager resources according to planned priorities or social needs. The voices of dissent were few and far between.

In seeking explanations for the lengthy delay before economic reforms began—as well as for the point at which reforms began—it is impossible to avoid the conclusion that the role of the donor community also contributed. Tanzania was among the most aid-dependent countries in sub-Saharan Africa, and its sheer dependence made it amenable to donor influence. World Bank economists considered Tanzania the most aid-dependent of African countries.[9] There are many different ways to measure aid dependency. Table 1 compares Tanzania's aid dependency with that of several other African countries by measuring foreign direct assistance as a percent of gross domestic product. This table shows that by the late 1970s, foreign aid constituted more than 10 percent of the Tanzanian economy. Tanzania's dependence on foreign aid grew steadily during the 1980s, from about one-sixth of GDP in the late 1980s to almost one-fourth during the first half of the 1990s.[10]

Mere figures do not convey the multidimensionality of Tanzania's dependence on the generosity of its donors. The donor financial presence was felt

Table 1. Average Net Inflow of ODA from All Donors (% of Recipient's GDP), 5-Year Intervals, 1970–2009

Country	(1970–1974)	(1975–1979)	(1980–1984)	(1985–1989)	(1990–1994)	(1995–1999)	(2000–2004)	(2005–2009)
Tanzania	5.03	10.79	11.43	17.62	24.28	12.62	12.61	13.03
Ghana	2.14	3.34	3.74	8.68	10.57	8.77	12.81	6.4
Kenya	3.69	4.41	6.51	8.57	12.19	4.36	3.63	4.73
Malawi	8.88	10.59	11.42	20.63	29.47	23.1	20.86	20.75
Senegal	5.33	6.84	10.76	12.56	12.29	10.84	9.25	8.13
Uganda	1.95	1.41	7.17	5.85	19.69	11.72	13.94	13.2

Sources: World Bank, *World Development Indicators*, www.worldbank.org; GDP 1970–1979, Global Financial Data, www.globalfinancialdata.com. Table prepared by Dr. Julia Kim.

everywhere, from direct budget supplementation, which enabled the government to pay its civil servants, soldiers, and suppliers, to sector-by-sector support programs that enabled the government to maintain infrastructure and provide public services, albeit at minimal levels. Tanzania's programs of education, healthcare, infrastructure, public transportation, disease control, and agricultural research—all were dependent on monies provided by donor countries. It is hypothetical to speculate about what socioeconomic conditions might have prevailed without this level of aid. Political scientists Robert Jackson and Carl Rosberg theorized that without donor support, aid-dependent governments such as Tanzania's might have ceased to exist in any meaningful sense of the term.[11] A more limited conclusion is that Tanzania would have been a much poorer country.

This level of aid dependency made Tanzania especially receptive to its donors' policy preferences. Academics disagree, however, about the effects of foreign aid on the policy frameworks of the countries that receive it. In the field of African studies, there is a lively scholarly debate about the impact of foreign assistance. On one side of this debate are the critics of foreign assistance who believe that it provides an enabling environment for a government's inappropriate policy choices.[12] In this line of thought, the resources that donors provide make it possible for governments to continue with policies that are not improving the well being of the country. Foreign aid also provided some of the wherewithal for the gluttonous rent-seeking behavior that formed the material basis and the financial incentive for authoritarian forms of rule. By raising the material stakes of holding onto power, foreign aid can increase the incentive for the governing elite to use any means at its disposal to maintain its ruling position.[13] Those like Dambisa Moyo who criticize the enabling effects of foreign aid further suggest that it may have negative effects on economic development. Among other outcomes, aid can create an atmosphere of cynicism about the choice of development projects, which governments may select less based on their economic benefits than because they can attract generous, long-term donor support.

The other side of this debate condemns the intrusiveness of aid conditionality and the accompanying tendency for donors to take control of the policy-making process out of the hands of the host government. Those who hold this position assert that the policy demands of the donor organizations go too far in compromising the sovereignty of independent nations. One author goes so far as to accuse the donors of "coercive adjustment policies."[14] The implication of this viewpoint is that foreign assistance should have fewer strings attached and that recipient countries should be freer to use their aid funds in ways they deem suitable and appropriate.

Both viewpoints portray foreign aid as a powerful determinant of a government's economic policy. In the case of Tanzania, both contain an element of truth. Between 1974 and the mid-1980s, Tanzania's donors were willing to provide enough financial support to enable the country to continue to function on a day-to-day basis and continue the strategy of state-led industrialization even though it was a demonstrable failure. There were several reasons for donor indulgence; indeed, different donors had different reasons for their willingness to provide ongoing assistance. Among the Nordic donors and Netherlands, there was sympathy for Tanzania's social ideal of an egalitarian and socially humane society. Among other donors, such as Britain and the United States, the willingness to continue aid grew out of a sense of Tanzania's importance as a third world country that remained steadfast in its determination to pursue a middle path between the communist bloc and the Western nations.

Sheer bureaucratic inertia made it difficult for Western countries to use their aid programs as a source of influence over government policy. Aid assistance is typically devoted to multiyear projects, such as building schools, installing water systems, improving rural roads, and providing health care assistance. Even direct budgetary support is normally committed on a multiyear basis so that a country can plan the size and deployment of its public work force. The prevalence of multiyear commitments made it practically impossible for the donors to make short-term changes in their aid packages. The tendency to approach aid on a project-by-project basis may also have enabled Tanzania's poor choice of policy because project-based assistance did not make adequate provision for a holistic appraisal of the causes of the country's economic decline. Much of the analytical work commissioned by bilateral donor organizations consisted of project-feasibility studies, and these reports did not often include comprehensive treatments of the shortcomings of government policy. It took several years for Tanzania's donors to conclude that project-based assistance could not improve economic conditions without major changes in the government's overall economic framework. Many of the donors simply accepted Tanzania's insistence that its economic difficulties were principally the product of a series of exogenous economic shocks, such as the drought conditions of the mid-1970s, the oil price increases of 1973 and 1979, and the costs associated with the break-up of the East African Community (EAC). In this narrative, poor policy choices were less important than a transient set of adverse circumstances.

All this began to change in the early 1980s when the voices of Tanzanian reformers became audible once again. The politics of reform during the final years of the Nyerere presidency, from 1981 to 1985, present an illuminating picture of a multitiered policy dialogue. The most visible disagreements were those between the Tanzanian government and the ILIs. During that period, Tanzanian reformers were caught in the middle: they worked intensively to generate reform programs that might have internal salability only to see their efforts collapse because the reforms they sought went too far for regime conservatives but not nearly far enough to satisfy the more stringent expectations of the ILIs, especially the IMF.

Despite these daunting circumstances, reformers within the government began to work on their own to generate reform proposals that might be able to gather support from the regime conservatives. In1981, they created a plan called the National Economic Survival Programme (NESP).[15] Even its advocates described the NESP as a series of moral exhortations rather than specific policy proposals. The Tanzanian government largely ignored it, and the donor community never took it seriously. Although the NESP had no impact on economic policy, its publication was a significant milestone. It showed that reformers could express dissenting views publicly without fear of losing their positions and without anxiety about arrest and imprisonment, an element of freedom that had been mostly missing since the treason trial a decade earlier. The willingness of a government ministry to publish a document calling openly for economic reform and the emergence of a public discussion about the reforms it proposed indicated that economic reformers had regained some footing. The NESP also provided a signal to the reform-oriented donors that they had a set of receptive dialogue partners within the government.

Neither the donor community nor the Tanzanian government was a unitary actor in this situation: among the donors, several Nordic countries were prepared to continue their financial assistance, thereby enabling the regime conservatives. The Tanzanian lobby against reform consisted of a coalition of institutional and social actors connected to the state industrial enterprises. The Office of the President was opposed to reform because the state industries seemed to fulfill the president's personal vision of a socialist industrial economy. Until 1984, the most powerful cabinet minister was still Kighoma Malima, who after leaving the Ministry of Finance had shifted to the Ministry of State for Planning and Economic Affairs, one of the more resolute antireform Tanzanian bureaucracies. His office aligned itself with the Ministry of Trade and Industry, whose assigned responsibilities placed it at the heart of the process of planned and protected industrialization. The Ministry of Labor joined these powerful units of the government in opposition to reform. It had much to lose if Tanzania were to move away from an economic strategy that prioritized state-controlled industries. Among other losses, it stood to lose the resources it obtained through its administrative control over the country's labor movement.

The World Bank and the Tanzanian government continued to have a conversation over the terms and conditions of a reform process throughout the early 1980s, but there was little basis for agreement. The two parties even lacked a common basis of discourse; each side seemed to have a different vocabulary. The Tanzanian participants used the terminology of their country's commitment to a nonexploitive, classless, and self-reliant society; the bank's representatives responded in the language of currency misalignments, the correlation between farm-gate prices and trade balances, and the crowding-out effects of large budget deficits. Their different vocabularies made communication difficult. By 1982, the misunderstanding was so deep that the representatives of the two entities were barely on speaking terms, an early indication of the extent to which Tanzania's dialogue with its donors could reach an impasse because each participant in the dialogue was convinced that the other could not understand its message.

In an effort to facilitate better communication, the World Bank provided funds to create an interlocutor group called the Tanzania Advisory Group (TAG). The idea was to have a few trusted individuals pave the way for a compromise document that both sides could accept and that might possibly set the stage for larger initiatives in the post-Nyerere period. The specific assignment of the TAG was to create a reform plan that could attract the support of both the government and the Bank.[16] What emerged from its efforts was a second internally generated set of recommendations called the Structural Adjustment Programme (SAP). By adopting the World Bank's economic terminology, if not its specific policy recommendations, TAG members hoped to send a positive signal to both sides. They wanted their Tanzanian colleagues to understand that an acceptable and comprehensive reform program could arise internally, thereby disarming those who were irritated at what they considered overbearing behavior by the Bank. They wanted the ILIs to understand that reforms could not go forward unless they originated from within the Tanzanian government.

During the TAG process, however, the Tanzanian reformers found themselves caught between the resistance to reform of the Nyerere coalition, on the one hand, and the growing impatience of the donor community, on the other. To placate their anti-devaluation colleagues within the government, the authors of the earlier NESP recommendations had omitted any reference to exchange rate reform. However, after 1981, the strategy of keeping the peace by avoiding the difficult issues was no longer available. The IMF representatives in Tanzania had begun to insist on a devaluation of between 100 and 250 percent. The gap between Tanzania and the ILIs seemed unbridgeable.[17] Within Tanzania, the divide between pro- and anti-reformers also seemed hopeless. Each group had powerful institutional actors. The principal institutional division on the Tanzanian side was between the President's Office, owing to the president's commitment to the centrally planned economy, and the Ministry of Finance, whose new minister Cleopa Msuya was an intense reformer. Under Msuya, the Ministry of Finance had become a gathering place for members of the younger generation of Tanzanian economists.

The principal issue was exchange rate reform, and the debate over this matter was a microcosm of the theoretical dialogue between development economics and orthodox approaches.[18] Those opposed to devaluation derived their views directly from the development economics textbook. For example, they disputed the notion that the world's purchases of Tanzanian exports, such as coffee, sisal, and cotton, would increase significantly in response to devaluation.[19] They used the idea of a backward bending supply curve to argue that Tanzania's export-oriented farmers were already operating at production levels that were optimal for their needs. Development economists insisted that once farmers had produced enough to satisfy their cash requirements, the price incentives afforded by devaluation would not make a significant difference. The opponents of devaluation also insisted that devaluation would harm the industrialization process, which was already exhibiting signs of great stress, by increasing the prices of necessary inputs. Finally, they expressed concern about the inflationary effects of devaluation, inasmuch as imported goods, which constituted a large part of urban consumption, would become more expensive.[20]

The proponents of currency reform argued that it would lead to an increase in Tanzanian exports as Tanzanian producers began to realize higher local currency prices for their products and as global consumers of Tanzanian commodities found the prices of Tanzanian goods attractive in hard currency. Currency reformers disputed the backward bending supply curve hypothesis and argued that the old idea of farmers with fixed cash needs was a discredited shibboleth. They insisted that increased producer prices would greatly increase production, as export-oriented farmers were more easily able to afford the labor and input costs of their goods. Reformers also sought to show that fears of inflation had little basis: since so much of the Tanzanian economy was already operating on parallel market exchange rates, most price inflation had already taken place. In fact, they argued, devaluation might actually lower consumer prices, because the improved flow of foreign exchange would make it possible to increase the domestic supply of imported goods.

There were also disagreements about other policy issues, such as trade reform and curtailment of the public sector. Tanzanian economist Samuel Wangwe has described how those favoring existing policies diluted the most important reforms in the SAP and, how, as a result, they became unacceptable to the IMF and the Bank.

> In particular, the [internal] revisions weakened proposals which made reference to price reforms, trade liberalization and public sector reform. The diluted version was presented to the IFIs but these considered the proposed programme insufficient in articulating economic reform, especially in terms of reducing distortions in goods and factor markets. Failure to reach an agreement with the IFIs also meant that many donors withheld their aid flows. The programme could therefore not be implemented because the external resource inflow which it had assumed did not materialize.[21]

The fact that both sides rejected the Tanzanian SAP, which grew directly out of the mediation efforts of a jointly chosen panel of experts, conveys the extent of the gap between Tanzania and ILIs.[22] Those who wanted assistance on terms that would allow the existing policy framework to continue intact dominated the Tanzanian side of the conversation. The ILIs were unprepared to provide financial assistance on that basis.

The mutual rejection of the SAP on the part of Tanzania and its donors is sometimes taken as a sign of the failure of the TAG mechanism. This is unfortunate because it had been able to achieve some minor success, especially in the area of exchange rate policy. The TAG efforts led to three currency devaluations: 12 percent in March 1982, 27 percent in June 1983, and 36 percent in June 1984. Although these devaluations appeared large in percentage terms, they were on a very small base and did little to bridge the gap between the official exchange rate and the parallel market rate. The TAG experience had other benefits as well. It had created an organizational model that enabled the government of Tanzania and the donors to communicate despite their intense disagreements over policy. In addition, the TAG devaluations, though modest, had conveyed an important message to the international community. A group of Tanzanian reformers not only were in agreement with donor concerns but were publicly prepared to move the country in a reform direction.

The 1984 devaluation was of particular importance. New minister of finance Msuya had announced it in the 1984 budget address. The donors knew Msuya was an influential reformer, and they concluded, correctly or not, that his budget address had the prior approval of the president. The annual budget address is an important event in Tanzania: it is widely reported in the Tanzanian press and widely discussed both among Tanzanians and throughout the donor community. Msuya was also on far better terms with the representatives of the donor community than Malima, whom some donors found irritating.[23] The shift of Malima's authority to Msuya was a signal that economic power had begun to shift from the reds to the experts.

Although the 1984 devaluation was not much greater than those of 1982 and 1983, it changed the tone of the government-ILI conversation. Key donors accepted it as the most the government could do while Nyerere remained in office and as a signal that more far-reaching policy changes would be implemented after that took place. One basis for optimism was that there was only one year to wait. Another was the unusually candid nature of Msuya's address, which described the weaknesses of the country's economy in extensive detail and contained additional reforms of real consequence. These included limited trade liberalization, removal of some agricultural subsidies, a substantial increase in the amount of grain Tanzanians could trade privately,[24] and cost-containment measures for some social services. The mood of the Tanzanian reformers was ecstatic: one official in the Ministry of Agriculture said, "Tanzania is going metric."

The dissolution of the TAG mechanism left things in a state of uncertainty. Despite the friendly signaling that was taking place with the sequential devaluations and despite the reformers' success in attaining leadership positions in key ministries, both the World Bank and the IMF concluded that the government was still not prepared to undertake the far-reaching steps necessary to improve the economy. The confused pattern that followed would be familiar to anyone who has had the opportunity to observe a country perched on the edge of economic reform. There was an element of strain between the Tanzanian government and the ILIs, which were insisting on broad-gauged reforms as a condition of ongoing financial assistance. The Tanzanian government was unable to comply because there were unresolved policy disagreements among different groups of key officials. The Tanzanian economy continued to stagnate, and rent-seeking behavior, especially in the area of the exchange rate differential, remained unchecked. Throughout all this, however, the Tanzanian government was able to turn to the Nordic donors and Netherlands for financial support that did not depend upon compliance with the reform conditions of the ILIs.

The tipping moment in donor politics came in November 1984, when the head of the Swedish aid agency delivered an address to a joint meeting between the government of Tanzania and the representatives of the Nordic countries. Scandinavian economist Kjell J. Havenivik, who has written extensively on Tanzanian economic affairs, quotes the key portion of the speech: "a basic assumption on the Nordic side at the outset of these deliberations, hence our working hypothesis, is that resources from our countries would serve to supplement, and not be a substitute for those emanating from an agreement with the Fund."[25] His statement represented a tectonic shift in the donor-Tanzania relationship; it was a signal that the members of the donor community who had been willing to subsidize the Tanzanian social experiment for two decades, were no longer prepared to do so. The donor community, which had been a significant factor in enabling the government to delay major reforms, had become a force for policy change. Almost overnight, donor enabling had given way to donor fatigue, or even, according to some accounts, donor irritability.

Exactly why this change took place is unclear. Donor enabling and donor fatigue are imprecise concepts. There is no established methodology for assessing how long donor generosity was a significant factor in enabling Tanzania to continue with a poor choice of policies any more than there is a scientific method for measuring the precise effect of a change in donor attitudes on government willingness to begin policy reforms. What caused the change in donor orientation? The conventional wisdom about the change in donor approach points to the rise of conservative governments in the United States under President Reagan and Britain under Prime Minister Margaret Thatcher as well as the rise of more centrist electorates in the Nordic countries. Tightened global circumstances after the oil price increase of 1979 may also have been an important factor. Several donor nations began to experience taxpayer resistance to large outlays of funds that did not appear to produce commensurate results. What is abundantly clear is that by the mid-1980s,

Tanzania's donors had reached the limits of their willingness to fund its chronically failing economic model.

Changes in the way the economics profession approached development were also a major factor. Just as the dominance of development economics explained the adoption of the import-substituting strategy in the early 1960s, a paradigm shift toward market-based theories of development explains the policy changes that took place in the 1980s. One of the earliest and most influential studies was a multivolume series co-authored and edited by Anne O. Krueger and Jagdish Bhagwati titled *Foreign Trade Regimes: Liberalization Attempts and Consequences*.[26] The series did not include a case study of Tanzania, but it did include a study of Ghana, the African country with which Tanzania is most frequently compared. Economist J. Clark Leith of the University of Western Ontario conducted the Ghana research, and his analysis of the reasons for the failure of Ghana's economic program spoke directly to the Tanzanian experience.[27] Leith's criticism of the ISI model was devastating. In a carefully understated conclusion, he noted that: "The combination of inflation and massive discrimination between activities was too much for the economy to withstand without suffering. It is difficult to distinguish clearly the individual influences at work, but there is a strong presumption that a significant share of the blame for reduced domestic savings rates, low productivity of investment, and poor export performance must fall on the control regime."[28] The impact of the Krueger-Bhagwati series, both in the scholarly community and in the world of applied policy, was considerable. It provided a compelling theoretical explanation for the failure of development strategies that depend on protectionism and central planning.[29] It further showed that development strategies that used free markets and free trade would yield greater and more sustained benefits in economic growth. After Krueger-Bhagwati, the subdiscipline of development economics, with its insistence on protectionism and central planning, lost its status as the authoritative theoretical basis for policy choice.

The Bank's shift in its economic approach to Africa came in 1981, with the publication of its seminal study, *Accelerated Development in Sub-Saharan Africa: An Agenda for Action*. This study, commonly referred to as the Berg Report after its principal author, Professor Elliott Berg of the Department of Economics of the University of Michigan, had an especially great impact on Tanzania, which it cited frequently, along with Ghana, as a leading example of poor policy choices bringing about poor economic results. By providing a convincing argument that exogenous factors, such as drought and terms of trade shocks, were not the principal reasons for economic decline, it under-mined Tanzania's official explanation for poor economic performance. In so doing, it ruled out a policy option Tanzanian officials had sought to keep on the table since the basic industries strategy of the mid-1970s: the idea that it was feasible to achieve economic recovery by improving the economic per-formance of the state-led industrial sector.

Immediately after the publication of the Berg Report, the Bank initiated a major change in its lending approach, moving away from an emphasis on project-based lending and toward requiring comprehensive policy changes as a condition for further loans. It also persuaded many bilateral donors that their project-based approach to development could not work until countries such as Tanzania made major corrections in their macroeconomic environ-ment.[30] By the mid-1980s, practically all the members of the Tanzanian donor community, including not only the ILIs but also an increasing number of bi-lateral donors, began to insist on market-based policy changes. The parsimo-nious explanation for the Nordic countries' 1984 change of approach toward Tanzania was simple; their aid officials had read, absorbed, and found them-selves in agreement with the orthodox economic principles that informed Berg's study.

Whatever the cause of the change in the donors' approach, Tanzania began to face a more challenging aid environment than had been the case earlier. To place pressure on the government, Tanzania's donors steadily re-duced their aid commitments during the early 1980s; between 1981 and 1985, net aid per capita fell from $90 to $60, a decrease of about 30 percent.[31] Sev-eral donors ceased their aid disbursements. It did not take long for Tanzani-ans to read the new environment and adapt to it. During 1984, a series of events signaled the government's willingness to change its economic ap-proach. The first was President Nyerere's announcement that he would not contest the presidential election of 1985; this was widely interpreted as his personal acknowledgment that the party would be free to nominate a presi-dential candidate who could negotiate a reform agreement with the IMF and the World Bank. The second was the budget address of June 1984, when Fi-nance Minister Msuya used his speech to the National Assembly to announce a set of economic changes that included currency devaluation, improvements in agricultural producer prices, and partial steps toward the liberalization of trade. By the time Tanzania's second president, Mwinyi, assumed office in fall 1985, there was no doubt about which direction Tanzania would take.

The debate about aid, then, poses two different questions and provides essentially the same answer to each. The first is why an inappropriate policy framework continued as long as it did even in the face of adverse circumstances. The second is why that policy framework began to change when it did. The answer to both questions begins—but does not end—with the role of the donor community. The answer to the first emphasizes the phenomenon of donor enabling and must include some reference to President Nyerere's remarkable ability to elicit donor support for his social vision even as the country's real economy crumbled into disarray. The answer to the second is donor fatigue and the donors' insistence on fundamental changes in economic policy as a condition for any further financial support.

The Tanzanian case provides evidence for both sides of the aid debate. During the twenty-year period from the mid-1960s to the mid-1980s, Tanzania was an example of donor enabling. Despite two decades of economic failure, the government continued to receive vast amounts of foreign assistance amounting to hundreds of millions of dollars per year. Tanzania was perhaps unique among African countries in the willingness of its donors to continue to provide vast sums of money for an array of economic needs ranging from direct budgetary supplementation to project assistance. Between the end of the 1970s and the mid-1980s, Tanzania was regularly receiving $500 to $700 million per year in foreign financial aid. The unconditional financial support of the Nordic countries and the Netherlands enabled Tanzania's poor choice of economic approach. Their decision to join other donors in insisting on economic reforms compelled Tanzania to adjust its policies accordingly. Tanzania now became a case study in the importance of donor pressure as a source of policy change. When that happened, Tanzania became an example of donor intrusiveness.

Tanzania's economic reform process has many similarities to Ghana's. Both countries came to independence with intellectually charismatic presidents who had created powerful nationalist movements and who favored a socialist economic outlook; after independence, both adopted a highly statist approach to ISI; in the political realm, both also made a transition to single-party rule. There were numerous other similarities as well. Both countries suffered from severe problems of political and bureaucratic corruption. Both countries adopted exchange rate policies that resulted in extreme overvaluation. Both countries repressed the export-oriented agricultural sector in search of resources to pursue the ISI strategy, and both countries suffered severe economic decline resulting from the adoption of inappropriate economic policies.

When the reform process began in the mid-1980s, the pattern of similarity continued. Both countries adopted the same set of core economic principles. These included the value of a market-based economy that featured private ownership of productive enterprises and appropriate fiscal and monetary policy to reduce budget deficits and lower inflation. Each reformed its misaligned exchange rate through a sequence of steps that began with official devaluations and then included structural reforms to ensure an equilibrium exchange rate. Both countries moved toward the adoption of a free trade policy that would enable internal markets to respond to global prices. To begin an economic recovery, both countries began to adopt structural adjustment programs under ILI auspices and with ILI support in the mid-1980s. The two countries also went through a comparable process divesting their state-owned enterprises toward some form of private ownership.

There was a glaring difference, however: Ghana appeared to "own" its reform program; Tanzania did not. Within the donor organizations, *reform ownership* is a frequent topic of discussion. This idea refers to whether the political and administrative leaders of a country become sufficiently invested in their country's economic reforms to participate proactively in the process, formulating their own strategic design for how various important reforms can best proceed. The concept of reform ownership is an elusive one since it describes the underlying attitudes of a country's public officials. Ownership has to do with the way the policy elite of a country approach economic liberalization. Whatever the exact meaning of the term, the notion of ownership had a particular resonance in the Tanzanian context. The donors believed that, unlike Ghana, Tanzanians did not own their reform process. They depicted Ghana as a nation where the political and administrative elites had embraced reform with a degree of alacrity that enabled the major aid organizations to take a secondary role in the strategic planning of the reform agenda. Tanzanians seemed reluctant and dispirited.

Many donor officials believed that Tanzania's leaders regarded policy reform as an external imposition. Some were openly convinced that Tanzanians' participation in the structural adjustment process derived only from a grudging acknowledgment that their government was so lacking in resources that it would collapse without foreign assistance. Donor officials complained constantly of the Tanzanian tendency to promise specific reforms only to renege when it came time for actual implementation. There was little confidence that Tanzania's willingness to undertake economic reforms grew out of an intellectual conversion to the orthodox economic principles that informed the process of structural adjustment. Using a metaphor from the academic world, some donor officials suggested that Tanzania was aiming for a passing grade in economic reform, just enough change that foreign aid would continue but little enough to leave the state-managed economy intact. Like many students whose goal is simply to pass, the Tanzanians sometimes skirted dangerously close to failure.

There are many explanations for the difference.[32] The most basic has to do with the length of time in office of the founder-presidents and the political parties they helped create. Kwame Nkrumah and the Convention People's Party (CPP) he formed were in power in Ghana for only nine years. Nkrumah became president of Ghana at independence in March 1957; a military coup overthrew him in February 1966. The military leaders who assumed power after the coup dissolved the CPP and repressed the entire cadre of political leaders associated with it. Except for a brief period of civilian rule from 1969 to 1971, party politics in Ghana ceased to exist. Between the mid-1960s and the early 1980s, Ghana did not have a dominant political party whose purpose was to sustain the founder-president's ideological beliefs and use them to explain their choice of policies. Indeed, the military heads of state who followed Nkrumah suppressed the philosophy of Nkrumah-ism and those they associated with it, even while they continued the state-managed economic system he had begun to put in place. Nkrumah died in 1972. By the time economic reforms began, he had been out of the country for nearly twenty years. Although some Ghanaians remembered Nkrumah and his party, sometimes fondly, his political presence in the country was a distant memory.

By comparison, Nyerere remained in a position of supreme power for nearly thirty years, more than three times as long. He became prime minister in 1961 and president at the end of 1962. Although he stepped down as president in 1985, he continued as head of the governing political party until 1990, and when he relinquished that position, he remained in the country and continued to be a formidable presence in its political process. Neither Nyerere nor the vast cohort of political and bureaucratic leadership associated with him and identified with his political viewpoint was ever overthrown. Tanzania being Tanzania, Mwinyi's ascent to the presidency in 1985 did not bring about a systematic purge of Nyerere elements from either the bureaucracy or the governing party. The CCM, which Nyerere had helped create and personally infused with the philosophical tenets of ujamaa, never ceased to exist as the CPP did. It remained the dominant institutional force in Tanzanian politics. High-ranking political leaders, bureaucratic officials, and university intellectuals who identified with Nyerere's philosophy continued to be an influential presence in Tanzanian society and its political system.

Their presence explains why seemingly necessary and obvious reforms often seemed slow and piecemeal in their execution, to the point where Tanzania appeared to its donors to be dragging its feet and implementing only as many changes as were utterly essential to keep aid funds flowing into the country, and then only under utmost pressure. Tanzania's ownership problem was the mirror image of the intellectual climate Czesław Miłosz described in his classic book *The Captive Mind*.[33] Miłosz described communist officials who were secretly captivated with the greater intellectual and political freedom available in bourgeois democracies. The Tanzanian government presented a mirror opposite picture. It had numerous public officials who, in their dealings with the donor organizations, paid lip service to free market principles, while in private they continued to harbor an admiration for the socialist values of the Nyerere era. The continuity of the Nyerere ethos is an important reason why the backstory of economic reform in Tanzania was one of rising tensions between the Tanzanian government and the representatives of donor organizations, sometimes to the point where personal relationships became subject to suspicion and strain.

From the Tanzanians' standpoint, the behavior of the donors seemed to be unduly intrusive. Tanzanian officials complained that the donors' conditions for economic assistance were not only far too numerous for any government to comply with but also that they were often contradictory. Tanzanians further complained that far too much of their time and energy was devoted to producing compliance reports and impact studies for the many different donor entities they had to deal with and that this subtracted from the time and resources they could spend actually implementing policy changes. In addition, some Tanzanians complained that the conduct of aid officials was sometimes overbearing. Telephone conversations about even the most minor matters, such as where a meeting would take place, took on multiple layers of meaning.

The great irony of the growing strain in the relationship between Tanzania and its donors during the early 1990s was that the government appeared to be making great strides in accelerating the pace of economic and political change. The National Assembly elected in fall 1990 appeared to embrace the need to move rapidly to approve the legislation needed for the transition to a market-based economy as well as to initiate the constitutional change to a multiparty political system. Within two years, it had passed a series of laws intended to bring about important changes in the economy and the political system. In 1991, the National Assembly passed the Cooperative Societies Act,[34] which began the restoration of the country's historic system of agricultural marketing cooperatives. The Assembly also busied itself with repealing some of the more conspicuously failed legislation of the Nyerere era, such as the Regulation of Prices Act of 1973,[35] which had created the ineffectual National Prices Commission. The following year, the Assembly passed a Foreign Exchange Act to create a system of foreign exchange bureaus that would provide an important step toward liberalizing currency transactions.[36] The Finance Bill of 1992 made far-reaching changes in the burdensome system of internal taxes that the Nyerere government had put in place.[37] The LART paved the way for divestiture of state-owned enterprises.[38] The Public Corporations Act of 1992[39] completed the legislative process to do so by creating a new government agency, the Parastatal Sector Reform Commission (PSRC), empowered to sell off the state-owned enterprises.

In addition to these laws, the National Assembly had also begun the process of restoring multipartyism with the Political Parties Act of 1992.[40] It had begun to restore the autonomy of the trade union movement with the passage of the Organization of Tanzania Trade Unions Act of 1991.[41] It had passed the very important Banking and Financial Institutions Act of 1991,[42] which facilitated the resumption of private banking. It had passed legislation creating a stock exchange, the Dar es Salaam Stock Exchange Company (DARSECO) in 1994.[43] Perhaps more important, this wave of reform activity appeared to be producing real results. The government was making significant progress in reducing the size of the public sector payroll, including the elimination of "ghost" workers. There was also progress in improving the real purchasing power of civil service salaries, especially at lower tiers in the salary scale, to reduce motivation for corruption. Between 1992 and 1995, foreign direct investment in Tanzania increased more than ten-fold, from $12 million to $150 million.[44] While much of this was investment in mining rather than industry, and some was reinvestment of the early proceeds of divestitures, its sheer magnitude reflected a new confidence in Tanzania's commitment to a market economy. Tanzanians pointed to the torrid pace of legislative activity in the early 1990s as evidence that contradicted the donors' insistence that they did not "own" their reform process.

Why, then, was there such a large misunderstanding between Tanzania and its donors? The E. C. Bentley quotation that opens this volume directs our attention to the oldest of truisms, the deceptiveness of appearances. What appeared to matter in early 1990s Tanzania was the National Assembly's approval of a sequence of laws that provided for far-reaching economic changes. What may have mattered even more was the extent to which corruption in the country's political-economic oligarchy degraded the meaningfulness of even the most extensive reform agenda. Economist Anna Muganda has suggested that the government's inability to control corruption was causing growing economic difficulties. "In particular, macroeconomic stability was not achieved due to the government's inability to control credit expansion to public enterprises, massive tax exemptions, poor revenue collections, and tax evasion. The large increases in tax exemptions was [sic] symptomatic of corruption and governance issues. Meanwhile, gains made earlier in reducing inflation were reversed: inflation rose from about 22 percent in 1992 to 37 percent in 1994."[45] Spiraling out-of-control corruption had lowered government ability to collect revenues owed, resulting in large deficits, in turn causing greater dependence on donor finance, a heightened rate of inflation, and lower real GDP growth.

The ILIs and the Tanzanian government were poles apart in their respective understandings of the reform process. Tanzania exhibited a form of fundamental attribution error. The ILIs had hoped to attribute the Tanzanians' openness to reform to an intellectual conversion from socialist beliefs to the principles of an open economy. A number of Tanzanians, especially some of the younger generation of economists, had made that journey. Many donor officials, however, became convinced that Tanzania's receptiveness to new policies derived from the acquisitiveness of the political oligarchy rather than an intellectual conversion to free markets. Economic liberalization was simply a new form of opportunity to acquire wealth and power. The Tanzanian atmosphere during the early years of the Mwinyi administration was, in effect, an economic free-for-all. President Mwinyi, whose popular nickname was "Bwana Ruhsa" (Mr. Permission), had encouraged the country's political leaders to acquire wealth. His unqualified endorsement of business activity seemed to imply blanket approval for entrepreneurial Tanzanians to enrich themselves by any means necessary, including predatory behavior toward the government itself.

This was the dissonance between what mattered and what seemed to matter. On the surface, the Tanzanian government appeared to be making substantial progress toward the reform of its economy. It was liberalizing trade, devaluing the exchange rate, licensing private banks, creating a stock exchange, reintroducing market pricing into the grain sector, injecting private sector competition into the procurement, processing, and marketing of export crops, removing consumer subsidies on maize, improving fiscal policy to lower deficits, removing subsidies on agricultural inputs, and, above all else, seeking to reassure investors by creating an overall climate of opinion favorable to private sector activity. To the donors, however, what really mattered was that all this was taking place in a manner that enabled a corrupt political elite to solidify its grasp on economic wealth and political power.

The misunderstanding between government and donors was so great that it caused discussions about mid-range issues to assume disproportionate importance. One issue, for example, was whether the NMC would have permission to create and administer a strategic grain reserve. From the government's standpoint, the NMC system had undergone a thoroughgoing reform. The government had stripped it of its role as the sole legal purchaser and distributor of milled grains and greatly reduced it in size. The only remaining question was whether the country should have a strategic grain reserve and whether the NMC would be the appropriate agency to manage it. Owing to the history of famine, the concept of food self-sufficiency is popular throughout Africa. Many African leaders, including Tanzania's, have raised the specter of "food shocks"—situations in which domestic production shortfalls coincide with high world prices for staple grains. They assert the value of a strategic grain reserve as a protection against future famine. The government proposal was that the NMC be permitted to use its remaining statutory authority to purchase grains for this reserve and that it be able to use its vast storage and transportation facilities to manage the reserve.

The disagreement over this proposal had a level of intensity that, by some accounts, far transcended the importance of the issue. Government officials claimed to be engaged in a technical discussion about the appropriate size of a grain reserve and the point at which NMC purchases would cease so that private merchants could become the principal actors in the grain markets. Tanzania's donors had a very different perception. Given the NMC's history as one of the country's most costly, corrupt, and inefficient economic institutions, World Bank spokespersons had favored its complete dissolution, advocating a complete return to free markets in the grain sector. They feared that the strategic reserve proposal was a pretext to enable the NMC to continue its role as grain purchaser of first resort throughout the countryside. Bank officials stated that private markets had served the country well in the period immediately after independence, when Tanzania was a significant grain exporter, and there was every reason to assume that a free market approach was best. From the ILI standpoint, the best strategic grain reserve was for the government to have sufficient cash reserves to buy grain on world markets when it needed to do so. In an interview, one Bank official insisted, "The best strategic grain reserve is a check book."

From the Tanzanian standpoint, the donors' interference in this matter was proof of donor over-reach and the donors' uncritical assumption that they needed to control every aspect of the government's reform program. From the donors' standpoint, the government's search for an ongoing role for the NMC was one more signal of its lack of will to carry out an urgently necessary reform. They mistrusted the government's intentions and privately believed that the idea of a grain reserve was a pretext for the NMC to continue as grain buyer of first resort, with all the attendant rent-seeking opportunities such a responsibility would provide.

The 1994 Aid Crisis

By the mid-1990s, the government of Tanzania and the ILIs were in almost exactly the same position as they had been a decade earlier, in the midst of a pattern of misunderstanding so recriminatory that it nearly produced a breakdown in aid. These relationships deteriorated to the point of rupture in 1994 when several donors became so disappointed in Tanzania's failure to comply with their conditions that they suspended aid disbursements. Personal and policy frictions were so acute that Tanzanian and donor officials were barely on speaking terms, and third party mediation once again became necessary as a desperate measure to salvage the reform dialogue.

The strain that arose has become the subject of a case study in dysfunctional aid dynamics. Thomas Theisohn and Philip Courtnadge have sought to show that the core element in the breakdown was the tendency for each party to create its own narrative of events.[46] This prevented each side from seeing merit in the other's point of view. The remedy Theisohn and Courtnadge suggested was the creation of an honest broker group to mediate the dispute. This was precisely what Tanzania and the Bank had done with limited success in 1982 in creating the TAG, which—despite its failure to attain major policy reforms—had improved the tone of the donor-government dialogue. In mid-1994, the Danish government initiated conversations with the government of Tanzania with a view toward creating an interlocutor mechanism similar to the TAG. The new dialogue group had the somewhat clumsy name, the Group of Independent Advisors on Development Cooperation Issues between Tanzania and its Aid Donors (hereafter, Advisors' Group). The chair of the Advisors' Group was Professor Gerald Helleiner, who had been a member of the TAG in 1982.[47]

Except for the fact that it took place in the midst of a far-reaching process of economic liberalization, the Tanzanian government-external donor relationship in early 1995 bore a striking similarity to that of a the early 1980s, when the donors had first begun to press for far-reaching reforms. Effective communication had all but ceased; policy reforms had stalled because of poor working relationships between government representatives and representatives of the major donors, and each side blamed the other for the atmosphere of mistrust. Even some of the key personalities were the same: the Tanzanian minister of finance during the early 1990s was Professor Malima, the person who had replaced Edwin Mtei in 1979. Malima's reappearance as finance minister was especially unfortunate. From the donors' standpoint, he was objectionable on several counts: he held the wrong economic views; he was personally difficult; and he presided over a ministry that had become so corrupt as to have worsened the country's fiscal performance. To the ILIs, Malima seemed to be an abrasive spokesperson for a one-sided Tanzanian narrative that blamed them rather than internal mismanagement for lingering problems in the economy.

The challenge to the Advisors' Group was to find a way to resolve the impasse. It might not have been much more successful than its predecessor, the TAG, had it not been for Helleiner's presence. Helleiner has a unique position in the history of Tanzanian political economy. He is not only a scholar of great stature but is alone in having enjoyed both the trust and the intellectual esteem of both the government of Tanzania and the donor community over an extended period. The report he produced, *The Report of the Group of Independent Advisors* (hereafter Helleiner Report), sheds invaluable light on the gulf of misunderstanding that had arisen between the donor organizations and the government of Tanzania.[48] It documents the extent to which strained personal relationships can jeopardize the working relationships necessary to move reform forward. Helleiner's Report conveys the government's viewpoint in blunt language.

Its [GOT] (Government of Tanzania) politicians and officials believe that the pace of change in Tanzania is as fast as is technically and

politically feasible. They feel that they are being singled out for disproportionate (and negative) attention by the international donor community. They perceive the problem of increased corruption as, in part,
a response to reduced real public sector wages and salaries; while
seeking to lessen it, they see the problem as no more severe in Tanzania than in other developing countries. They regard the donors as
"driving" Tanzanian development programmes and intruding exces-
sively upon matters of domestic policy, and they resent their inability
or unwillingness to share information.[49]

Tanzanian officials further believed that the donors were imposing impossible expectations in the sheer number of reports they were expected to produce, the number of meetings they were expected to attend, and, of utmost
importance, the burdensome and sometimes contradictory aid conditions
they were expected to comply with.

There is an element of truth in the Tanzanians' position. One World Bank
official acknowledged the daunting task Tanzania faced in simply managing
its donor relationships, noting that the Tanzanian bureaucracy was required
to produce approximately 2,400 quarterly reports per year for its donors, and
to receive about one thousand donor "missions."[50] The Danish economist Ole
Therkildsen has pointed out that during the 1980s, Tanzania had more than
two thousand development projects, all of which required some measure of
coordination between the Tanzanian government and donor organizations.[51]
Some Tanzanian officials also felt that donor officials were treating them with
condescension, and they began to resent the tone of paternalism they perceived in their discussions with donor representatives. Some also objected to
the lack of trust inherent in all the requirements they had to comply with,
believing that the sheer burden of donor conditions was impeding further
progress in liberalizing their economy.

The donor community had an altogether different narrative, one that
blamed the Tanzanian government for the stalled reform effort. The Helleiner
Report states this view as follows:

the government of Tanzania has lost its momentum and its sense of
direction, has little sense of direction, has little sense of ownership of
its major programmes, and is unable to exercise fiscal control because
of declining administrative capacity and increasing corruption. After
more than thirty years of support, donors are disappointed with the

Tanzanian performance record and regard their continued support for the GOT as politically unsustainable among their own electorates. They do not believe that the government is doing all it can in terms of revenue collection and is therefore inordinately dependent upon their aid.[52]

The key terms in the donor narrative were lack of ownership, lack of political will, and corruption. From the donor standpoint, Tanzanians did not own the measures to make a successful transition to a market economy; they had merely accepted the reform conditions as an unavoidable necessity for receiving financial assistance. Although donors acknowledged they had indeed assumed a great deal of oversight over the implementation of specific policy changes, this was necessary, they argued, principally because the Tanzanians had failed to do so themselves.

The donors and Tanzanians found themselves quibbling over a range of economic issues, such as the size of the government deficit, the trajectory of currency devaluation, the pace of divestiture, or compliance with conditions attached to trade liberalization. But the real source of donor disquiet was the extent to which corruption was causing the government to fall short of its ability to collect enough revenue to come close to a budgetary balance. Behind the scenes, the donors believed the reform process was being manipulated in such a way as to enable Tanzania's political-economic oligarchy, which had already gained a firm grasp on the nation's most important economic and political institutions, to entrench itself still farther. There was an uncomfortable sense that what motivated Tanzanians' willingness to reform was not an intellectual conversion to the magic of the marketplace, but the growing realization that a market-based system provided greater opportunities to acquire wealth than the state system had.

The Advisors' Group offered several measures of the effects of corruption. One was the extent to which corruption had lowered the government's revenue performance. Tanzania seemed to compare poorly with other African countries. From 1990 to 1992, the Tanzanian government averaged approximately $22 per capita in annual revenue. In comparison with a set of five other African countries that included Ghana, Kenya, Uganda, Zimbabwe, and Malawi, this was a woefully inadequate amount. Tanzania's revenue collection, for example, was only about half of Malawi's ($43), about 40 percent of Ghana's ($53), and less than a third of Kenya's ($75). Only Uganda managed less revenue collection per capita ($10).[53]

The government of Tanzania had also shown during this period that it was less able than other countries to limit or reduce the extent of its indebtedness in hard currency to foreign banks. To measure this borrowing, the Bank calculates the amount of external debt that is public and publicly guaranteed (PPG) as a percentage of a country's GDP. Figure 1 compares Tanzania with Kenya and Ghana in this respect.[54]

Many countries wrestle with indebtedness, but Tanzania's donors believed that much of this problem could be addressed by bringing corruption under control. Some of the bilateral donors, for example, singled out the problem of extreme corruption at the Port of Dar es Salaam, where corruptly obtained tax exemptions and undervaluation of imports reduced the customs revenue the government was able to collect. Indeed, the immediate trigger event for the 1994 crisis was a massive and widely publicized corruption scandal at the Port of Dar es Salaam. Early in 1994, the Tanzanian government had

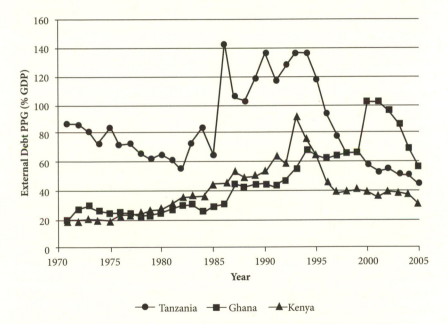

Figure 1. External debt stocks, public and publicly guaranteed (PPG) as % GDP (1971–2005). This graph sheds valuable light on the aid crisis by showing that during the decade from the mid-1980s to the mid-1990s Tanzania's debt hovered around 140 percent of GDP. This was substantially greater than for the comparison countries. Calculated and prepared by Dr. Julia Kim from World Bank, World Development Indicators, www.worldbank.org (external debt stock PPG, current U.S.$); Global Financial Data, www.globalfinancialdata.com (GDP, 1970–1979).

contracted with two foreign agencies to assist in the monitoring of its international trade and in the collection of the tax revenues that were owed on this trade. With the information provided by these agencies, the Tanzanian auditor general estimated that the Tanzanian government had suffered a revenue shortfall at the port of about $200 million, about one-quarter of the government's total projected revenue. This loss was caused by the fact that the Ministry of Finance, under Malima, had issued approximately two thousand tax exemptions to Tanzanian businesses and individuals. Even the President felt called upon to make a public statement acknowledging the magnitude of the corruption problem: "There is evidence to suggest that there is significant abuse of the Investment Promotion Centre exemptions. Treasury discretionary exemptions need to be sharply curtailed. The abuses hurt the legitimate business community, which is investing in this country, and the abusers must be caught and prosecuted. No exemption will be effective in future unless it is gazetted and published in a newspaper."[55] Tanzania's donors were especially angry that a large portion of their financial assistance was simply making up for revenues the government had lost to malfeasance.

The Advisors' Group had a limited but important success: it provided a catharsis in the relationship between donors and the Tanzanian government. By changing the tone of the donor-government dialogue, it helped to restore a more amicable working relationship between the two parties. President Mwinyi, embarrassed by the need to make a public statement about the extent of corruption in the Ministry of Finance, transferred Malima to another ministry and replaced him with a former military officer, Lt. Col. Jakaya Kikwete, who had a reputation as an effective advocate of reform and for personal incorruptibility.[56] The prime minister at that time was Msuya, who, as finance minister in 1984, had given the key budget address announcing the government's early reform intentions. The rise to prominence of political leaders known for their pro-reform views improved the government-donor conversation. In the aftermath of the Advisors' Group experience, the two parties were able to converse with one another with less rancor and acrimony.

The Advisors' Group restored a working relationship between Tanzania and its donors, but it did so by leaving their deeper disagreements unresolved. One had to do with how long a reform program should take to enable a country to transition from state controls to a market orientation. The Tanzanian reform exercise was approximately eight years underway when the 1994 aid impasse arose. Mwinyi had assumed office at the end of 1985; he had begun to initiate policy changes in early 1986 and signed an IMF agreement in August. The Advisors' Group process began in mid-1994, about eight years later. Tanzanians insisted that they had accomplished a great deal in a short time. From their perspective, the donors' impatience was unwarranted. Some Tanzanians believed that the donors were pressuring their government into undue haste in the implementation of economic changes that would affect the shape of Tanzanian society for generations to come.

Tanzanian participants in the aid dialogue also raised, as a matter of fundamental concern, the role of democratic debate in a reform process. Although the Tanzanian government was still a single-party system,[57] it was a broadly popular one with a lively and pluralistic internal dialogue over the merits of the various policy choices. Tanzanian participants pointed out that, unlike Ghana, their government was not a military dictatorship or a personal autocracy that could impose its will by force. A number of Tanzanians believed that if the ILIs insisted on treating the government as a unitary actor capable of making speedy and binding decisions on major issues, this could force a tendency to stifle dissenting views. Even donor representatives acknowledged that the democratic argument carried great weight; some agreed that Tanzania's democratic discussions should have been given a greater effect on the pace, timing, and sequence of its reform process.

The Advisors' Group experience revealed another, sometimes unspoken aspect of the donor-recipient relationship: the extent to which the two parties are essential to each other. The concept of aid dependency does not apply only to the recipient country; it describes both recipients and donors. Host countries need the financial assistance and technical support donors can provide. The donors need responsive recipients. To justify their costs and expenditures, they need to be able to show beneficial outcomes from their investment of taxpayer funds. The mutuality of need makes it difficult for either party to disengage.

The Advisors' Group process culminated in a grand but unspoken bargain. The government of Tanzania accepted the need for timely and credible progress in implementing further economic reforms. The donors would accept that that they could do very little, short of interference in Tanzania's domestic affairs, about Tanzania's entrenched political-economic oligarchy, which orchestrated the economic transition in a way that ensured its continued control of the economy and the state. Some aid officials have maintained that it is not the responsibility of the foreign community to dislodge the CCM from its grip on political power. This grand bargain has now been in place for nearly twenty years. It has been the basic building block in Tanzania's reputation for political and economic stability. However, it has done little to erase the corruption that pervades the Tanzanian political system, the inequality between the governing oligarchy and the vast majority of Tanzanians, or the likelihood that the CCM would keep control of the country in the near future. Since the 1994 crisis, foreign aid in Tanzania has been both enabling and intrusive at the same time.

Chapter 5

The Path to Economic Reform
II: Internal Alignments

There are two critical weaknesses in the aid debate. The first is its reliance on an oversimplified, two-actor model, the tendency to view the reform dialogue as one between unitary agents on each side. The Tanzanian reality was far more complex. During the long period of delay between the 1974 economic low point and the initiation of a reform effort in the mid-1980s, both the donors and Tanzanian leaders showed internal divisions in their approach to the country's economic policies. The second weakness is that both sides exaggerate the impact of donor influence: one side holds the donors almost exclusively responsible for a continuity of poor policy, the other for an assertive intrusiveness that provides an explanation for policy change. Each is an overstatement.

Tanzania's donors could not have begun to bring about significant changes unless the country's internal political alignments had undergone a corresponding shift in favor of policy reforms. This was not a smooth or speedy process. It would be naïve to believe that an economic crisis produces a collective change of heart on the part of a country's top leaders, who now come to understand that their crisis calls for fundamental policy changes. The relationship between an economic crisis and a government's decision to move forward with a program of economic reform is not a simple matter of cause and effect whereby political elites recognize their policy mistakes and adjust their policies accordingly. If that were so, Tanzania would not have experienced such a prolonged interlude between the low point of its economic crisis and the beginning of policy changes: it would have initiated reform efforts years earlier.

The ensemble of causal factors that launches a policy change is a cryptic mix of external and internal elements and of intellectual and material considerations. The immediate causal connection between an economic crisis and the start of reforms is weak: an economic crisis strengthens the arguing position of those who favor alternative policies and weakens the policy arguments of those who wish to preserve the existing framework. However, the strength of policy arguments is only one factor in providing a convincing explanation of exactly when a reform effort begins. The societal dynamic by which an economic crisis brings about reforms is less obvious and more gradual: a crisis gradually strips away the social basis of support for those who wish to continue the existing policy arrangements.

Any policy framework creates economic winners and losers. It seems axiomatic that social groups that are doing well, even if an economy as a whole is in decline, will be more reluctant to accept economic reform than those that are doing poorly. As an economic crisis deepens, it inverts the ratio of winners to losers: the winners decline; the losers increase. As yesterday's winners become today's losers, their social support for the system will decline correspondingly. As it grows in size, the coalition of economic losers is able to exert growing pressure on the government to change its policies. This was exactly what happened in Tanzania. In the first years of the ISI system, the social groups connected to the state-sponsored industrial sector were winners. As such, they were prepared to support the policy and the various measures the government needed to take to implement it. However, as the economic crisis deepened, it converted more and more of these groups into losers and critics of the system.

The clearest example of this phenomenon is the Tanzanian labor movement. The socioeconomic history of labor movements in Africa is so important that it is time for labor studies to replace ethnicity studies as a focus of African area research. Like so many parts of the Tanzanian story, the evolution of labor's relationship with TANU/CCM, from an uneasy nationalist cooperation to political mistrust, deserves a separate political narrative. Major parts of the Tanzanian labor movement had never aligned themselves with the government's insistence on socialist industrialization. These included agricultural workers, who were directly dependent on the prosperity of the agricultural sector, and transportation and dockworkers, who moved the crops from the fields to the cities and ports. The idea that Tanzanian workers had an economic interest in industrialization applied at most to Tanzania's industrial workers and then only for a short period. The common expression for describing the political alignment that emerges under ISI is *peronista coalition*, a term drawn from the experience of the Argentinian dictator Juan Perón. It conveys the idea of a political alliance of industrial labor and capital, both of which benefit from the subsidies provided by taxes on agriculture. Tanzania's labor history suggests that this was never a very strong coalition to begin with. By the 1970s, it had become a coalition of the unwilling.

One of many ironies in the political economy of Tanzania lies in the fact that a socialist government committed to promoting the country's industrial sector never fully enjoyed the support of its industrial workers. As early as 1969, it lost what little worker support it seemed to have. There had always been a strong sense of divergent interests between Tanzanian workers and their country's nationalist movement. Before independence, Tanganyika had a classic form of labor organization that consisted of politically unaligned unions that felt free to pursue the interests of their members. In the mid-1950s, Tanganyika had about two dozen small union organizations with a total membership of approximately fifteen thousand. In 1955, approximately seventeen of these organizations came together to form the Tanganyikan Federation of Labor (TFL). By the time of independence, the TFL had grown to about 180,000 members, an extraordinary increase in membership but still less than 2 percent of the total population. Despite the small numbers, several of the TFL unions, including those representing dockworkers, railroad workers, and plantation workers, were powerful and well organized. Because of their economically strategic position, these unions' ability to leverage the economy was disproportionate to their small numbers.

During the nationalist period, the TFL adopted an arm's length political strategy that offered support for TANU's nationalist goals while, at the same time, maintaining organizational independence. The TFL derived its approach from the classic pattern of free union movements in the United States and Western Europe. This model stressed the need to preserve the unions' strategic options, including collective bargaining, strikes, work stoppages, formation of mutually supportive alliances between unions, and, perhaps most important, flexibility to operate freely in the political sphere by supporting or opposing different parties. TFL leaders shared the core premises of free trade unionism, the most important of which was that the socioeconomic interests of union members were not necessarily identical to those of the wider population.

After independence, the fragility of the TFL-TANU alliance became more and more apparent. One source of disagreement was the pace of Africanization.

How long would the TANU government allow non-indigenous Tanganyikans to hold jobs that might otherwise go to Tanzanian workers of indigenous descent? Union leaders viewed the newly independent political environment as an opportunity to advance the interests of union members. From their standpoint, the same set of union tactics that had been available to support the nationalist cause should now be available to advance the well being of unionized workers.[1] A series of strikes around the time of independence brought this cleavage into sharp focus. Union leaders tended to press for an unequivocal commitment to Africanization. TANU leaders, however, tended to be cautious on the Africanization question, seeking ways to balance a commitment to Africanization with a concern for how quickly university graduates with the technical and managerial skills required by a modern government might become available.

Once in power, TANU leaders who had welcomed union support during the nationalist era began to take a critical view of workers' rights. From their standpoint, a strike by strategically powerful unions, such as the railroad workers or dockworkers, could easily cripple the nation's entire economy, lowering the welfare of all Tanzanians. The unions might well improve their members' material position by engaging in these activities, but this could be at a great cost to the well being of the 95 percent or more of Tanzanians who were not members of numerically small but economically powerful unions. To prevent the unions from exercising their traditional rights, the Government of Tanganyika passed a series of laws that greatly enhanced its ability to constrain trade union activity. These included the Trade Unions Ordinance (Amendment) Act, no. 51 of 1962,[2] the Trade Dispute (Settlement) Act, no. 43 of 1962,[3] and a broad law creating greater government authority over union membership and strike participation passed in 1964.[4]

The government formally banned the TFL in February 1964, alleging that TFL leaders had supported the army mutiny a month earlier. Later in the year, it placed the union movement wholly under the control of the Ministry of Labor by passing the National Union of Tanganyika Workers (NUTA) Act of 1964.[5] Within two years of independence, the government had brought the country's trade union movement under the administrative and regulatory jurisdiction of the Ministry of Labor. The areas of disagreement between the TANU government and the unions included a dispute over the desirability of state-led industrialization. Union leaders had always been among those who had doubts about Nyerere's inclination to pursue a socialist development strategy. Many believed that a market economy would afford unions greater freedom to negotiate with private employers over wages and benefits. In a private economy, the government's role would be limited to arbiter of last resort. Since the government would have no direct stake in the outcome of labor negotiations, unions could use the entire array of tactics at their disposal to pursue the interests of their members.

Despite their doubts about state-led industrialization, some union leaders were prepared to accept it because it offered workers a series of trade-offs that worked out slightly in their favor. Workers would lose union autonomy and, along with it, the right to engage in independent work actions such as strikes. They would also lose the right to support opposition leaders and organizations. In return, however, they received substantial economic benefits. These included secure jobs in protected industries and the improved purchasing power afforded by an overvalued exchange rate that cheapened the cost of imported consumer goods. Urban workers would also benefit from the higher living standards afforded by agricultural pricing policies that reduced the cost of food staples. In addition, they would enjoy a lax disciplinary environment for infractions such as absenteeism, tardiness, pilferage, or disruptive behavior. Since the industrial workers' principal employer was a benevolently inclined government administering a system of industrial protections, they did not need to concern themselves with the squeeze on wages that might arise from the profit motive or a competitive industrial environment.

During the early years of industrialization, the expansion of the industrial sector meant increased employment opportunities and a buoyant environment for salaries and promotions. Workers were sufficiently well off that some Tanzanian officials and a few university intellectuals began to complain of the emergence of an *aristocracy of labor*, suggesting that the widening socioeconomic gap between the affluent industrial workers and the impoverished majority of Tanzanians might undermine the president's ethos of social equality.[6]

The worker prosperity that led to fears of a worker aristocracy did not last very long. As the state-managed industrial economy ground down, the economic conditions of industrial workers grew steadily worse. The steady drop-off in industrial capacity utilization meant that even a benevolent socialist state had to accept the need for layoffs and furloughs among workers who could no longer be productively employed. The financial insolvency of many industries also meant wage payments were often late; some workers went unpaid for long periods. Rising rates of inflation also eroded the purchasing power of workers' salaries. The rising prices in parallel markets, where workers had to obtain many of their essential goods, also lowered living standards, as did inflation, which threatened to erase such prized perquisites as retirement and death benefits. The decline in public services also had its greatest effects on industrial workers. Because the worker areas of Dar es Salaam are far from the parts of the city where the industries are located, the decline in public transportation became a critical source of difficulty. Access to medical services became similarly degraded. As unemployment rose and real wages declined, workers became acutely aware that the government-sponsored NUTA was less an organization to promote worker welfare than a government vehicle for controlling worker dissent.

The tipping moment for Tanzanian workers arrived in fall 1969 when the government arrested the minister of labor Michael Kamaliza and placed him on trial to face the accusation that he had plotted the overthrow of the government. Kamaliza had been a highly respected figure in the Tanzanian labor movement. During the late 1950s, he was the leader of the Transport and General Workers Union (TGWU), one of the largest of the constituent unions in the TFL. He subsequently rose to become president of the TFL. In 1961, when he agreed to become minister of labor and preside over the country's labor movement, many accepted his insistence that this decision grew out of a genuine desire to make the newly independent government work for the benefit of unionized labor. As minister of labor during the 1960s, he had emerged as a defender of the NUTA model, which ended the autonomy the labor movement. Many Tanzanians believed that if he had participated in a treasonous plot, this would have come about because of his disillusionment with the NUTA system and, possibly, with the broader socialist framework that seemed to require such tight controls over unionized labor.

Throughout the 1970s, Tanzanian workers were at most captive participants in an economic system over which they had no control, which they were powerless to change but still somewhat reluctant to oppose openly. To the extent that there was worker support for the government's framework, it derived partly from fear of the possible effects of reform rather than any benefits workers might have been receiving. Despite the falling purchasing power of workers' salaries and all-pervasive anxieties that the ongoing economic decline might cause additional factory closures and layoffs, there was a countervailing fear that liberal economic changes might only make conditions worse. Some employment, even under increasingly desperate conditions, seemed preferable to the all-but-certain unemployment that would ensue if the state divested itself of the factory system and subjected it to free market forces.

A second and vitally important social group that experienced the economic conversion from winners to losers was mid- and low-range state employees. During the early years of expansion of the state sector, lower civil servants had enjoyed many of the same sources of upward socioeconomic buoyancy as industrial workers. Rapidly expanding employment opportunity in fast-growing government ministries, such as planning and financial affairs, trade and industry, labor, and lands, housing, and urban development, created numerous job opportunities and expanding opportunities for promotion to upper management. The ready availability of imported consumer goods and foodstuffs whose prices were lowered by the overvalued currency further buoyed the living standards of public sector employees. Many state employees also enjoyed very generous fringe benefits that included publicly provided housing and special access to government hospitals and clinics. Even lower level civil servants seemed to find ways to supplement their official income through rent-seeking and white-collar pilferage.

Economic decline had exactly the same effect on public sector employees as it did on industrial workers. Inflation was eroding the real purchasing power of their salaries. Although rent seeking seemed to be all pervasive throughout the Tanzanian bureaucracy, there were many public officials whose positions did not afford rent-seeking opportunities or whose rent-seeking opportunities were limited. Custodial and service personnel in government office buildings, clerical and technical personnel in government positions that did not afford contact with the public, mechanics and technicians who maintained government vehicles, and teachers in primary and secondary schools—all these had fewer opportunities to engage in rent-seeking.[7]

One of the most pivotal sources of political change in Tanzania was the price structure of the parallel marketplace. Rising prices in parallel markets converted many public employees from supporters to opponents of the system. Owing to goods scarcities, many civil servants had to spend a part of their working day scavenging parallel markets for items that might or might not be available in sufficient supply to satisfy family needs. Their well being worsened as the prices in parallel markets placed the goods they needed further out of reach. By the early 1980s, virtually any commodity Tanzanians needed or wanted—from the smallest watch batteries to air conditioners and portable generators—was still available in the parallel marketplace but at unaffordable prices. Although currency overvaluation should normally have cheapened the cost of these goods, scarcity meant that many items were outside the price range of even middle-class Tanzanians. As wages stagnated and prices skyrocketed, even heroic efforts at inventing rent-seeking opportunities were not sufficient to arrest the decline in middle-class living standards. The enduring symbol of middle-class decline became the inoperable family automobile, stored on cinder blocks, awaiting spare parts that might never again be available or affordable. Deepening and seemingly irremediable poverty changed the political outlook of this entire social class.

The downward mobility of Tanzania's public sector employees was an especially acute problem for the governing party. The CCM had always self-identified both to the Tanzanian public and to its international audience as a mass party whose members came from all walks of life in Tanzanian society.[8] While there may have been some element of truth in that claim, the fact was that the core membership of the party, the real backbone of its organizational structure, were always Tanzanians with some public sector connection. Tanzania's unionized workers had never aligned themselves very closely with the governing party and Tanzanian farmers, both large and small, objected to the high levels of taxation and control inherent in the government's economic model. Immediately after independence, Tanzania began to face a problem common to many African countries: the governing party could not maintain the enthusiasm and high levels of active membership that had been characteristic of the late nationalist period. The political scientist Henry Bienen described post-independence Tanganyika as a "no party" state.[9]

To deal with the decline of the party, Tanzania's political leaders had decided that the classic Whitehall-Westminster model of government, with a legal separation between the civil service and political wings of government, was not applicable to a single-party developing country.[10] Civil servants were encouraged to become party members and party members who wished to become civil servants enjoyed great advantages in doing so. After that, the CCM became a party of civil servants and employees of public sector institutions with a veneer of mass membership among other social strata. When that stratum of Tanzanian society was doing well, as in the mid- to late 1960s, the party enjoyed their loyalty and affection. When the living standards of civil servants began to fall, along with those of other Tanzanians, public sector employees began to evince doubts about the system. It is helpful to distinguish between a tipping point, which refers to a single moment, and a tipping process, which has more gradual effects. Among the several processes that tipped mid-1980s Tanzania toward market-based policies, one of the most important was the governing party's growing inability to maintain the uncritical support of the mid- and lower level civil servants who provided its core membership.

Other elements of the statist coalition underwent a similar political transition. There was growing opposition to the statist economy among the influential technocratic elements that had emerged with the early growth of the state-sponsored industrial system. This group included the engineers, technicians, equipment managers, accountants, and personnel officers who were essential for complex industrial production. So long as the state-industries were benefiting from an inflow of subsidies and protections, employment opportunities for these groups expanded, and they enjoyed rising real wages, job security, and generous benefits. When the industrial sector began to deteriorate, however, the white-collar technocrats suffered alongside everyone else. Like industrial workers, they began to experience heightened levels of unemployment and the diminishing real value of other benefits. The same was true of the many small businesses that provided services for the large factories, such as the companies that provided catering, uniforms, and office equipment.

Urban consumers, though not organized as an interest group, also experienced a status reversal. Early in the industrial process, urban consumers—and this included state employees—benefitted from overvalued exchange rates that cheapened the prices of imported goods and from agricultural policies that lowered their cost-of-living by suppressing the prices of food staples. As consumer goods become less available in formal markets that operated according to official exchange rates, however, the exchange rate subsidy began to disappear. Indeed, workers on fixed wages tended to be among the first casualties of economic decline. The parallel markets, where Tanzanians obtained many of their consumer goods, adjusted their prices for the real exchange rate and for the element of risk. Over time, consumer goods that had been relatively affordable became affordable only to the most affluent. The same was true of the cost of food staples, which also rose as faltering agricultural production led to scarcities of these items. When consumers began to suffer the deprivations of economic decline alongside other social groups that depended upon the new industrial sector, the government began to confront an urban environment of political discontent.

Elite Dynamics

World Bank economist Yvonne Tsikata has compared Tanzania's reform efforts with those of Ghana, pointing out that Ghana's reforms came earlier and were more all embracing.[11] However, Ghana was a military dictatorship during the early period of economic reforms, and although Tanzania was a single-party system, it had a political process that sustained open discussion in the party and the government. There were institutional pockets of reformism just as there were institutional pockets of resistance. The foremost anti-reformer was President Nyerere who, throughout his period in office, remained a proponent of socialism and the need for a state-led economy. There has never been any suggestion that he ever wavered from his belief in these ideas. Throughout his presidency, he used his formidable political power to appoint leaders who shared his views and dismiss those who disagreed with him. At times, he used his legal authority to imprison political opponents. His ability to control the government was virtually absolute. Nyerere won reelection to his final five-year term as president in fall 1980. Despite repeated overtures by the international community as well as the rising chorus of reformist voices in his own government, he refused until the end of his presidency to initiate the policy changes that might lead to liberalization of his nation's economy.

The impression that Nyerere's departure from the presidency ushered in a new era in the Tanzanian policy process is only partly true. The 1985 election was a tipping point for Tanzania but only in the limited sense that Nyerere was willing to step aside and allow a reform-minded president to assume office. Mwinyi was well disposed toward reform and began to use the powers of the presidency to begin the process. He could launch a number of reforms from the president's office, and he could encourage private sector activity by changing the tone of political discourse. However, he did not have the towering political stature Nyerere had enjoyed. The circumstances of Mwinyi's early years in office, which included the hovering presence of the former president, did not permit a wholesale sweep of Nyerere-era officials. As a result, many leaders Nyerere had appointed to important positions continued in positions of power from which they were often difficult to dislodge. The early years of the Mwinyi presidency presented a somewhat perplexing picture: a liberalizing president chosen for that office by a political party whose leadership still included many influential figures doing well under the old system and who were unconvinced of the need for market-based reforms. The party was presided over by a revered former president whose commitment to the existing system was widely shared among elected and administrative members of the governing elite.

The key institutional source of the delay was the way in which the CCM nominated its candidates for the National Assembly. The CCM chose its candidates for the National Assembly through a system of party nomination that empowered the party's highest tier of leaders to make the final choices over who could stand for office and who could not. The nomination procedure required prospective candidates to apply first to district-level selection committees, which selected a panel of five possible nominees. The district committees then submitted their recommendations to the party's National Executive Committee (NEC), which had the final authority to choose the two candidates who would be allowed to stand in each constituency. It had always been customary throughout Nyerere's presidency for the same person to hold the positions of head of state and head of the party. This enabled the head of state to have a decisive influence over his party's selection of candidates for the National Assembly and minimized the possibility of a political division between the executive and legislative branches of government. Many Tanzanians had considered this arrangement a binding precedent and expected Nyerere to step down as head of the party at the same time he left the office of head of state.

That did not happen, however. After stepping down as president in 1985, Nyerere had insisted that he remain head of the party, thereby splitting the two roles. This weakened the legislative authority of President Mwinyi because he was not in a position to influence the selection of the party's assembly candidates for the 1985 general election. From 1985 to 1990, Tanzania effectively had two heads of state: one, Mwinyi, was head of the government and favorable to reform; the second, Nyerere, was head of the party and at best a reluctant reformer. Since the constitution made the party the supreme organ of government, Nyerere's position of authority was constitutionally superior to that of the head of state. According to Tanzania's constitutional theory during this period, the party had supreme authority to choose the country's policy approach, and the National Assembly had the responsibility to translate the decisions of the party into the law of the land. While the president might well be inclined to move the country along the path of economic reform, his authority was technically subordinate to that of the party.

The political outcome of the split leadership scenario was a reluctant National Assembly. Nyerere had selected or approved the nomination of the members of the National Assembly who gained election in 1985—and who would hold office between 1985 and 1990. His position as head of the party had longer-term implications. If he should choose to stay on, he would control the nomination process for the 1990 election as well. The lesson was clear: for the entire five-year period from 1985 to 1990, any National Assembly members who gained a reputation for opposing Nyerere's economic views might be placing their seats at risk. This explains why the reform record of the National Assembly between 1985 and 1990 was poor and why the only reforms that went ahead expeditiously during that period were those that the executive branch could accomplish on its own. The process of building a reform coalition within the legislature could not begin until Nyerere had stepped down as head of the party, and one person, President Mwinyi, would hold the two most powerful positions in the country, head of government and head of the party. Nyerere's departure as head of the party in 1990 set the stage for a wave of reformist legislation, a certain indicator of the extent to which he had held up the legislative side of the reform process before that time.[12]

To avoid a head-on collision with the Nyerere elements in the National Assembly, the Mwinyi administration pursued an alternate reform strategy, one that did not depend on its willingness to pass reform-oriented laws. Mwinyi's early initiatives included the first phases of exchange rate devaluation, granting permission for the import of used clothing—a highly popular measure owing to the failure of the state's clothing industry—and reducing the number of items under the control of the NPC. Mwinyi's most important source of power was his ability to control political symbolism.. He could change the national discourse away from the virtues of socialism and stress the benefits of a market economy. The president's political strategy was to build social constituencies outside the legislature as pressure groups for eventual legislative action. Some aid officials and Tanzanians criticize the Mwinyi administration for encouraging a somewhat lawless transition to a market economy, one that took the form of unchecked corruption on the part of high-ranking officials. In assessing this criticism, it is helpful to keep in mind that the National Assembly still had control over Tanzania's legal environment, which consisted, for the most part, of laws passed during the Nyerere era. Since the National Assembly was under the influence of the former president, corruption was one of the only mechanisms available to create a set of interest groups for a market-based economy.

Tanzania's political pattern from 1985 to 1990 contradicts its usual image as a country with an all-powerful executive branch. During that period, it offered an example of the checks and balances that arise in a divided government. Tanzania had an executive branch occupied by a strongly reformist president, Mwinyi; a constitutionally supreme governing party, the CCM, still headed by the country's arch anti-reformist, Julius Nyerere, and a party hierarchy densely populated with officials who shared Nyerere's views. It also featured a legislative branch whose members owed their nominations to the former head of state. As a result, many of the economic reforms that required legislative approval tended to proceed slowly during the first term of the Mwinyi Presidency. Only when Nyerere's departure from the party permitted a reunification of the two positions was Mwinyi in a position to exercise influence over the nomination process. At that point, the National Assembly became more amenable to reform initiatives emanating from the president's office and began to pass the torrent of reform legislation that began with the Cooperative Societies Act of 1991.

Throughout the 1980s, the pattern of power relationships in Tanzania exhibited the classic factional divide between "reds" and "experts." The former group wished to retain the older policy framework with its insistence on government ownership, central planning, and strict regimentation of the agricultural sector. The latter emphasized the benefits of market forces and the need to dismantle the government's costly, unproductive, and corrupt mechanisms of control and regulation. The policy disagreements between reformers and anti-reformers were often but not always a reflection of their deeper institutional interests. Each of these factions consisted of a cluster of institutional and social actors. The balance of power between the two groups was such that Tanzania's transition toward a more open economy was slow and piecemeal. It also meant that the timing, sequence, and thoroughness of economic reforms in Tanzania had less to do with a unified effort to attain an optimal economic changeover than with the shifting power relationships between the different domestic actors involved in the process.

The reds coalition largely consisted of the wide array of political and bureaucratic actors that benefited from the existing system of economic controls. In Tanzania, the most powerful of these was the governing party itself whose top leadership exhibited a frame of mind that confounded aid officials. One highly placed World Bank official described this unusual frame of mind in the following terms:

At the outset of the economic recovery program, economic decision-making was dominated by a political party that remained firmly wedded to its socialist principles and was primarily concerned with economic recovery. There was no consensus on the need to move to a more liberal, market based economy. The background, orientation, hardened attitudes, and ingrained habits of those entrusted with implementing the reforms clearly meant that the reform process would, at least initially, be difficult and slow.[13]

Even while acknowledging the desperate state of the country's economy and the imperative need for economic improvements, the highest-ranking party officials appeared to disconnect the policy measures required for an economic recovery from the socialist ethos to which the party was officially committed. It was as if the measures required to improve the operation of the economy were separable from the party's commitment to a socialist economic system. Although government officials might acknowledge that some of the state's major economic institutions, such as the NMC or the NPC, had performed poorly, the dialogue they sought had to do with what might be required to improve the performance of the existing system, not how to replace it with market forces.

There is sometimes an image that a reform exercise is a well-orchestrated whole, with a core actor or group of actors with sufficient authority to give the reform process a systematic quality. That would be very rare. There is a common understanding that the minister of finance and resident representative of the World Bank can orchestrate a reform process. However, even if those two key individuals work closely together, their ability to influence the behavior of other key players is limited. A Ministry of Finance is only one actor within a government; it has limited ability to orchestrate the actions of other ministries. The minister of finance, working closely with the World Bank resident representative, can signal the beginning of a new economic era, but the process of changing economic policies often exhibits a silo pattern whereby a different group of policy actors controls each separate area of policy reform. In Tanzania, there was one circle of actors concerned with exchange rate reform; another, with international trade; still others, with agricultural reforms, including reform of land ownership; and a different set of actors engaged in divesting the state-owned enterprises. The silo effect meant that reforms in the silos controlled by economic reformers tended to proceed much more quickly than those still in the hands of regime conservatives. It also resulted in a tendency for each area of reform to have its own distinct trajectory separate from any planned connection to other areas of reform.

Further complicating matters was a divided pattern of authority within the Tanzanian bureaucracy. During the period of single-party rule, which lasted until the early 1990s, the governing party had embedded itself in the bureaucracy. The CCM effort to rejuvenate itself by recruiting civil servants had saturated the civil service with devoted party members. The Tanzanian bureaucracy had a dualistic system of authority and rank. The first was the usual tiered system of administrative ranks with promotions based on merit. The second consisted of parallel units of the party called *ten-house cells*. These existed in each agency of the bureaucratic hierarchy. The party's system rewarded ideological loyalty and party activism. Each party cell had its own leader, elected by the party members in the cell. Any government office, therefore, might have both an office manager with bureaucratic authority and a ten-house cell leader with authority based on election by the party members who worked there.

The presence of a party apparatus embedded in a government bureaucracy meant that it would be inaccurate to describe Tanzania's internal conflicts over reform as pitting a reform-oriented bureaucracy against a conservative and still ideologically driven political party. Since the cell leaders often perceived economic reforms as threatening to party dominance, they could be a source of resistance to reform even in ministries that had a reformist outlook. Many bureaucratic officials who favored economic reform believed, often correctly, that it was impossible to gain promotions within the administrative hierarchy without the endorsement and support of their ten-house cell leader, who sometimes occupied a lower position in the formal bureaucratic hierarchy. The constitutional supremacy of the party made it especially difficult to resolve the inherent strains between the two forms of hierarchy. Since the party was officially the supreme organ of the Tanzanian government, the dual pattern of authority was a source of uncertainty about where final decision-making authority might rest and insecurity about advocating a policy change that might not have party approval. Donors who did not understand the internal effects of this binary system sometimes concluded that the bureaucracy was simply sluggish and resistant.

Overall, however, the reds versus experts cleavage did correspond closely, if not entirely, to the major bureaucratic divisions in the government. Not surprisingly, the ministries with the deepest stake in the system of state controls were the most reluctant to change it. One example was the Ministry of Lands, Housing, and Urban Development, which had grown massively in size and resources because of the nationalization of rental housing in 1967. Its jurisdiction over rental housing made it the country's largest landlord: it was responsible not only for assigning apartments by prioritizing the list of applicants but for the maintenance and repairs of the countless apartment buildings that had been nationalized. The opportunities for rent seeking in this ministry were extraordinary. Since the government fixed the rents on apartments in Dar es Salaam at 1967 levels, the depreciation in the value of the Tanzania shilling caused by inflation meant that the official rental cost of most apartments shrunk to levels that were inconsequential relative to incomes. At parallel market exchange rates, the Tanzania shilling cost of many apartments amounted to only one or two dollars per month. The difference between the government's monthly rental charge for an apartment and its real market value created incentives for ministerial officials to find ways to capture the difference. They were inventive in doing so. By the late 1970s, the key money cost of obtaining an apartment was equivalent to several years of rent. The under-the-table payments for having an apartment repaired could also be considerable. If reforms were to result in reassigning responsibility for rental housing to the private sector, this ministry would lose both its administrative reason for existence, with all its attendant budgetary resources, and the lucrative opportunities for side payments that went along with it.

The Ministry of Trade and Industry also had much at risk if reform were to go forward. Since it presided over the management and operation of the state-sponsored industrial sector, it could maintain itself on an especially grand scale, with a payroll that included large numbers of civil servants who had responsibility for funding, constructing, staffing, and operating the state industries. This ministry was also responsible for issuing the lucrative subcontracts to the firms that provided the support services required by the state industries, including accounting and payroll, laundering, transportation, custodial work, and catering. The tendering of service contracts was notorious for the scale of the rent-seeking opportunities it provided. As the institutional locus of the government trade policy, the Ministry of Trade and Industry also presided over implementation of the cumbersome system of trade protection. Ministries with responsibility for trade policy tend to oppose reform because liberal changes take away the rent-seeking opportunities that arise from their authority to authorize trade licenses and foreign exchange. The opposition of Tanzania's Ministry of Planning and Financial Affairs to a market model was obvious: in a market-driven economy, its principal areas of authority would become superfluous.

The list of bureaucratic entities opposed to reform was practically endless. It included the NMC, which stood to lose a large part of its bureaucratic resources as well as the lucrative opportunities for rent seeking that derived from its authority to administer the distribution and sale of key food staples if the reform process shifted these areas of responsibility back to the private sector. The NMC would lose the opportunity to staff and profit from the national network of village-level buying stations, processing centers, and storage warehouses. The crop-marketing authorities would also have their authority and resources substantially diminished if private sector actors or primary cooperative societies resumed their historic areas of responsibility. Given the extensiveness and influence of bureaucratic sectors that were cool toward reform, it is not surprising that the early stage of the reform process was slow.

The reformist or "experts" coalition was not without powerful actors of its own. After Mwinyi's succession to the presidency in 1985, it began with the office of the president, which, under Tanzania's system of strong executive authority, was the most powerful institutional entity within the government. The list of reform-oriented institutions also included the Central Bank (the Bank of Tanzania) and the Ministry of Finance, which had firsthand insight into the economic damage wrought by the country's inappropriate monetary, exchange rate, and fiscal policies. Reformers within the government enjoyed the support of a younger generation of academic economists at the University of Dar es Salaam who, through their friendships with government officials and the force of intellectual persuasion in their scholarship and their consulting reports, helped to reinforce the new climate of opinion. The reformist views of Tanzania's liberal economists enjoyed the added weight of their ability to align themselves with powerful international actors such as the World Bank and International Monetary Fund.

The Ministry of Agriculture, one of the largest in the government aligned itself strongly with the reformist coalition. Ministerial officials had firsthand exposure to the economic damage done to the rural sector by the government's unrelenting tendency to use agriculture as a source of tax revenues and to the harmful economic effects of insecurity over land entitlements caused by the socialist villages program. As part of the early wave of reform efforts, the Ministry of Agriculture in 1982 had issued its own reform document, the *Tanzania National Agricultural Policy*.[14] One of Tanzania's leading economists, Professor Simon Mbilinyi, chaired the ministerial study group that produced this report and several of the country's most prestigious economists including Lucien Msambichaka and Benno Ndulu were members. Their voices carried great weight within the government. In sometimes outspoken language, the ministry's report criticized a pattern of agricultural decision-making motivated by ideological objectives, such as communal farming, and by concerns for other sectors rather than by an interest in maximizing agricultural productivity and in increasing agricultural exports to improve foreign exchange earnings. In its rebuke of fifteen years of failed agricultural policy, the *Agricultural Policy* report stated that the CCM government had departed from its own basic principles, which had accorded high priority to development of the rural economy and called for restructuring the country's investment priorities back toward the agricultural sector.

The division between reds and experts sometimes had no apparent connection to institutional rivalries; it could spring from the way in which different members of the political elite viewed their best interests. One example was divestiture of state-owned manufacturing enterprises. Some members of the oligarchy were eager for privatization of the SOEs, seeing this as an opportunity to expand their private sector holdings into areas of economic activity still under government control. Some of the most powerful and well-off Tanzanians were aware that if they could manage divestiture strategically, they could acquire ownership of state firms at bargain basement prices. Other members of the oligarchy, sensing the imminence of multiparty competition, viewed SOEs more in terms of their long-term political advantages. Since even poorly performing state industries could still hire employees, qualify for preferential access to foreign exchange, and award subcontracts to firms that provided services, they could be a significant source of political patronage.

Sometimes the interaction between the government and civil society organizations could decisively affect the trajectory and outcome of a reform effort. On occasion, civil society organizations frustrated the implementation of major economic reforms that had navigated the tortuous pathway through intragovernmental divisions and received legislative approval. One major example has to do with changing the traditional social or communal basis of land holding to introduce private forms of land ownership. This issue is of monumental importance throughout sub-Saharan Africa, and since colonial times, it has been the subject of countless official and scholarly studies. Tanzania is a leading example of how deep-rooted, complex, and controversial this topic can become. More than perhaps any other topic, the issue of land rights in Tanzania deserves a separate book-length study.

The controversy over land entitlements in Tanzania has largely pitted two broad viewpoints against each other. On the one hand, economic reformers have long believed that the country's historic system of land ownership, which vested root title to land in the government but accorded traditional communities an entitlement status that amounted to communal ownership and control, needed to be altered to provide ownership rights to individuals and families. This would create a market environment and ensure that land be put to its highest and best use. On the other hand, some scholars favor the preservation of certain forms of traditional entitlement, such as those that safeguard the rights of pastoral communities. In this viewpoint, a market in land might not only give rise to landlessness and inequality in agricultural areas, but could also deprive migrant pastoral communities of their access to historic grazing land. There were also deep concerns about gender equity. Among some, there was a strong conviction that if the Tanzanian government were to proceed with a system of individual entitlements, it should take steps to provide the right to inherit and own land to women, who often did not have these rights under traditional systems.[15] Both sides agree that as Tanzania's population has grown and land has become more valuable, market-like transactions over rights to land have become more commonplace even in areas where the nominal ownership is communal. The difficulty is that since these informal market transactions have been unsupervised and unregulated, they are somewhat anarchic.

On the issue of land ownership, the Ministry of Agriculture also aligned itself with the reformers. Its 1982 report had recommended a system of individual and family titles so that Tanzanians could be more secure in their land entitlements and plan to invest in their farms on a long-term basis.[16] During the 1990s, reform-minded Tanzanian officials, influenced by the growing influence of the property rights school of economic development[17] and by donor opinion, concluded that Tanzania would gain considerable economic benefits by shifting rural communities away from social or communal ownership of land in the direction of individual land ownership.[18] To initiate the process, the government appointed a presidential commission to document Tanzania's existing patterns of land holding and to make recommendations about how to provide a legal basis for a transition to private ownership on parcels of land that individual Tanzanians had previously held through communally assigned use and occupancy rights.[19] Professor Issa Shivji, a globally renowned Tanzanian scholar who held the prestigious Julius K. Nyerere Chair in Pan African Studies at the University of Dar es Salaam, chaired the study commission, which included members of the Tanzanian National Assembly. After the report of the presidential commission was published, the Tanzanian National Assembly began to frame legislation that would establish a system of individual titles to land. In 1999, it passed two laws whose purpose was to initiate a changeover from communal ownership to individual title deeds. These were the Land Act of 1999 and the Village Land Act of 1999.[20]

The social coalition opposed to these laws, which was described by one observer as Tanzania's "odd couple," brought together urban intellectuals, mostly academics and journalists, and rurally based traditional authorities. In 1994, the urban intellectuals opposed to individual ownership rights had formed a protest organization called Land Rights (Haki Ardhi),[21] which became a powerful force in opposition to the new laws. The urban opponents of land reform believed that private land ownership would result in increased landlessness and rising inequality.[22] They pointed to high rates of alcoholism and social despondency among individuals who had lost their rights to land in those areas of the country where there was an existing system of individual leasehold. They also called attention to the desperate conditions of families that had become impoverished when these losses took place. The opponents of land reform also drew attention to the potential for adverse environmental outcomes if the occupants of land did not have a communal responsibility to pass it on intact to subsequent generations.

The urban opponents of land reform found themselves in common cause in with traditional authorities, whose motivation was somewhat different. For a variety of reasons that included traditional forms of rent seeking, such as the gifts that customarily accompanied a grant of communal rights, rural community leaders were reluctant to surrender their control over land allocations. Leaders of Muslim religious organizations also expressed themselves in opposition to legal reforms that would offer women the right to inherit property. Western donor organizations, concerned about their relationship with Islamic countries, treated Muslim opposition with utmost seriousness. The opposition of these groups, combined with the daunting bureaucratic difficulty of creating a nationwide system of land registries that could administer a title-deed system, has frustrated any significant movement toward the implementation of a private deed system.

The product of so many internal divisions among Tanzanians was a constantly shifting political landscape of changing alignments and coalitions. The process of reform that resulted seemed lacking in any ordering principle. Beneath the shifting surface, there was a discernible trend: the forces of reform were becoming ascendant. Progress in this direction was painfully slow and sometimes seemed to stop altogether as a result of political obstacles within the government, but by the end of the 1980s, there was no longer any doubt about what direction the country was about to take. However, those who assume the inevitability or irreversibility of this outcome or who assume that any single force vector, such as donor influence, could have produced it, gravely underestimate the complex and difficult struggle that had gone on in the government. They also underestimate the huge political obstacles reformers had to overcome to ensure the reform process.

The untidiness of the political process has proven frustrating to economists, some of whom wished to prescribe an optimal reform sequence.[23] Some economists, for example, recommended that divestiture of SOEs should precede trade liberalization so that the newly divested companies might have the benefit of a period of protection while navigating the challenging transition from public to private ownership. A cocoon of protection, they believed, might have the additional advantage of making these companies more attractive to private purchasers. Some economists also recommended that divestiture should precede full currency devaluation so that newly privatized industries could have the benefit of a partial exchange rate subsidy while they went about the costly process of recapitalizing plant and equipment.

There was very little optimality about the sequencing of Tanzania's reform process. Contrary to economists' preferences for optimal sequencing of reforms, exchange rate devaluation and trade liberalization preceded the divestiture of state-owned enterprises. The disorderliness of the process, with its ever-changing alliances, its infinite variety of political actors, and its unpredictable outcomes has also proven frustrating to scholars, some of whom wished to discover an overriding explanatory variable. There was no answer to the frequently quoted but doubtless apocryphal request of some donors, "just tell us what buttons to push."

The Role of the Parallel Economy

The political leaders who presided over the old system and who benefited from it were among the last to surrender their attachment to it. The tendency for a country's political elite to resist reform even in the face of appalling economic conditions underscores one of the key political challenges faced by advocates of reform everywhere. The presence of an economic crisis does not mean that high-ranking members of the political elite are suffering from that crisis. They may even be profiting from it. In Tanzania, as in other countries undergoing economic difficulties, economic hardship was highly selective in its effects. Large- and small-scale farmers, industrial workers, and the middle and lower ranks of public sector employees were suffering deepening poverty; the higher-ranking members of the political elite were not. Jonathan Barker has referred to this phenomenon as the *paradox of development*, the idea that meaningful reform would require political leaders to change the socioeconomic order from which they personally derived great benefits and in ways that might diminish those benefits.[24]

Barker's paradox illuminates much about the Tanzanian reform process. The economic policies of the political elite were imposing costs on others, not themselves. Throughout the country's economic crisis, those occupying the highest levels of the government and bureaucracy lived very well. They enjoyed luxurious housing in the exclusive residential areas of Dar es Salaam. They had preferential access to imported goods including luxury items. They had government vehicles and government staff at their disposal and could send their children to exclusive private schools. They also had opportunities for international travel with generous per diem expenses paid in hard currency. Owing to the rent-seeking opportunities afforded by the very scarcities of goods and services their policies were creating, members of the elite also had abundant cash, and every prospect of continuing personal affluence even as the country's broader economy deteriorated.

Barker's paradox spotlights the element of elite perversity when it comes to the need for economic reform. Political and economic elites do not have an obvious interest in changing their countries' economic policies. Indeed, to the extent that reform involves a transfer of power and resources from government actors to an impersonal marketplace, they have every interest in opposing it. Although Tanzania's economy was in a desperate state, the policy framework that had brought it to that point continued to provide generous benefits to the highest-ranking members of the governing elite, the Tanzanian 1 percent. Barker's paradox raises perhaps the most challenging question for scholars of Tanzanian political economy: how did the governing elite, which had benefited so greatly from the state-centered policy regime, morph so quickly into a social class that favored a market-based system?

There is no theoretical answer to Barker's question. The answer, at least for Tanzania and possibly other countries that embark upon economic reform, lies in the empirical realm. In Tanzania, it had to do with the role of corruption in making the political-economic oligarchy the major stakeholder in the country's rapidly expanding parallel economy. By the early to mid-1980s, many Tanzanian officials had begun to participate in the parallel economy not simply as consumers but as investors. At first, their involvement was the

urban version of a subsistence survival strategy. As the official economy declined, many members of the governing elite found that the only way to survive was through rent-seeking activities that could provide the additional
income necessary to purchase goods in the parallel marketplace, where prices
were constantly increasing owing to scarcity and inflation.[25] It did not take
long for many to discover that the pathway to even greater rewards lay in
participating in the booming parallel sector as business entrepreneurs actively involved in the production and retailing of goods. Some of this participation was blatant and overt. Sometimes elite members concealed their
involvement in the parallel economy through various forms of hidden partnerships or by vesting ownership in other family members.

For a great many Tanzanian officials and for ordinary Tanzanians, the
most glaring fact of everyday life had always been the dissonance between the
country's buoyant ethos of socialism and the economic hardships of daily
existence. When it comes to coping with hardships, Tanzanians are endlessly
inventive. Many public officials began to engage in private sector activities
early in the economic decline.[26] Some turned to garden farming to satisfy
urban demand; others raised chickens or operated small food kiosks. Some
state employees used their private vehicles as taxis or as commercial trucks.
Still others operated parallel market retail businesses of various kinds. The
close-knit extended family provided an ideal social vehicle for this economic
strategy. By having different family members involved in different economic
sectors, Tanzanians could diversify their portfolios and minimize their exposure to the collapse of public sector enterprise. Whatever the mechanism, the
families of many high-ranking political and administrative officials as well as
numerous members of Tanzania's mid-level elites began to engage in what
social anthropologists have termed *straddling*—finding ways to derive their
family income from multiple sources. Tanzanians began doing what people
everywhere do under conditions of economic stress: seeking to secure and
stabilize their family income by diversifying their portfolio of economic
activities.

The widespread practice of economic straddling by members of the Tanzanian middle class provides a compelling answer to one of the most frequently asked questions in the field of contemporary Tanzanian studies.
How did one of modern Africa's great socialist parties, which had presided
over a daring socialist economic experiment lasting for nearly twenty years,
transform itself so readily into a party of economic liberalization and structural adjustment? The answer lay in the socioeconomic transformation of

Tanzania's state-based political elite, which by the mid-1980s had simultaneously become, by way of straddling, a class of private entrepreneurs. The middle and upper level civil servants may have derived their official incomes from positions in the public sector or in state-controlled corporations. However, they often derived the larger portion of family income by creating and operating profitable side businesses in the parallel marketplace. As a result, Tanzania's public sector middle class had acquired a powerful economic interest in the broader legitimization of private sector activities. The countless thousands of other business entrepreneurs who operated productive enterprises in the informal sector joined them, creating a formidable constituency for reform.

One of the many contradictions in Tanzanian society during this period was the extent to which civil servants whose official responsibilities had to do with the management of a state economy were sustaining themselves and their families with income from their private sector businesses. Although Tanzania's leadership code had a formal prohibition against government employees earning secondary incomes from any sources, many officials were active participants in the parallel marketplace. A composite portrait of a typical urban Tanzanian family during this period might well show one member as a civil servant, teacher, or parastatal manager, a spouse engaged in trade or operating a small private sector retail business, and a brother or brother-in-law generating income in the transportation sector with a taxi or pick-up truck. The core ingredient in this family economy, however, was the public sector connection since this connection made it all possible. An official salary, even a small one, provided the initial finance for the side businesses and it was essential in reducing the risk of arrest or imprisonment.

Participation in the parallel marketplace changed the economic interest of Tanzanian public officials: the deeper their participation in this marketplace became, the greater their material stake in the normalization of the private sector. As Tanzanians found themselves compelled by circumstances to seek income in the parallel sector, they developed an economic interest in the creation of a political environment in which this activity would become legal. In 1986, when economic reforms began to erode the state-managed economy, and when President Mwinyi encouraged public officials to enrich themselves in the private economy, the most discernible reaction on the part of many public officials was a sense of relief. Few regretted the passing of the old order. Among many, there was eagerness to take up a new set of opportunities.

The scale of the parallel economy reveals much about the magnitude of this social process. This requires some untangling of the terms *parallel* and *informal economy*. The conventional way to understand the term informal economy is that it consists of small-scale producers, service providers, and merchants who provide goods available in larger, more elaborate enterprises. Thus, an individual who brings her car for service and repair to a dealership, which records and taxes the transaction, is dealing with a formal sector enterprise. The same person bringing the same car for repair to a roadside mechanic, who does not record or tax the transaction, is dealing with an informal sector enterprise. In Tanzania, one of the more salient differences had to do with the legality of a business activity. An informal entrepreneur is generally operating legally; a parallel market entrepreneur may be operating in a legal gray area. A small workshop converting discarded automobile tires to footwear might well be operating legally. However, if a public official owned this workshop, it might be in violation of the party's ban on multiple incomes.

This usage is close to that provided by Bagachwa and Naho in their seminal article on this topic.

> The term informal sector refers to very small-scale units producing and distributing goods and services and consisting of both employed workers and independent self-employed persons in both rural and urban areas. They are informal in the sense that they are for the most part unregistered, unrecorded in official statistics; and participants have little or no access to organized markets, to credit institutions, to formal education and training or to many public services. . . . Parallel market activities involve illegal production and trade of goods and services that are legal in themselves, and therefore have an alternative legal market.[27]

The taint of illegality was why so many public sector employees operated their side businesses through their spouses or other close relatives. In Tanzania, the terms parallel economy and informal sector have so much in common that they are almost interchangeable. By the early 1980s, there were so many public officials participating in the parallel economy that, from the standpoint of political effects, there was no meaningful distinction between the two. The key features of the parallel economy were its large size, great diversity, and increasing economic importance for large numbers of Tanzanian households, many of which included a public sector employee who provided start-up capital and a measure of political protection.

The exact magnitude of the informal sector is virtually impossible to measure because most transactions were unrecorded and untaxed. However, this is a matter of some importance since the size of the parallel market was an indicator of the extent to which privatization of the economy had taken place even under the umbrella of state control. The most common measurement of the size of the parallel marketplace is a comparison with the size of the country's formal GDP. For Tanzania, even these estimates have varied widely. The economists Alexander H. Sarris and Rogier van den Brink surveyed a number of efforts to measure the size of Tanzania's parallel sector. Combining these with their own measurements, they concluded that the Tanzanian parallel economy was somewhere between one-sixth and one-half the size of the official economy.[28] Bagachwa and A. Naho refer simply to the *second economy*. According to their estimates, Tanzania's second economy accounted for at least 20 percent of GDP in the early 1980s and probably more.[29] Whichever figure is closer to the correct one, the basic reality was that untold numbers of Tanzanians had become economic migrants into the parallel economy on both its supply side and its demand side. Bagachwa and Naho showed that a large proportion of Tanzanian families were obtaining much of their income through their private sector activities just as they were obtaining a large proportion of the goods they needed to purchase in the parallel marketplace. They concluded, "Over time the second economy has become a major source of livelihood, employment, and incomes for the majority of the households."[30] For all families in this position, economic liberalization would be a welcome change. It would help eliminate the element of legal risk involved in parallel market activity and create a wider horizon of economic opportunities.

Following on the Bagachwa and Naho study, Tanzania's Economic and Social Research Foundation (ESRF) conducted a comprehensive study whose purpose was to create an inventory of research on this topic. The estimates recorded by the authors of the ESRF report varied widely but practically all suggested that the parallel economy was between 30 and 50 percent of official GDP.[31] Some estimates were even higher and placed the parallel economy at as much as 75 percent of official GDP. The authors of the ESRF report settled on an estimate of between 60 and 70 percent of official GDP but warned that even these numbers could significantly understate the size of the parallel economy. It would be difficult to overstate the significance of this research. If the ESRF analysis was even close to correct, it affirms that Tanzania was well on the way toward becoming a largely privatized economy well before the beginning of formal economic reforms. On the eve of economic reforms, the Tanzanian government no longer had a choice as to whether to accept a transition to a market-based economy. For all practical purposes, the Tanzanian government's only choice was whether this transition would take place in an orderly manner under the legislative and administrative oversight of the state, and with the financial and technical assistance of the donor community, or whether it would take place in the unruly further expansion of the unregulated, untaxed, and somewhat anarchic parallel sector.

One of the more powerful motivations for economic reform was the element of lawlessness that had begun to emerge in parallel markets. Markets capable of providing clothing, alcoholic beverages, cigarettes, and luxury goods outside the legal framework governing the economy are just as capable of trafficking in arms, currency, and narcotics. Tanzanian officials were becoming alarmed that parts of the parallel economy operated as a front for money laundering and international traffic in other contraband goods. As long as the parallel market remained outside the administrative jurisdiction of the government, those forms of trade would be especially difficult to eliminate. Legalization of the private economy might not eliminate trade in these goods but it could help the government gain a greater element of control.

How could all this have taken place so quickly? The answer is that it did not. Whereas economists have called attention to the effects of ISI on the agricultural sector of nations such as Tanzania, there has been less documentation of its tendency to suffocate urban, small-scale manufacturing enterprises. Recall that, at independence, societies such as Tanzania had a vast array of small businesses that produced and delivered an extraordinarily wide variety of goods and services. There were literally thousands of small workshops, many with fewer than a dozen employees, producing an array of products including kitchen utensils, pottery, plastic containers, cigarettes, clothing, and even alcoholic drinks. Local firms produced wooden products such as tables, desks, beds, and dressers. Small enterprises converted discarded tires into shoes and sandals; some firms remanufactured discarded oil drums into lamps, stoves, and charcoal braziers; others used discarded items to manufacture a host of products, including agricultural implements such as hoes, shovels, harvesting tools, and storage containers. Some informal sector firms even produced large items, such as the passenger sections of local buses, the cargo sections for trucks, or the trailers farmers use to transport agricultural produce. Still others specialized in the repair or remanufacturing of an array of automobile and truck parts including transmissions, motors, generators, and alternators. Other firms remanufactured refrigeration and air conditioning equipment, office machines, and virtually any other imported item that would be expensive to replace.

During the period of economic decline, Tanzanians rediscovered their entrepreneurial skills; they did so by straddling multiple sectors and by enlarging the scale of their involvement in the parallel economy. They did so under the daunting conditions of an economic environment where official regulations, political restrictions, and an atmosphere of rampant public sector corruption made it difficult to operate. Moreover, they did so in the shadow of giant state-owned corporations that enjoyed huge advantages in taxpayer-provided subsidies, protection from foreign (and domestic) competition, and access to hard currency at preferential rates. Members of Tanzania's private sector had known all along that they were perfectly capable of producing all the goods on the standard ISI list, including beer, cigarettes, soft drinks, shoes, plastic products, and construction materials. They knew from firsthand experience that the cardinal mistake of the Nyerere administration was its belief that only large, monopolistic state enterprises could bring about an industrial revolution.

The policy framework that implemented the import-substituting industries had a suppressant effect on this entire sector. This happened in several different ways. First, the ISI industries had an unfair competitive advantage over the small-scale informal sector firms that were producing comparable goods. Thus, for example, the new import-substituting textile factories, which enjoyed massive input subsidies, import preferences, and trade protections, tended to crowd out the small local clothing firms that did not enjoy such extensive propping up by the government; the same was true for import-substituting cigarette factories, breweries, soft drink plants, shoe manufacturers, and plastics firms. The government provided so many subsidies for the state firms that it was difficult for unsubsidized manufacturers to compete in the same marketplace. The giant, government-sponsored import-substituting firms enjoyed a huge set of policy advantages that enabled them to crush the much smaller informal sector ones. Owing to overvaluation of the currency, imported replacement parts and equipment for all those goods tended to become cheaper than remanufactured parts. Why purchase a remanufactured transmission or rebuilt engine when a 2,000 percent overvaluation of the currency made it possible to purchase a new imported one at a fraction of the price? The many small-business firms that had suffered from this sort of economic discrimination during the ISI period became a constituency for economic reforms that would level the playing field.

The significance of the parallel sector was that it had first preserved and then enlarged and enriched Tanzania's bourgeoisie. Although the official ties of many members of this class were to the Tanzanian state, their deeper economic interests lay with other parallel market entrepreneurs. The obstacle to their further evolution as a more fully developed capitalist class was that the state sector, though badly degraded, constrained their ability to diversify and enlarge their business activities. To achieve their further evolution, the parallel sector entrepreneurs had to reform the country's policy framework in such a way as to move the state sector out of the way. They had difficulty engaging in overt lobbying because so many parallel sector entrepreneurs were state employees and because Tanzania was still an officially socialist nation. However, as would-be, large-scale entrepreneurs, the many Tanzanian families that derived a portion of their family income from the parallel marketplace were an important, if latent, constituency for economic reform.

In the simplest terms, Tanzania always had a complex and robust private sector waiting in the wings. The less frequently told story of economic recovery in Tanzania and in other countries that went through a generation-long experiment in centrally planned industrialization is that so many of those small manufacturing enterprises managed to survive despite the adverse circumstances of the state-dominated policy environment. They did so by becoming a parallel economy, that is, by finding ways to occupy niche portions of the economy, where they could continue to produce goods and deliver services that the large state enterprises could not. As the ISI firms began to fail in their assigned purpose, the economic space for these small local firms began to open up. One of the many hidden consequences of the ISI experiment had been its opportunity cost; the damage done to the small-scale, privately owned productive enterprises that might well have evolved into larger enterprises if the large state enterprises had not taken over the resources and markets that would have been necessary to do so. The owners and operators of those firms were deeply aware that if Tanzania should ever fully liberalize its economy, they would be in a strong position to expand their business activities.

When the state enterprises began to fail, the Tanzanians who were already successful private entrepreneurs in the informal marketplace were eager for the opportunity to revive their business skills and apply them to the economic areas where competition was difficult because of the state presence. As it became more and more apparent that the era of large state industries was

ending, many informal sector entrepreneurs became a constituency for extending free market opportunities into sectors of the economy occupied by
state industries. The principal source of difficulty in doing so was the continuing presence of the state sector where state-owned and -managed corporations, though practically bankrupt and inactive, were still in the way.[32]

The political difficulty for parallel sector firms was that they were not able
to organize as an effective interest group and this was a constraint on their
ability to pressure the government for liberal reforms. The political restrictions that accompanied Tanzania's single-party system made it difficult for
this (or any) segment of Tanzanian society to vocalize its economic discontents. Even in the absence of formal political outlets, however, Tanzanians
managed to share and convey their dissatisfaction with the state economy.
Though lacking opposition parties, Tanzania was not so oppressive that people were afraid to speak with one another. Economic hardship became a
bonding experience and individuals experiencing difficulty began to feel an
almost spontaneous solidarity with one another.[33] When they did, their conversations were often about the economic difficulties they were experiencing.
A major topic of conversation was the responsibility of the political elite for
leading the country into that situation.[34]

Much of the internal political pressure for economic reform came from
this group of Tanzanians. For this large, rapidly growing and increasingly influential community of entrepreneurs, the parallel economy had a built-in
constraint; namely, its inability to expand beyond a certain point so long as
the state sector still had legal standing. Their problem was one of scale. Parallel markets could provide many goods and some services but, even in a highly
corrupt environment, parallel market entrepreneurs had to be concerned
about their exposure to official monitoring and legal sanctions. A small kiosk
selling gray market cigarettes and soft drinks or used clothing was feasible; a
full-scale brewery, cigarette factory, or textile plant was out of the question
until there were basic policy changes that legitimized these activities.

The Ministry of Agriculture, again aligning itself with the policy reformers, had already taken the position that further efforts to impose the bureaucratic system of regulation and control were likely to be both futile and
counter-productive. Its widely circulated and widely read study of the parallel
market in grains stated this in explicit terms:

> Government could try to increase roadblocks, fines, prison sentences
> and Party monitoring to shut down all of part of the trade. The cost of

providing enough enforcement to provide an effective deterrent would be huge, however, and the probable result of such a policy would be high prices and interrupted supplies for consumers, unreliable markets for farmers, resentment and anger by both parties, and higher profits for successful middlemen. This option is considered to be both effective and counter-productive.[35]

The report concluded that legitimization of the parallel market was the only realistic policy option. Many government officials believed that this conclusion applied to all sectors of the parallel economy and not to the grain sector alone.

Tanzanian political leaders and policy makers in the 1980s had become profoundly aware that their nation's economy really consisted of two distinct economies: an official economy and a parallel one. The former was shrinking and in extreme stress. It supplied a diminishing fraction of the goods that Tanzanians actually consumed and was increasingly unimportant relative to the scale of real economic life in the country. The parallel economy was expanding rapidly, provided a growing proportion of family income, and supplied most of the goods that people actually needed. For increasing numbers of Tanzanians, the parallel economy was their economy. Tanzanian leaders were also aware of the affluence of the proto-bourgeois economic class that was profiting from its parallel sector activities. Many were already members; others aspired to join.

Tanzania's transition to a market-based economy, then, was not a matter of a socialist state legitimizing private sector activity where very little existed; it was a matter of writing into law the fact that the nation's economy had already been largely privatized by the widespread proliferation of parallel markets. And it was not a matter of encouraging Tanzanians to take up private sector opportunities; countless thousands of Tanzanians had been engaged in that sector before socialism ever began and had continued to do so during the socialist period. By the time official economic reforms began in the mid-1980s, Tanzania already had a free and open economy.

Chapter 6

Cases in Economic Reform

By the mid-1980s, it appeared that Tanzania had the major ingredients in place for sustained reform. A reform-minded president had replaced Julius Nyerere. A new economic paradigm that emphasized market forces had discredited the older idea of state-sponsored industrialization. Following on the diffusion of this paradigm in the form of the Berg Report, the donor community had come together in its insistence on policy reforms as a precondition for economic assistance. An influential segment of the country's political leadership and many of its most prestigious economists had begun to advocate reforms both within the government and to the Tanzanian public. An overwhelming majority of Tanzanians appeared eager for reforms to take place. Some of the earliest reforms, such as the import of used clothing, were highly popular; the used clothing markets that appeared everywhere were a welcome sign of better days to come. Whatever their feelings toward Nyerere personally, Tanzanians were aware of the economic and political costs of his failed economic experiment. De facto liberalization of the economy had already taken place through the expansion of the parallel economy, which had become almost as large as or larger than the official economy. Perhaps most importantly, many members of Tanzania's political elite had become participants in the parallel economy: their personal economic interests went toward reforms that would acknowledge and regularize their status as a rich and powerful social class.

Despite these considerations, Tanzania's reform process was unsystematic, piecemeal, and painfully slow. The question this poses is very simple: why was that so? Case studies of policy reform provide an opportunity to develop answers. This chapter examines three areas of policy change; exchange rate devaluation, trade liberalization, and divestiture of SOEs, in order to portray some of the key dynamics of the process, four of which are especially noteworthy.

The first is uncertainty of outcome. When economic reform takes place in developing countries such as Tanzania, it is neither swift nor sure nor is it a universal solvent that systematically cleanses the economy of the policy features of the old regime. Nor is there a single moment when all the major actors join in a new policy consensus that assigns pride of place to the creation of a more open economy. If a developing country's transition to a market economy seems inevitable, that is a retrospective viewpoint. Nothing is irreversible. The political conflicts that arise are often so intense and so evenly balanced that reforms may come to a halt as political elements favorable to the older system assert themselves.

The second characteristic of reform is the multitiered pattern of political forces that comes into play. In Tanzania, the levels of interaction began with the dialogue between the government and the donor community, especially the IMF and the World Bank. However, as Chapter 4 showed, it would be a mistake to view either the donors or the Tanzanian government as unitary actors. For reform to occur, both sides had to undergo an internal dynamic of change. The donors had to put internal divisions behind and present a united insistence on liberal changes. However, they could not have brought about reform without a corresponding shift of opinion among strategically placed Tanzanians. Even when both sides had become united, civil society actors could emerge to play a role on important matters. The cumulative effect of all these levels of interaction was that the dynamic of change was not swift, sure or unilinear.

The third characteristic of reform in Tanzania had to do with the importance of institutions. As Tanzanians pointed out during the aid crisis of 1994/95, Tanzania was not a military dictatorship or personal autocracy that could impose its will on dissenting elements. It had a constitutional system that made for divided authority. Contrary to its persona as a country with an all-powerful executive president, Tanzania during the first half decade of reform had a system of checks and balances that divided power between its executive and legislative branches. This limited the government's ability to act expeditiously, even when it came time to introduce needed economic changes. The idea that a ministry of finance, even with the support of the World Bank, could orchestrate the behavior of other ministries was a vast overstatement of its authority.

The fourth important characteristic of economic reform concerned the all-pervasive impact of corruption. Throughout Tanzania's history as an independent nation, corruption has transformed well-intended plans into bad outcomes. This remained as true during the period of reform as it had been during the era of socialism. The idea that a market economy might reduce the opportunities for official corruption was a myth. It would involve very little exaggeration to suggest that the public officials who presided over reform tended to judge every aspect of policy reform to some degree based on its effect on their rent-seeking opportunities. The members of Tanzania's political-economic oligarchy did not embrace economic reforms out of a theoretical epiphany about the benevolence of the marketplace. They did so because they could manage the transition to a liberal economy in such a way that it did not diminish their ability to hold public office and use it as a gateway to personal enrichment.

Case 1. Exchange Rate Reform

Exchange rate devaluation showed that when the executive branch could act on its own initiative, reform could proceed readily. Devaluation was among the first reforms to go forward because the president, acting with the minister of finance and the governor of the central bank, could change the nominal exchange rate without the need for legislative approval. When further steps toward exchange rate reform required legislative action, as in a law required to create foreign exchange bureaus, this did not take place until the early 1990s, after a more reform-minded National Assembly had taken office and agreed to pass the Foreign Exchange Act that created the foreign exchange bureaus.[1]

Exchange rate reform was of paramount importance for many reasons. The policy of overvaluation, which grew out of the desire to provide subsidized capital for new industries, had numerous negative effects. It was a root cause of stagnation in the agricultural export sector since it lowered the prices received by export-oriented farmers. Indeed, no other area of government policy had so clearly demonstrated the extent to which the import-substitution strategy rested on an economic bias against export-oriented agriculture. The capital subsidy from overvaluation caused the industries to place too great an emphasis on capital-intensive methods of production rather than methods that would take greater advantage of Tanzania's potential for low cost labor. Overvaluation resulted in foreign exchange scarcities that gave rise to parallel markets, which then undermined the government's ability to provide trade protection for the infant industries. In addition, it was one of the more significant sources of rent seeking among corrupt members of the political elite.

The Berg Report had treated overvaluation as a root cause of stagnation in the export crop sector throughout sub-Saharan Africa, and donor officials viewed overvaluation as one of the causes of Tanzania's downward economic spiral.[2] For the IMF and the World Bank, as well as for many bilateral donors, the direction of change in a country's exchange rate provides the most easily read indicator of the changing power balance between a country's reformers and anti-reformers. Devaluation is fundamental. Without it, agricultural exports would continue to stagnate. Without a recovery of agricultural exports, foreign exchange would continue to be scarce. And without an improvement in foreign exchange earnings, there would continue to be import starvation throughout the economy in areas as wide ranging as the imports necessary for educational and health services as well as industrial and agricultural inputs. For the Tanzanian reformers both inside and outside the government, the ILIs, and many of the bilateral donors, policy reform had to begin with a remediation of the overvalued exchange rate.

Tanzania's exchange rate experience also illustrates the proposition that economic reforms are sometimes an official acceptance of an existing reality rather than the first steps toward building a new one. Despite heroic efforts to maintain an overvalued exchange rate, which at one point included stringent currency controls for visitors entering and leaving the country, major portions of the Tanzanian economy had already devalued. Official currency devaluation did not so much change the exchange rate at which countless economic transactions were taking place as it acknowledged the prevalence of a parallel market exchange rate that was already setting prices throughout the economy. The list of economic activities where the shadow market exchange rate set prices included the distribution of food staples, the import and retail distribution of consumer goods, and the import and distribution of inputs for small-scale productive enterprises. Privately provided services, such as transportation and a growing portion of the country's medical services, were also setting their prices based on the devalued Tanzanian shilling cost of their inputs. Even those portions of the Tanzanian economy that still appeared to be conducting business by using the official exchange rate were doing so to a lesser degree. The growth of "unrecorded" agricultural exports, for example, meant that many agricultural producers were finding ways, through informal channels, to obtain the devalued shilling equivalent of global prices for their commodities.

Tanzania's internal dialogue over exchange rate policy was as old as the Tanzania shilling itself. The Tanzanian government had created it in the spring of 1966 when the three East African governments, acting in concert, created separate national currencies to replace the East African shilling. Their purpose was to break away from the East African Currency Board, an independent tripartite agency that had set the East African shilling at a fixed rate to the U.S. dollar. To create its new currency, the Tanzanian government passed the Bank of Tanzania Act in early January 1966,[3] and the newly created central bank began to issue the Tanzanian shilling in June that year. For about a year, Tanzanian banks, like those in Kenya and Uganda, accepted both currencies on a strict one-for-one basis, which meant that, for that brief time, the Tanzanian shilling was pegged to the old East African shilling as well as to the national currencies of its two neighbors.[4]

This meant that the three national currencies should have been on a par, but even then Tanzanians, perhaps reacting to their government's early pronouncements of a socialist economic agenda, began to show a decided preference for the Kenya shilling. As early as spring, 1967, just a few months after the Arusha Declaration, Tanzanians were prepared to pay a premium price for Kenya shillings or U.S. dollars.[5] Two things happened. The first was that Tanzanian overvaluation created a profitable niche opportunity for currency entrepreneurs who could trade across currencies. Tanzanian government officials were among the first to discover the profitability of obtaining hard currency at the official rate and selling it at the devalued rate that prevailed in parallel currency markets. The second outcome was that parallel currency markets seemed to spring up everywhere: in Dar es Salaam, in Nairobi, at the borders between the two countries, and in global currency trading firms such as Deak-Perera. All these markets began to devalue the Tanzanian shilling from the very first moment of its existence.

The two leading World Bank authorities on the Tanzanian shilling believe that the divergence between the official exchange rate and the parallel market rate grew very rapidly. The economists Daniel Kaufman and Stephen O'Connell have stated, "In the two decades following the Arusha Declaration, the exchange rate in Tanzania's illegal parallel foreign exchange market rose at a rate of nearly 2.5 percent per month, more than three times that of the official exchange rate. By early 1986, the parallel rate exceeded the official rate by more than 800 percent."[6] Tanzania's exchange rate difficulties illustrated the rapidity with which rent seeking could transform the purpose and the outcome of a government policy. Some development advisors had been prepared informally to accept a modest amount of overvaluation, perhaps about 5 or 10 percent, as an effective means of taxing agricultural exports and subsidizing industrial inputs. That sentiment was behind the creation of a separate national currency. Before long, however, Tanzania's currency misalignment was so great that the country's industrial policy could not explain it. The best explanation was private wealth seeking on the part of Tanzanian officials who could take advantage of the differential between the official and parallel rates. The greater the differential, the greater the profitability. By the late 1960s, many government officials had a stake in currency overvaluation that had little to do with the success or failure of their government's industrial strategy.

As the currency premium for other currencies grew, it began to have significant effects on the economic behavior of Tanzania's most important export-oriented farmers, the coffee growers in the Kilimanjaro region of the country. The economist Richard Mshomba has estimated that between 1977 and 1986, "the producer price of coffee Arabic in Tanzania was, on average, only about 20 percent of the producer price of the same type of coffee in Kenya."[7] This differential was so great that Tanzanian coffee farmers began to find ways to trade their coffee in Kenya so that they could receive payment in the more highly valued currency. The larger the discrepancy between the official exchange rate for the Tanzanian shilling and the devalued exchange rate in parallel currency markets, the more pronounced this behavior became. Mshomba has calculated that, on average, about 4,000 metric tons of Tanzanian coffee, with a market value of about eight million U.S. dollars, was smuggled into Kenya annually during this period, while during the same period Kenya had a coffee boom, part of it consisting of unrecorded coffee exports from Tanzania.[8] Two categories of economic winners emerged from coffee smuggling: the border officials who turned their heads as truckloads of coffee moved from Arusha to Nairobi, and Kenya, which gained substantial earnings of foreign exchange from the transshipment of Tanzanian coffee.

During the 1970s, the gap between the official exchange rate for the Tanzania shilling and the parallel market rate escalated so rapidly that estimates of its magnitude varied greatly. It is almost never possible to know with certainty the differential exchange rate between the parallel rate and official rate for a currency. Parallel currency markets are, by their very nature, somewhat hidden from view, and therefore difficult to observe on a systematic basis.

Parallel market rates are also highly variable because they include spot market transactions, which change from one to the next. The only certainty is that when the Tanzania-Uganda War ended, in spring 1979, Tanzania was experiencing such an acute scarcity of hard currency that the differential between the official and parallel markets rates spiraled upward. Tanzanian officials privately acknowledged that parallel currency markets in the Tanzania shilling were offering four or five times the official exchange rate; that is, thirty or forty Tanzania shillings per U.S. dollar at a time when the official rate was still 7.14 Tanzania shillings per U.S. dollar.

Casual visitors to Tanzania reported an even greater gap between the nominal exchange rate and the parallel market rate, possibly as much as several hundred Tanzanian shillings per U.S. dollar. The widest gap between the parallel and official market rates for the shilling emerged during the mid-1980s. IMF economist Roger Nord estimates that between 1986 and 1988, the parallel market rate for the Tanzanian shilling was 800 percent greater than the official exchange rate.[9] Throughout this period, parallel currency spot markets—those involving Tanzanians who were desperate to send hard currency overseas—were offering as much as twenty to thirty times the official rate. Exchange rate differentials of that magnitude are not sustainable because they offer too great an incentive for currency profiteering. Rent seeking in currency markets provides one of the more powerful explanations for the failure of the ISI strategy. The Bank of Tanzania was never able to discipline its allocations of hard currency according to the investment pattern specified in the government's sequence of multiyear development plans.

Tanzania had a parallel form of hard currency auction long before the Central Bank created an official one in the early 1990s. The bidders in this auction were those holding large stocks of Tanzanian shillings they wanted to use to acquire hard currency. Many were high-ranking political leaders. Since some were prepared to pay almost any price to deposit hard currency in overseas accounts, their implicit competition with one another drove up the parallel market price of the U.S. dollar. This forced a wider and wider wedge between the official and parallel market rates, heightening the incentives and opportunities to take advantage of the difference. The effect was painfully obvious. Much of the hemorrhage of foreign exchange found its way into overseas accounts, greatly reducing the supply of hard currency locally available for legitimate development purposes such as industrial expansion or infrastructure rehabilitation. Tanzanians with political connections to the Central Bank were draining off much of the country's supply of hard currency while the government was entreating its donors to provide hard currency for day-to-day fiscal requirements.

Tanzania's rent-seeking entrepreneurs did not originate in the exchange rate differential: there were too many other rent-seeking opportunities available for that to be true. However, the exchange rate differential gave a huge impetus to the emergence of currency entrepreneurs who could become rich by taking advantage of the hard currency scarcities and import shortages created by the overvalued exchange rate. The way to great riches in the Tanzania of the late 1970s was to use one's political connections to obtain a hard currency allocation at the official rate and then find ways to sell that currency—or the imported goods it could purchase—at the parallel market rate. The result was an economic abyss that demoralized Tanzanians, infuriated the donor organizations and provided validation for the recommendations of the reform-minded economists.

By 1979, the stage was set for a collision over exchange rate policy between the ILIs and the Tanzanian government. Tanzanians were not a unitary voice on this matter: reform-minded officials were already inclined to agree with the IMF that their currency should be devalued. The Tanzanian minister of finance during this period was Edwin Mtei, one of the country's prominent reformers. His extraordinary autobiography provides a dramatic account of what transpired.[10] During spring 1979, Mtei invited the IMF to send representatives to Tanzania to discuss economic reforms. As a signal of good intentions, he devalued the Tanzanian shilling about 33 percent, from its initial rate of about 7.14 shillings per U.S. dollar to about 9.6 shillings prior to the IMF visit. The gesture failed miserably. The gap between the parallel market rate, which had climbed to two or three hundred shillings per U.S. dollar, and an official rate that was still less than ten shillings per dollar was far too great to satisfy the IMF. The Mtei devaluation, though appreciated as a symbolic gesture, was too small to prevent the continuing hemorrhage of hard currency into the rent-seeking currency market, much less begin to address the broader economic crisis caused by the drop in exports. The IMF demanded a more realistic devaluation; President Nyerere flatly refused and fired Mtei, replacing him with Kighoma Malima, a professor of economics at the University of Dar es Salaam, who aligned himself with the anti-reform group.

The exchange rate collision between Nyerere and Mtei was a vignette of the internal politics of economic reform during the period following the Ugandan War. At one level, it was a collision between a charismatic socialist president and an intellectually brilliant, technocratic minister, the ultimate "red" versus the ultimate "expert." Embedded in their disagreement was the conflict between two irreconcilable visions of how Tanzania should evolve: one viewing its destiny as a classless socialist state; the other as a market-based democracy. Nyerere's ability to switch finance ministers in the midst of an IMF dialogue also spoke worlds to the power imbalance between him and any other Tanzanian politician.

The Nyerere-Mtei episode also revealed the magnitude of the policy gulf between the government of Tanzania and the IMF. Nyerere had a personal resentment of the ILIs and their tendency to condition their assistance on policy changes, which he perceived as interfering in Tanzania's internal affairs. He expressed his animosity toward the IMF in a 1980 article in *Development Dialogue*.

> Tanzania is not prepared to devalue its currency just because this is a traditional free market solution to everything and regardless of the merits of our position. It is not prepared to surrender its right to restrict imports by measures designed to ensure that we import quinine rather than cosmetics, or buses rather than cars for the elite. My Government is not prepared to give up our national endeavor to provide primary education for every child, basic medicines and some clean water for all our people.[11]

The fact that Tanzania's parallel marketplace offered an abundant supply of cosmetics and luxury goods for the elite while the official marketplace exhibited scarcities of medicines and clean water did not appear to be part of the president's thinking on this matter. His disagreement with the IMF was not a pragmatic conversation over how much devaluation would be required to stimulate agricultural exports, or how much overvaluation might provide a subsidy to the state industries. It was a dialogue of polarized visions of Tanzanian society.

When the World Bank created the TAG process in the early 1980s, it drew valuable lessons from the Mtei experience. Perhaps the most important had to do with political style. Nyerere rejected the Mtei devaluation of 1979 because the fanfare and publicity that accompanied it, which included front-page pictures of Mtei personally greeting the IMF delegation, was an affront to presidential authority. The TAG understood the need for quiet diplomacy. It operated in a low-key manner and sought to gain presidential assent for its activities. In the course of its brief existence, the members of the advisory group met privately with Nyerere to make a special appeal for flexibility on the exchange rate question. Their presentation to the president emphasized the "technical" nature of minor devaluations that would provide some relief for hard-pressed agricultural exporters while, at the same time, offering no serious threat to the exchange rate subsidy needed by the state industries. As part of the low-key approach, the Ministry of Finance was discreet in its implementation of the 1982 and 1983 devaluations. It did not hold press conferences or make public pronouncements that embarrassed the president. It is revealing that the Tshs 12.5 rate achieved by the TAG was one that Mtei had been able to persuade the IMF to accept in 1979 but that Nyerere rejected when he dismissed Mtei.

If devaluation had a single tipping point, it was Nyerere's departure from the presidency at the end of 1985. With the election of President Mwinyi, the donors began placing pressure on the new administration to devalue quickly. The exchange rate relief provided by the 1984 Msuya devaluation had been at most a signal of good intentions; any economic relief it provided was symbolic, temporary, and limited. It did not come remotely close to bridging the gap between the nominal exchange rate and the parallel currency market, which by early 1986, had once again climbed to an unsustainable level of about 800 percent.[12] Within months of assuming office, the Mwinyi administration conveyed its willingness to do what the Nyerere administration had never been willing to do; comply with the donors' insistence on meaningful changes in the exchange rate. In April 1986, the Mwinyi administration devalued the Tanzania shilling from a rate of 17 per U.S. dollar, where it had stood since the Msuya budget address of 1984, to 40 per U.S. dollar, a devaluation of nearly 250 percent.

The Mwinyi devaluation, though important, was only a first step: an official devaluation did not alter the way the country's exchange rate was determined. The exchange rate was still set based on a directive from the minister of finance to the governor of the Central Bank, which the country's commercial banks would be legally obliged to accept. Although Tanzania had signed its first post-Nyerere IMF agreement in the summer of 1986, structural changes in the determination of the exchange rate were slow in coming. Institutions mattered and Tanzania's institutional arrangements stood in the way of structural changes. Throughout President Mwinyi's first term in office, 1985-1990, the National Assembly was resistant to passing the legislation required to bring about structural reforms. As a result, the most Mwinyi could accomplish was a series of nominal devaluations initiated by the president and the minister of finance. These reduced but did not eliminate the parallel market premium, which remained at about 60 percent until the early 1990s.[13]

The absence of any provision for market determination of the exchange rate was a source of friction between the Tanzanian government and the donor organizations, such as the IMF, which wanted structural changes such that market forces and not decrees from the executive branch would determine the value of the currency. The first step in that direction did not occur until 1992, with the creation of exchange rate bureaus. The government of Ghana had created these at the end of 1989, and Tanzania adopted the Ghanaian model in 1992, with the passage of the Foreign Exchange Act.[14] Currency exchange bureaus receive permission to exchange currencies in both directions; that is, they both buy and sell local currency at prices that are posted directly outside their place of business. To obtain their supply of hard currency, the exchange bureaus had to obtain licenses that permitted them to purchase it at periodic auctions held by the Central Bank. As the exchange bureaus and other licensed participants in the auction competed against one another for hard currency, their bidding increased the Tanzanian shilling price of foreign exchange. The bidding process not only devalued the Tanzanian shilling further, but also introduced a structural element into the devaluation process.

The currency exchange bureaus were visually dramatic evidence that a new economic era had arrived. For the casual visitor to Tanzania, the change was extraordinary. The opportunity to walk into a legitimate business office and transact currency at posted rates was light years from the secretive and risky transactions that were the principal features of the old parallel currency market. Tanzania began this part of the reform process by licensing approximately 200 independent exchange bureaus. On the assumption that each bureau employed approximately five to ten workers, the exchange bureau system generated wage employment for between one and two thousand people—about the number of workers employed in a fairly large industry.

The most widely accepted indicator of the effectiveness of a devaluation process is the real exchange rate (RER). The RER measures changes in the price of a basket of goods over time in a given country as contrasted with the price of that same basket of goods in another country or group of countries. The RER reveals whether or not the changes in a country's nominal exchange rate represent a genuine—as opposed to a simply numerical—devaluation.[15] The convention in RER graphs, such as that shown below, is that an upward sloping line indicates a depreciation or devaluation of a currency; a downward sloping line indicates an appreciation in the value of a currency. Figure 2 depicts Tanzania's RER from 1970 to 2010. This graph shows that although there was significant progress toward devaluation during the second half of the 1980s, when the president's office implemented official devaluations, and the early 1990s, when the government created the exchange bureau system.

The portentous feature of this graph, however, was the tendency for the line to begin sloping downward again during the early and mid-1990s, indicating a recurrence of overvaluation. If there were value in a single-factor explanation of the aid crisis of 1994/95, this graph could provide it. During its first term, the Mwinyi administration's successive devaluations had earned it a reputation as one of sub-Saharan Africa's most engaged reformers. These devaluations, alongside other changes, had gained the admiration of World Bank officials, one of whom described Tanzania as a "resolute" reformer.[16] The reappearance of overvaluation as shown in this graph, however, contradicted that view. The extent of overvaluation was not nearly as great as it had

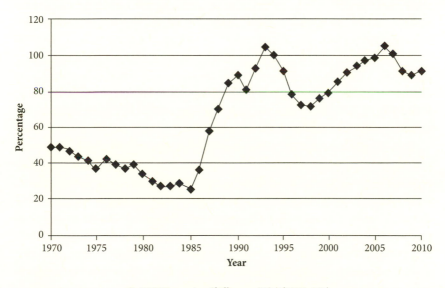

—◆—RER Tanzanian Shilling vs. US $ (1994=100)

Figure 2. Tanzania real exchange rate (Tanzanian shilling vs. U.S.$) (1994=100). Calculated by Dr. Julia Kim from World Bank World Development Indicators, www .worldbank.org. RER = (Official Exchange Rate × U.S. Consumer Price Index) / Tanzanian Consumer Price Index.

been during the Nyerere years but by the mid-1990s, the Tanzanian shilling had appreciated by nearly 40 percent.[17] To donors who interpret a country's RER as a litmus test of the government's true intentions—and this was practically all the major donors—the return of currency overvaluation constituted indisputable evidence that the Tanzanian government was backsliding on reform.

There were two important questions. The first was how this could have happened, given that an auction at the central bank was determining the nominal exchange rate. The second was why it happened. The answer to the first question was simple: it had to do with the ease with which a government can manipulate a currency auction system. The Tanzanian government found that it could influence the exchange rate by restricting the number of licensed bidders and by imposing limits on the amount of local currency they were permitted to spend at any single auction. Both these limitations artificially lowered domestic demand for hard currency, thereby producing overvaluation. The Tanzanian government had imposed other restrictions as well. One was that Tanzanian citizens using the bureaus as a source of hard currency were limited in the amount of hard currency they could purchase. Still another limitation was that the exchange bureaus had to operate strictly through cash on cash transactions; they could not offer hard currency to Tanzanians for promissory notes. The government refused the ILIs informal suggestion that the exchange bureaus might evolve into mini-banks that could lend foreign exchange on a longer-term basis. The donors concluded that internal pressures were taking advantage of the manipulability of the auction process to reverse exchange rate reform.

It proved more difficult to determine why this was happening. Some donors were suspicious and mistrustful of Tanzania's intentions and a number of donor representatives sought the answer in the persistence of older economic views. Although the Tanzanian government had begun to implement economic reform in the mid-1980s, large and influential parts of the governmental apparatus never seemed to exhibit "reform ownership," that is, the will to participate proactively in creating a market-based reform program.[18] Some donors inferred that Tanzania still had an economic culture that favored state industries and that made it permissible for government policy to privilege this sector over others.

Although this may have been partly true, it was a minor part of the problem. The currency appreciation of the mid-1990s did not have its principal causal root in the 1960s ideology of state-sponsored industries. That development strategy had lost its ability to shape the official viewpoint a decade earlier in the aftermath of the Berg Report. The novel feature of the 1990s overvaluation was that it had emerged as part of the broad transition toward a more open economy. It revealed the political muscularity of a growing class of politically well-connected private investors for whom inexpensive hard currency could provide a significant economic boost. The members of this class had specific economic interests that would benefit from overvaluation.

The first was Tanzania's manufacturing sector. Tanzanian investors wanted to acquire the state-owned industrial firms that the government had scheduled for divestiture. The industries that were first on their list were, for the most part, the ISI firms whose purpose was to produce consumer goods for the domestic market. These industries exhibited the perennial problem of inward looking firms: they required costly imported inputs to conduct business but their markets were domestic consumers spending local currency. Because these industries had deteriorated to the point where they could barely operate, they were in desperate need of recapitalization. Some were still using worn-out machinery purchased in the 1960s. One of the largest cost factors, therefore, would be the expense of importing the machinery and other capital goods necessary to put those firms back into operation. As part of its liberalization effort, the government had begun to allow exporters of nontraditional products to retain a large portion of their foreign exchange earnings. However, the ISI firms did not have an export orientation and, therefore, could not acquire foreign exchange through that mechanism. Overvaluation provided a partial remedy for this dilemma. By cheapening the capital cost of refurbishing these firms, overvaluation would provide a significant benefit to the new owners.

The second area of investment opportunity was commercial real estate. Because of long suppressed demand during the socialist period, Tanzania has been experiencing a real estate boom. In Dar es Salaam and other major cities, there has been a rapid expansion in the construction of high-rise office buildings, condominium complexes, housing developments, shopping centers, and luxury hotels as well as refurbishing for sale or rent of much of the country's older real estate stock. By the 1990s, commercial real estate investment had become one of the most profitable investment opportunities for Tanzanian entrepreneurs. Tanzania's real estate investors were in exactly the same position as prospective investors in the old ISI firms; that is, they were in need of large amounts of hard currency but without any significant means of obtaining it. Real estate investment was similar to investment in domestically oriented factories; that is, it could be highly profitable but would not generate nontraditional export revenues sufficient to defray start-up capital costs.

The construction of a modern high-rise office building, a luxury shopping mall, or a new housing development, for example, requires a large initial outlay in hard currency to finance the cost of an endless array of imported items. These include the construction equipment itself as well as the many other critical items such as elevator systems, plumbing fixtures, air conditioning machinery, and computer and office equipment. Investors would need to acquire even mundane goods such as kitchen and dining accouterments in international markets to satisfy the demanding tastes of a global clientele. For those who had to incur these costs, overvaluation would make a significant difference in eventual profitability. By the 1990s, Tanzania's emerging class of real estate investors had become a powerful lobby for a currency policy that cheapened their foreign exchange costs.

The Advisors Group had one of its great successes in negotiating the exchange rate. Tanzania agreed to initiate the final step in the devaluation process, licensing a number of private banks that would have permission to engage in currency transactions with one another. They would also have the authority to provide hard currency to their customers at the exchange rates they charged one another. The common term for this policy is the London Inter-Bank Offered Rate; most economists consider it the best approximation of an equilibrium exchange rate. The RER graph in Figure 2 shows the reform effect of the Advisors Group; after 1996, the Tanzanian shilling was on a trajectory toward an equilibrium exchange rate. Within the ten-year period 1986-1996, the government not only achieved a radical devaluation of its currency but brought about a structural change in the way the exchange rate was determined.

The principal barometer of the success of this policy is the differential between the official exchange rate and the parallel rate; by the late 1990s this differential had narrowed to 5 percent or less, well within the boundary of economists who accept modest overvaluation as a beneficial prop for the industrial sector. In the midst of an ongoing dialogue over other aspects of economic policy, the Tanzanian government and the ILIs mutually accept that exchange rate policy has become a nonconfrontational issue.

Case 2. Trade Reform

Tanzania's policy of import substitution required an extensive pattern of trade regulation that included rising taxes on exports, restrictions on the import of consumer products scheduled for domestic production, and a set of import priorities that privileged the import requirements of state industries above those of other economic sectors. By the end of the Nyerere era, Tanzania had constructed an elaborate edifice of trade regulations including tariffs, quantitative restrictions, and outright bans to regulate imports as well as numerous taxes on exports. Importers had to secure licenses that, at least in theory, accorded with the industrial priorities identified in the multiyear plans. Obtaining an import license was only the first step: the licensee then had to obtain a hard currency allocation from the Central Bank, which had great difficulty meeting the currency needs of the many new industrial producers. Exporters faced a bewildering array of export duties and surcharges as well as the burden of an unfavorable currency environment.

The economic difficulties that resulted from these restrictions were commonplace in societies that had pursued state-led ISI strategies. These included balance-of-payments deficits on trade and rising foreign indebtedness owing to the pincer effect of stagnant exports and costly industrial imports. There were fiscal difficulties because so many exports went unrecorded and therefore escaped taxation. The tendency for members of the political elite and other well connected Tanzanians to engage in parallel currency markets to sequester funds in overseas accounts further aggravated the hard currency scarcities. The trade pattern that ensued was illogical in the extreme. Much of Tanzania's dwindling stock of hard currency went toward the import of costly inputs for industries using only a small fraction of their installed capacity. The hard currency costs of the state firms included not only expensive machinery and raw materials but also a host of other expenses including patent rights, royalty fees, and management contracts with foreign companies. The currency allocations for these imports displaced, at least in official markets, the items people wanted and could use, from agricultural inputs to basic consumer goods such as clothing, food, and automobile parts. By the end of the Nyerere period, every important sector of the official Tanzanian economy exhibited import starvation: schools and hospitals lacked needed supplies, farmers lacked needed inputs, and consumers lacked just about everything. Essential public services ranging from trash collection to road repair operated minimally if at all.

The purpose of trade reform was to improve upon all this. From the standpoint of trade reformers, the optimal result of reform is a freer trade environment. The structural adjustment process in sub-Saharan Africa and other developing regions during the 1980s and 1990s incorporated the free trade principles that have informed economy theory since David Ricardo first developed the notion of comparative advantage in his classic 1817 work, *Principles of Political Economy and Taxation*. The principal arguments for free trade begin with the proposition that it imposes an efficiency discipline on the internal allocation of economic resources. Free trade results in the most productive use of a society's land, labor, and capital. Its proponents also point to the rapid diffusion of new technologies, which help ensure that an economy deploys all factors of production, including labor, in the most productive manner.[19] Modern economic theory embraces the idea of free trade to such a wide degree that the central question addressed by today's economic reformers is how to dismantle trade restrictions to evolve the society toward a freer trade environment.

Tanzania presented a powerful case for the proponents of free trade. Corruption in trade management had seized control of a vital economic process and changed it in ways that made it unrecognizable to those who devised it. One of the major causes of the failure of its industrial experiment was the unanticipated spread of rent seeking throughout the system of trade management. Rent seeking became pervasive in the process of granting trade licenses and in the issuance of foreign exchange for the import of industrial goods. It also gave rise to the spread of parallel markets in traded goods since public officials with access to resources and influence could augment their incomes by engaging in these markets. By the 1970s, corruption had undermined the developmental intentions behind Tanzania's extensive system of trade controls, which had taken on a size and shape bearing little resemblance to the economic planners' original designs. As Anne Krueger had anticipated, trade restrictions began to arise because of the rent-seeking opportunities they provided rather than because of their potential to nurture industrial growth.

The difficulty Tanzania faced was that corruption had produced a disconnect between the goal of a protectionist trade policy and the reality of what was actually taking place in the economy. The market for clothing, beer, and cigarettes offered an example. The early planners intended for these industries to provide the leading edge of Tanzania's industrial revolution. The early planners selected them based on low demand elasticity among consumers. Since imported items would be unavailable, Tanzanian consumers would have no choice but to obtain these items from local industries even if the goods were poor quality and expensive. As industries given high priority for the first stage of ISI, this set of consumer goods industries enjoyed many forms of protection including quantitative restrictions and outright bans as well as high protective tariffs. To staunch the flow of imports, the government denied import licenses to the trading companies that dealt in competing commodities.

Rent seeking in the trade area undermined the planners' intention. Tanzania was never able to calibrate the level of allowable imports in a way that would create market space for domestic production. Entrepreneurs who could find ways to acquire imported items could sell them at scarcity prices. Since corruption made it possible to evade tariff barriers and quantitative restrictions, there was always an unregulated supply of imported products in the parallel marketplace. The basic idea of low demand elasticity among consumers was correct, but it did not take into account the corruption-induced porosity of trade barriers. It only meant that Tanzanians willing and able to pay a price premium could always obtain the goods they desired outside the official economy. The Tanzanian industrial experiment failed for many reasons including moral hazard and overcapitalization. However, a basic reason for the failure was that local demand found its supply in the uncontrolled flow of goods into the parallel marketplace.

Contraband imports of beer and cigarettes as well as a host of other items did not cause the failure of the ISI industries; they were symptomatic of the failure of the model rather than its cause. But the mere existence of a vigorous cross-border trade between Tanzania and neighboring countries suggests the futility of attempting to implement an economic strategy that required a regulatory capacity that did not exist: namely, the ability to exert effective control over what imported goods were available in the domestic economy and at what prices. Tanzania's attempt to enforce its trade restrictions was an exercise in futility: when there were profits available to those with the will and ability to evade the country's trade regulations, many did so. When the system was finally reformed, it was partly out of recognition of the sheer impossibility of having sought to impose such a restrictive system in the first place.

There are unresolved and unresolvable theoretical issues about the relationship between corruption and trade. Krueger's classic 1974 article on rent seeking sought to show that corruption tended to undermine economic growth by shifting the allocation of economic resources away from productive activity and toward the pursuit of rent-seeking positions.[20] Economist Jagdish Bhagwati, however, has taken a different viewpoint about the impact of corruption on trade and development. He has sought to show that corruption in the trade sector might have beneficial results. Taking free trade as an optimal economic arrangement, Bhagwati showed that, by inducing large loopholes in the protectionist system, corruption would produce a freer pattern of trade than that specified in the formal, legal framework.[21]

Their debate over this matter has a great bearing on Tanzania. If development economics with its insistence on the developmental benefits of protection was a poor idea to begin with, then little was lost because of the tendency for corruption in the trade system to foster the emergence of a parallel marketplace that provided a healthy element of competition for the state industries. Corruption, in other words, brought the real pattern of trade closer to free trade by contravening the protectionism of official policy. If Bhagwati is correct, corruption hastened the demise of a trade system that should never have been attempted in the first place. It improved the economic state of affairs by facilitating the import of beneficial but otherwise scarce goods. Corruption in Tanzania's trade system satisfied Bhagwati's criteria for positive benefits: it led to a freer pattern of trade and enabled the import of some needed production inputs to both the agricultural sector and private production firms that found a survival niche in the parallel economy. As bad as economic conditions had become, corruption may have resulted in a better performing economy than if the highly protectionist formal trade framework had actually been closely followed.

Corruption, however, may have given Tanzania the worst of both worlds regarding its trade policy. Just as it subverted the intentions of protectionism by creating a free trade environment in the parallel economy, it also undermined efforts to liberalize trade during the mid-1980s. Tanzania's official trade liberalization effort began with the Msuya budget address of June 1984, which announced a program of "own-financed" imports. The idea of this program was simple: Tanzanians with legitimate bank accounts overseas could use these accounts to import goods on a "no questions asked" basis. The rationale for this program seemed compelling: numerous Tanzanians, such as students or professional people, had lived and worked abroad for varying periods; while doing so, many had legitimately accumulated hard currency savings in other countries. Theoretically, imports financed from these savings would not be an economic drain on the currency reserves generated by exports and, therefore, should not require a currency allocation from the Central Bank.

The "no questions asked" provision seemed politically essential. Owing to the Sokoine anti-saboteurs campaign of the early 1980s, many Tanzanians were still fearful that the government might arrest and imprison them if it suspected that they were in illegitimate possession of imported goods. A "no questions asked" provision would provide an important reassurance of immunity from official harassment for those who took advantage of their overseas accounts. At first glance, the idea seemed to work: overnight, Tanzanian began to experience a surge of imports.

The own-financed imports program offers an excellent example of the way in which the government's inability to control corruption undermined a reform effort that seemed to have sound theoretical merits. In theory, the own-financed imports should have helped to abate inflation by alleviating the scarcity of imported goods. The more abundant supply of imports should also have softened pressure on the Tanzanian exchange rate by satisfying some of the pent-up demand for imported goods. Proponents of the own-financed imports policy also believed that the own-financed program would help to abate the culture of evasion that had arisen from the need to obtain essential goods in illegal markets. Whatever its theoretical merits, the own-financed import scheme had perverse economic effects: it created a heightened incentive for corruption in exchange markets, and, owing to the "no questions asked" provision, the government was in an even weaker position to control corruption in trade than in other economic activities. Many government officials had long attempted to conceal a portion of their gains from rent seeking by converting their Tanzania shillings into hard currency accounts overseas. Since any Tanzanian with an overseas account could now make vast profits on the import of scarce foreign goods, there was a renewed scramble to create such accounts or, in the case of numerous Tanzanian officials, to add additional sums to their existing overseas deposits. For members of the Tanzanian political elite, it had never been difficult to ship money abroad or use it to bring goods into the country. The legal immunity afforded by the "no questions asked" provision made the process even easier because Tanzanians did not have to explain how they had acquired their overseas funds.

Offered an opportunity to profiteer from the sale of imported goods, strategic civil servants sought ways to expand the scale of rent-seeking behavior; their implicit competition to convert their local currency rents into hard currency funds that could be deposited overseas led to added devaluation pressures on the Tanzanian shilling in parallel markets.[22] In theory, the own funds import program should have reduced the discrepancy between Tanzania's official exchange rate and the parallel market exchange rate since the added supply of imported goods ought to have lowered the parallel market demand for hard currency. In practice, the own funds scheme had the opposite effect. Inasmuch as Tanzanians now had an added incentive to build up their hard currency holdings overseas, the parallel market premium for hard currencies grew larger rather than smaller. Between 1984 and 1986, the parallel market premium for the U.S. dollar increased from about 300 percent to nearly 900 percent.[23] The greater the parallel market premium became, the greater the incentive for corruption since the goods imported into the country through the own funds scheme could be resold locally at prices reflecting the higher parallel market exchange rate.

The Tanzanian government and the World Bank quickly became aware that legitimately acquired overseas funds could not possibly account for the high volume of imports taking place under the own-financed scheme. Within a short time, these imports amounted to more than a third of all the country's imports.[24] The conclusion was inescapable: the own funds import scheme had contributed to increased corruption in the form of smuggled exports. The reason was that the own-financed approach to trade liberalization was asymmetrical: it offered some liberalization on the import side without providing any corresponding liberalization as regards export earnings. Since it was still illegal for Tanzanian exporters to retain more than a fraction of their hard currency earnings, they had an incentive to keep their earnings in overseas accounts rather than bring them into the country. The most advantageous way for Tanzanian exporters to participate in the own-financed program was to under-invoice their exports and then accept part of their payment abroad in the form of a hidden deposit into an overseas account.[25]

The own-financed imports policy had other perverse effects as well. By lowering the volume of officially reported export earnings, it reduced the tax revenues collected from those exports.[26] This resulted in increased fiscal starvation of public sector services.[27] The own-financed program also gave rise to additional layers of cooperation between the private business people who were exporting and importing goods and the public officials who could see to it that this went on without interference. Private exporters and importers could not have shipped their products overseas or hidden their domestic earnings without the collusion of public officials. Public officials found ways to join with private entrepreneurs in profitable import or export ventures that required government agencies such as the Tanzania Revenue Authority to look the other way. Tanzania's pattern of close partnerships between private entrepreneurs and influential officials did not originate in the own-financed import scheme. It had come into being long before, and was taking place in many different economic sectors well before the own-financed import program began. The own-financed import scheme, however, reinforced the pattern of economic collusion between private and public sector actors, further blurring any meaningful distinction between public influence and private wealth.

The basic goal of the trade reform effort was to replace the protectionist trade framework of the ISI period with a more open trade regime. Part of this effort has involved replacing quantitative restrictions with uniform tariffs that do not discriminate between different economic sectors. Tariffs have a somewhat ambiguous status among advocates of structural adjustment. Any tariff is inherently somewhat protectionist, but many economists concerned with development accept tariffs so long as these are low, relatively flat, and utilized for the purpose of revenue generation rather than as a means to cushion domestic enterprises from international competition. The donors favor a free trade environment commonly referred to as an *open general license* (OGL). This is a policy that permits open trade to begin with a positive list of permitted commodities but moves toward a negative list that merely specifies prohibited goods such as weapons, drugs, or nuclear waste.

Since progress toward OGL would move the country along toward removing the wall of protection around protected industries, the donors' goal was to move Tanzania toward an OGL system as quickly as possible. The World Bank recognized that that the country's agricultural exports were recovering too slowly to permit a robust resumption of consumer imports and that import scarcities during a period when Tanzanians' shilling incomes were increasing, might lead to a high rate of inflation, thereby undermining the devaluation process. To address these challenges, the Bank and other donors pledged external hard currency funds to cover a part of the cost of the anticipated increase in the flow of imports. The idea was that an abundant flow of imported goods might help inhibit inflation and, at the same time, help improve the government's fiscal position by boosting revenue collection through tariffs on the incoming goods. In this vision of trade liberalization, the external financing of import flows would only continue until there was a sufficient recovery of the export sector to permit Tanzania to cover the cost of imports on its own.

The OGL program did not proceed as smoothly as the donors had hoped. In fact, it may well stand out as one of the great examples of unintended outcomes, all of them negative in their economic effects. Perhaps the most obvious of these was the sheer scale of the program. Within a short time, the OGL program expanded to cover a larger and larger share of Tanzanian imports; by the early 1990s, funds provided by the World Bank, the IMF, and other donors financed more than 25 percent of Tanzania's imports. A program intended to help encourage trade liberalization by providing interim financial support for some imports had quickly become the largest single source of funding for imported goods.[28] By 1991, Tanzania was financing a larger proportion of its imports with funds borrowed from the ILIs than any other single source of foreign exchange, including own-financed imports.

A trade support program of that magnitude could not fail to have ripple effects on other aspects of the country's policy reform. One difficulty was that the ready availability of ILI funds to cover the cost of imports seemed to lessen the urgency of policies intended to promote a more timely recovery of the export sector. The donors' support for the OGL program may have contributed to the appreciation of the currency that was taking place in the early 1990s and this represented a continuation of the country's long-standing tendency to discriminate economically against producers of exportable agricultural commodities. The easy availability of donor funds lessened the urgency of Tanzania taking its own measures to increase foreign exchange earnings; for example, by devaluing the currency to increase producer prices for exports.

The donor-financed OGL program may also have helped seal the doom of some state industries. Some Tanzanians insist that, contrary to the image of all-inclusive failure, a few of the state industries might have been strong enough to survive if they had had a modest level of protection long enough to adapt to the country's rapidly changing economic circumstances. The donors, however, conditioned their support for the OGL program on a requirement that the Tanzanian government expand the number of goods that could be freely imported. Their list included practically all the goods in the ISI sector. Because of this pressure, the OGL program led to an abundant inflow of cigarettes, beer, paper products, clothing, and shoes. The Bank's financial support for the program put the government in the position of competing with itself. On the one hand, the government was still expending a certain amount of effort and resources to sustain parts of the import-substituting sector, if only to make some ISI industries more valuable to prospective purchasers. On the other hand, it had begun to obtain and use vast amounts of donor funds to import goods that were competing in the marketplace with the products of its own ISI factories.

One of the burning issues in the field of political economy is the optimal sequence of economic reforms. Many Tanzanians continue to believe that, to be successful and grow, domestic manufacturing firms would require some level of protection from foreign competition. Although mistakes were made during the pre-reform period with respect to both the form of ownership (state) and the form and duration of protection (quantitative restrictions, long term), there is a lingering attachment to the idea of protection as a valid boost to the manufacturing sector. According to this logic, trade liberalization should have awaited the divestiture process so that newly privatized industries could be afforded a limited period of protection while they navigated the transition from public to private ownership. The OGL program, which provided large amounts of donor funding to finance a rapid resumption of consumer goods imports, foreclosed that possibility. In so doing, it diminished the potential economic value of ISI industries because they had to face stiff import competition well before the divestiture process had gotten underway.

The economic spokespersons of countries undergoing liberalization often call attention to the problem of cross-conditionalities, situations in which one area of policy reform may conflict with another. The OGL program may offer an example because it complicated the government's effort to divest itself of ownership in the SOEs. Although the World Bank did not apply the terminology of economic shock to the OGL program, the import boom financed by the Bank and the Fund constituted a significant blow to the state industries. The World Bank and IMF were financing such a large flow of imports that the prices of imported goods tended to decline. This helped to reduce inflation but the low prices for imported items made them even more attractive to Tanzanian consumers than the goods local industries could produce. The counterfactual argument is not far out of reach. Without donor intervention to boost imports, the prices of imported goods would have risen and rising prices would have afforded an element of natural protection to domestic industrial firms. Because the donors were subsidizing the hard currency costs of imported goods, however, this did not occur.

Given the appalling economic performance of the state industries, there may have been little chance that any could survive in an era of market liberalization. However, the OGL program, because it led to a massive flow of imported goods, seemed to foreclose any remaining possibility of survival for even the best domestic industries. By facilitating a flow of imports, the ILIs were taking away much of what remained of the value of the consumer goods industries, making them even more difficult to sell to private investors. Import liberalization and divestiture of state firms were getting in the way of one another.

Despite the linked problems of corruption and the perverse economic outcomes of the early efforts at trade liberalization, the ten years of the Mwinyi administration were a period during which the government of Tanzania made substantial progress in evolving its economy away from the rigid protectionist emphasis of the post-independence decades and toward freer trade. There is little doubt that ordinary Tanzanians have benefited from the freer trade atmosphere. When the Mwinyi government began to allow the import of used clothing, a category of imports that earlier trade restrictions prevented as a protection for the state-owned wearing apparel industry, this became so popular that Tanzanians began to refer to it colloquially as "Asante, Mwinyi," or "Thank you, President Mwinyi." Since the used clothing arrived in large bales, it generated employment opportunities for thousands of Tanzanians who had to sort the bales by category of clothing, transport it to sales points across the country, and then market it to eager consumers. And although Tanzania's importers and exporters continue to complain about the costs of corruption at the country's major ports and about the cumbersome paperwork and endless bribes[29] necessary to clear their shipping containers, they regard the current trade regime as a major improvement over the rigid protectionism of the statist era.

Since the mid-1990s, when the aid crisis was resolved, Tanzania and its donors have agreed that trade policy must be judged against a free trade standard. The trade dialogue between Tanzania and its donors has largely been of a technical nature. The Tanzanian government has officially accepted that it needs to move toward a freer trade environment and the donors have accepted that this is a genuine statement of government intentions.[30] In 2003, the Tanzanian government officially accepted the principle that export-led growth was critical to the country's overall economic development and to poverty alleviation, and in 2005 Tanzania rejoined the EAC, aligning its import duties with those of its companion countries.[31] The principal topics of discussion have to do with whether the export sector continues to carry an undue burden of taxes and whether taxes and duties on trade continue to provide too large a share of government revenue. Free trade theory has replaced development economics as Tanzania's economic orthodoxy.

The disquiet that arises in considerations of trade reform is that the economics profession does not have a unanimous consensus on free trade. Some of the world's most prestigious economists, including Nobel Prize winners Paul Krugman and Joseph Stiglitz, have called for a critical reexamination of the proposition that free trade is the optimal approach for developing countries that remain dependent on primary commodity exports.[32] Their research suggests that a heterodox approach, one that combines elements of protection with elements of free trade, could provide superior developmental benefits for societies at an early stage of development. A recent surge of interest in the views of the Harvard University economist, Alexander Gerschenkron, is a part of this trend. There is a sympathetic reexamination of his belief that late industrializers face different problems than early ones and that the differences call for a more active role by government.[33] The economist Ha-Joon Chang, for example, has sought to show that late industrializers could derive an economic boost by providing protection for carefully selected infant industries. He shows that this policy worked for early industrializing nations, which did not face the challenge of global competition when they went through an industrial revolution. For late industrializers, needing to deal with a global marketplace dominated by powerful multinational firms, the benefits of a period of protection might be considerable.[34] These views suggest the need for a more critical approach to the widely prevailing assumption that free trade is the best policy for all countries at all stages of their development.

Case 3. Divestiture of State Owned Enterprises

Of the many different areas of economic reform, the divestiture of SOEs is the most intensive in its need for legislative action. It affords an important example of the extent to which institutions matter in determining the timing and outcome of reform. To begin the process, the National Assembly had to pass legislation creating a tripod of financial institutions that would be responsible for moving divestiture forward. The first legislative step was the Loans and Advances Realization Trust Act of 1991, which created an eponymous agency, LART,[35] whose mandate was to extract the maximum return from the disposal of SOE physical assets and from the liquidation of their debts to the banking system. The next step was to create the agency that would have primary responsibility and legal authority for divesting Tanzania's SOEs to private or mixed ownership. The government created the Parastatal Sector Reform Commission (PSRC) by passing the Public Corporations Act of 1992.[36] The third was a stock exchange, which would enable newly formed private companies to raise capital by selling shares. The Tanzanian National Assembly passed the Capital Markets and Securities Act in 1994 to create a stock exchange, which it named the Dar es Salaam Stock Exchange Company (DARSECO).[37] This entity was somewhat slower to develop fully: DARSECO did not fully incorporate until September 1996 and did not begin actively trading shares until 1998. Taken together, LART, PSRC, and DARSECO formed the institutional tripod for the divestiture process.

Since the authority to create these institutions resided in the legislative branch, divestiture could not begin until after the 1990 general election, when the Tanzanian National Assembly became more amenable to economic reform. To the donors, the delay in divestiture seemed to symbolize the reluctance of Tanzanian political leaders to proceed with reforms that might diminish their ability to control valuable economic assets. The ILIs had vocalized this concern repeatedly in their meetings with Tanzanian officials. However, as Chapter 5 showed, President Mwinyi and his supporters were not in a political position to go ahead with economic reforms that required legislative action. Mwinyi did not enjoy the degree of control over the assembly that Nyerere had, and he and his supporters were concerned that the National Assembly might stall or defeat any major reform bills they brought forward while Nyerere was still head of the party. Although the ILIs perceived this as foot-dragging on important reforms, it was better understood as Mwinyi's pragmatic reluctance to pursue a legislative battle he might well have lost.

The divestiture process also had to include fundamental changes in the legal basis of the trade union movement. The government would need to emancipate the trade unions from their status as adjuncts of the Tanzanian state and restore organized labor to its historic position as a free movement able to negotiate independently with private employers. Under the NUTA legislation of the early 1960s and the successor legislation that created the Union of Tanzanian Workers (JUWATA) in 1977, Tanzanian trade unions were still under the administrative jurisdiction and political control of the minister of labor. That legislation proscribed strikes and other forms of worker action and gave the authority to choose labor leaders to the minister of labor instead of regular members. The government had justified the OTTU/JUWATA framework with the theory that it would be unfair for union members who owed their livelihood to taxpayer funds to engage in strikes that could harm taxpayer welfare. The reformers understood that the old arguments for a state-administered union movement would lose force once these industries were in private hands. A state-controlled union might be a logical fit for a state-owned industrial system. A privatized industrial system required a return to more traditional trade union principles.

To create a freer trade union movement, the National Assembly in 1991 passed legislation that established a new union called the Organization of Tanzania Trade Unions (OTTU).[38] While retaining the overall structure of a single nationwide trade union movement, OTTU detached the movement from the administrative and political supervision of the Ministry of Labor. The new labor law also created a much more permissive environment for the formation of separate unions that could organize according to different industrial sectors. OTTU came into being in 1992 and began immediately to encourage the formation of separate sub-unions; within only a year or two, there were eleven separate industrial unions. OTTU was also a more democratic body: the highest OTTU official in the union was an elected executive director, not the minister of labor, and individual union leaders were also to be democratically elected, restoring some element of organizational control to the rank and file. The OTTU act also gave individual unions greater latitude in determining their relationship with the parent union: the eleven industrial unions actually seceded from OTTU in 1995 to form the Tanzanian Federation of Free Trade Unions (TFTU). Perhaps most importantly, the OTTU legislation also restored to individual unions the right to negotiate directly with employers as well as the right to strike over work actions.

With the creation of the PSRC in 1992, thorny economic questions arose. The first was what exactly constitutes an SOE for purposes of divestiture. There were several competing answers. For the economists who believed that the root cause of economic decline was the decision to adopt ISI, the concept of a divestible SOE referred narrowly to the manufacturing firms that arose during the ISI experiment. The list of these firms is by now familiar and includes the enterprises that produced beer, paper products, cigarettes, textiles, shoes, soft drinks, plastic goods, and certain construction materials such as concrete. These firms cried out for early divestiture because they were incurring large operating losses despite the fact that they enjoyed a host of costly economic subsidies. Because the industrial firms were unable to pay their bills to the state-owned utilities that provided telephone service, electricity, and water, they were causing large operating losses in other public corporations as well. Divestiture of the consumer goods industries had an urgent quality. Many of these firms still had authority to borrow funds that had government guarantees and some were still using this authority to obtain loans from domestic and international banks even though their productive performance had all but ceased.

Some ILI economists, however, believed that Tanzania's openness to divestiture offered an invaluable opportunity to extend the operation of market forces to wider areas of the economy. From their standpoint, it was too restrictive to limit divestiture to the industrial firms. Banks and hotels, for example, seemed to be obvious targets for divestiture. During the period of socialism, Tanzania had nationalized its tourist industry and banking system, thereby adding a number of hotels and the National Bank of Commerce (NBC) to the list of SOEs. Since many of these firms were operating at large net losses, the government agreed to add them to the divestiture list. A number of economists within the donor community began to seek an even wider definition of the SOEs that would be candidates for divestiture, calling for public utilities, for example, to be included in the process. This would mean that the government corporations that provided water and electricity, telephone and postal service, waste disposal, and transportation services such as the ports and harbors authority, the national railroad, and the national airline would also face privatization.

Disputes about which enterprises the divestiture list should include aroused intense debate both within the government, between reformist and conservative elements, and between the government and the donor community. There were those who wished to add to the divestiture list the subsidiary businesses of institutions that would remain in public hands. The University of Dar es Salaam offers an instructive example. Free market advocates in the donor community believed the mission of the university was to provide education. They argued that private companies should take over the university's subsidiary operations such as its residential facilities, dining facilities, and transportation operations. In the end, one of the explanations for the slowness of the divestiture process was the inordinate amount of time required even to compile a list of the economic entities that would be considered for divestiture, much less establish priority categories.

The final list of SOEs considered suitable for divestiture was extraordinarily long and included about 400 businesses, from public utilities to small tourist hotels. The sheer length of the list raised difficult questions of its own. There is a vast distance between an in-principle commitment to divestiture and the practical steps required to implement a sale of assets for such a large and diverse group of institutions. There were intense discussions over the question of how the PSRC should sequence the divestiture process. Should it begin with the largest SOEs whose financial losses were greatest? Should it begin with the smaller and less complicated SOEs that would be easier to sell? Should divestiture begin with the businesses that promised the greatest immediate benefits in generating employment opportunity such as the railroad, port authority and national airline? Should it begin with the more economically promising SOEs such as the brewing, soft drink, and cigarette industries that might be more attractive to prospective buyers? Should it begin with the SOEs that had the greatest foreign exchange potential such as tourist facilities? Because of poor record keeping both in the SOEs and in the banks that had lent them money, there was no way to create a comprehensive audit of the financial records necessary to answer these questions. As the level of mutual frustration rose, some members of the donor community began to advocate a fire sale approach: simply dispose of the SOEs at rock bottom prices to any buyer who might come along. Their impatience added to the strain between the donors and the Tanzanians.

Other participants in the divestiture dialogue, including both Tanzanian economists and some members of the donor community, advocated a more methodical approach. Their most convincing argument was that divestiture actually has two fundamental objectives. The first is to privatize a country's productive enterprises as quickly as possible so that they become profitable and begin to generate growth and employment. The second is more normative in nature; it consists of building a culture of financial prudence and fiscal responsibility. Policy reform begins with the implementation of policies that will reduce fiscal and trade deficits, resolve exchange rate disequilibria and foster the emergence of healthy private markets. But it is also about creating a political culture that inhibits these problems from arising again. This vitally important dimension of the reform process has received far too little attention from policy reformers and scholars. The omission is regrettable because the first objective may not enjoy long-term success without the second. Without a surrounding culture of accountability, there is little assurance that policies that led to such poor outcomes in the first place will not happen again. Creating a culture of prudence was particularly important in Tanzania because its ISI sector had proven to be so susceptible to rent seeking and moral hazard behavior.

The issue that provided the best opportunity to build this culture was what to do about the outstanding debts of the SOEs: their unpaid loans from the banking system. Tanzania's early economic planners had conceived SOE indebtedness as a necessary but transitory feature of state-sponsored industrialization. The new factories would need time to go through the steps necessary to begin production: to construct plants, acquire and install machinery, train workers, obtain licenses and use-rights on patented machinery, and conclude subcontracts with local suppliers for everything from office furnishings to catering services. The planners assumed that several years might go by before any of these firms could begin to realize earnings on investment by beginning the actual production and marketing of a good. In the meantime, these industries would need financial support from the banking system.

The dilemma that confronted the Tanzanian government was how to finance the process of creating industries until production began. Banks might be reluctant to provide financing for industries that were dependent on large public subsidies and might not begin to produce goods for some time, or whose goods might be unattractive to consumers. The answer was that government would become the guarantor of the loans required to meet these industries' start-up expenses. There was a three-way relationship. SOEs would become the borrowers; banks, whether private or public, would become the lenders. Government would become the ultimate guarantor of the loans. No one asked what might happen if the SOEs defaulted on their indebtedness because the theory did not anticipate industrial failure. Had anyone done so, the answer would have been that the Tanzanian taxpayer would have to indemnify the banks for their losses through an annual budget appropriation. The possibility that the SOEs' financial obligations would become the basis for spiraling budget deficits seemed negligible. Leading economists had insisted that ISI had a sound basis in scientifically proved economic theory.

The failure of that model is the reason why governments such as Tanzania's needed to create institutional mechanisms whose purpose was to extract as much monetary recovery as possible from the defaulted debt even though this might take longer than the crash sale approach some were advocating. LART had exactly this purpose. LART and the PSRC shared the purpose of facilitating the divestiture process. However, they diverged in matters of timing and strategic approach. Whereas the PSRC's responsibility was to arrange a timely sell-off of state assets, LART's responsibility might require holding on to those assets long enough to extract any residual cash value they might have.

The question many students pose about this indebtedness is utterly pragmatic. Why have LART? Why didn't the Tanzanian government simply "forgive" these debts? After all, in Tanzania, these were not international debts to foreign private banks, the ILIs, or bilateral donors; they were simply local currency debts owed by one set of SOEs, the industrial companies, to another, the various branches of the state-owned National Bank of Commerce. Hadn't taxpayers already borne much of the cost of these enterprises in the form of negative growth rates, severe inflation, goods scarcities, high unemployment, and other hardships? In addition, wouldn't simple forgiveness greatly accelerate the divestiture process, thereby satisfying ILI insistence on speedier action?

There is no strictly economic answer to those questions. Forgiveness of domestic debt would have been a possibility and might have had some short-term advantages. It would have dissolved the banks' obligation to carry these loans on their books as nonperforming assets. This could make it possible for banks to begin lending again. Even within the donor community, some were prepared to accept a sort of "that was then and this is now" point of view toward SOE indebtedness. The best answer to the forgiveness question has to do with the need to create a prudential economic culture: responsible governmental actors do not simply default on their debts even if they have the legal authority to do so. The principal reason is that doing this might create the sort of precedent that would make it easy for a successor government to repeat the process. The principle that mistakes should not be cost-free is not narrowly economic; it pertains to a far wider circle of behaviors. To learn that lesson for the future, responsible government actors find a way to work through their accumulated indebtedness in such a way as to create an ethos of accountability that will bind future generations.

LART and comparable organizations such as Ghana's Non-Performing Assets Realization Trust (NPART) have the responsibility to deal with the after-effects of the moral hazard problem, the huge overhang of unpaid parastatal debts to the banking system. LART's responsibility was to deal with the way moral hazard in the form of irresponsible SOE borrowing from the banking system had devastated any economic promise the SOEs might have had. Whereas the purpose of the PSRC was to dispose of the SOEs and privatize the economy as rapidly as possible, the purpose of LART was to make it clear that irresponsible indebtedness was not cost free. The PSRC and LART, therefore, had different short-term objectives. For the PSRC, the goal was privatization because it would lead to a more efficient economy and a higher rate of growth. The economic assumption underlying LART was that the SOEs represented a government investment of taxpayer funds and the government therefore had a responsibility to its taxpayers, at least to the extent of doing everything possible to demonstrate that this would not happen again.

PSRC and LART officials had different terminologies that revealed their differences in approach. PSRC administrators sometimes referred to the SOEs in terms of their "scrap value." Its focus of attention was on the different modalities of divestiture, which included outright sale, sale of shares, liquidation, joint purchases, and long-term lease arrangements. LART proponents understood that quick sales at bargain-basement prices would leave the government with a larger volume of unpaid debt. The LART terminology referred to the embedded value that still resided in the SOEs. Even if the industrial companies appeared to be no more than the derelict relics of a failed economic experiment, its responsibility was to search for that value and monetize it. Those familiar with the LART process understood that there could be monetary value in the industries' physical location, which was often adjacent to a railroad spur or roadway, or in their connections to the country's essential utilities such as the electricity, water, and sewage system. There might even be a monetary value in the physical layout of a company such as its office area and factory floor.[39]

LART and the PSRC sometimes came into conflict over the best method for structuring the divestiture of an SOE. There were about 400 of these, ranging in size and character from large manufacturing firms and banks to small hotels in the tourist sector. With that many SOEs to dispose of and with unremitting donor pressure on the Tanzanian government to show quick results, the PSRC seemed to have an institutional preference for sales that could be accomplished quickly because they did not obligate the buyer to assume the heavy responsibility for a firm's past indebtedness. For LART to do its job properly, however, it had to attempt, at least, to ensure that the structure of an SOE sale obligated the prospective buyer to assume some responsibility for a portion of the firm's indebtedness such as pension obligations to retired workers. If LART could induce prospective buyers to divert a fraction of future profits toward paying these debts, it would reduce the long-term debt obligation of the government. This would free government funds for needed social purposes. To accomplish its goal, LART sometimes took companies into receivership, a legal status that was not directly compatible with the PSRC motivation to achieve a fast sale. The recovery of funds would not make it possible for LART to lower the burden on past taxpayers who had already suffered through the ISI experiment. However, in transferring any funds it might recover to the Tanzanian Treasury; it would help to ease the burden on future taxpayers.

The challenges inherent in the LART process were overwhelming. To do its job well, LART should have undertaken a comprehensive audit of all the assets and liabilitiesof the state companies scheduled for divestiture. However, Tanzania had such a severe scarcity of licensed auditors and accountants that this might have taken years to accomplish and even the most patient reformers could not justify that timetable. The sheer volume and poor quality of SOE paperwork also made the process difficult. Record keeping was so poor that it was often difficult even to locate all of a company's loan documents, which made it next to impossible to compute its aggregate debt to the . banking system. Sometimes undiscovered loan documents requiring government indemnification seemed to appear months after LART had completed a debt inventory. Serious problems of authentication arose as some of these documents seemed to have been the products of forgery and corruption. Sometimes loan documents that did not comply with the timetable specified in the LART legislation were altered to make them appear eligible for government guarantees.

To do its job thoroughly, LART would also have to function as a sort of anti-corruption agency because there was great political pressure to enable members of the political elite to acquire SOE assets at sharply discounted prices. As the Warioba Commission Report made clear, however, there was no agency in the Tanzanian government, including LART, which was immune to the corruption process. Because LART operated beneath a veil of confidentiality, it is difficult to assess how well it performed. Some informants believe the confidentiality principle concealed a lackluster performance; others call attention to the fact that LART had responsibility for the most challenging part of the divestiture, monetizing nonperforming assets (bad debts) that had sometimes been in default for many years.

The third leg of the divestiture tripod was the Dar es Salaam Stock Exchange, first known as DARSECO. Economists have long called attention to the advantages of a stock exchange. It can make a major contribution to divestiture by providing a fast and transparent market for sale of state properties. A stock exchange could also bypass the laborious and time-consuming process of auditing the physical assets and paper liabilities of the SOEs; it could generate a quick cash return at a current market value determined by those prepared to take the risk. Under optimal conditions, a stock exchange could provide a means of disposing of the indebtedness of the state companies.

Brokerage firms could bundle the SOEs' defaulted paper into bonds for sale at discounted prices to investors prepared to purchase high-risk securities. There is an element of fairness about a stock exchange since participants understand that there are risks as well as rewards and choose to invest with that awareness in mind. A stock exchange could also have great value as vehicle for public education; it would provide a powerful symbol of the government's commitment to a new way of managing the economy.

The technical difficulties in creating a stock exchange were daunting. Tanzania had been a socialist society practically since independence in the early 1960s. Its commercial code consisted for the most part of older British laws set in place during the colonial era when the economy was small and many modern forms of transaction did not exist. Since Tanzania became a socialist country following independence, the CCM government had never assigned a priority to bringing the colonial era commercial code up to date. With the transition to a market economy, the government needed to revisit colonial era laws and pass new legislation relevant to the global market realities of the 1990s. Although stock markets may appear to be the epitome of free market forces, they cannot even begin to operate without a large body of regulatory legislation. The government had to consider laws pertaining to such matters as insider trading, due diligence, best practices for sales and purchasing agents, the boundaries between civil and criminal infractions, and the standard of legal proof for violations of market rules.

Existing legislation on these matters, if it existed at all, was inadequate. Tanzania had no current laws on its books that would provide a workable regulatory framework for a host of basic questions. Should the government require Tanzania's brokerage firms to enlist the assistance of independent ratings agencies? What regulations might be necessary to enable the brokerage firms to handle complex financial instruments such as derivatives, credit default swaps and collateralized debt obligations? Should the government even permit these during the early years of operation? Should the government allow a secondary market in the defaulted loans to the banking system? Would it permit international investors to trade on the Tanzanian exchange, thereby permitting a flow of foreign investment in the newly divested Tanzanian companies? Would it permit Tanzanian brokerage houses to handle international transactions so that Tanzanian investors could purchase stocks in internationally traded companies?

A government that creates a stock exchange must also create and staff the supervisory agencies necessary to see to it that its laws and regulations are enforced. This requires a judicial system equipped and staffed to handle complicated financial cases. There was a critical shortage of trained and experienced personnel. Some donor representatives believed that the creation of a stock exchange should await a donor investment in the expansion of the business and business law programs at the University of Dar es Salaam to provide training for the accountants, brokers, auditors and attorneys who would handle stock transactions. Creating a stock exchange also meant the need to create and license the brokerage firms and other financial institutions that mediate between buyers and sellers. As with so much else in the divestiture process, there was a vast gulf between a theoretical perspective that assigned a prominent role to open financial markets, on the one hand, and the practical, legal, and legislative steps required to bring such a market into operation, on the other.

The most challenging questions, however, were social, not technical or legal. Even Tanzanians who favored the transition to freer markets raised doubts about the distributional effects of a stock exchange in a predominantly smallholder society. In their view, stock markets can function well in industrial societies where there is a large middle class and large institutional investors with the capability of monitoring market behavior and where a sizable proportion of the population has disposable cash income. Even there, participation in stock ownership does not often extend beyond the upper reaches of a society's social structure. In a small agricultural society such as Tanzania, no more than a tiny fraction of the population would be able to participate in equities markets. Stock ownership would exacerbate the country's social inequalities. The combination of technical challenges and social doubts explains why the stock exchange was the last of the three core divestiture institutions to become operational and why its role in the divestiture process, indeed in the economy as a whole, has remained limited. Even today, nearly twenty years after it began operations, the Dar es Salaam Stock Exchange does not have a significant impact on the Tanzanian economy. It conducts trades in less than twenty companies, only a small number of which grew out of the divestiture of the industrial SOEs.

The Tanzanian government and its donors view the outcome of divestiture differently, a reflection of the unresolved issues that followed the aid crisis of 1995. Tanzanian officials point to divestiture as a success story, further evidence that they have made rapid progress in a short time. Within a decade of beginning divestiture, the PSRC had disposed of more than half, about 210, of the firms on the divestiture list. Of these, about 170 represented outright sale of shares or assets.[40] These included many small or medium-sized SOEs that produced readily marketable goods such goods as beer, cigarettes, and cement. Because Tanzania is a highly popular tourist attraction, the list of successfully divested firms also included a number of tourist hotels. In 1996, the government of Tanzania agreed to include public utilities on the divestiture list. Within a decade, private investors had assumed ownership of Tanzania Telecommunications, Dar es Salaam Water and Sanitation, and portions of the Harbor Authority. Divestiture reduced the size of Tanzania's public sector payroll by more than 100,000, lowering total government employment from about 360,000 positions to about 250,000.

Donor officials accept that the government has done a great deal but view the divestiture process differently. They point to features of the process that confirm their fears about the extent to which uncontrolled corruption has influenced economic reform. One was the government's willingness to extend guaranteed lines of credit and borrowing authorizations to bankrupt companies. From the donors' standpoint, there was little chance that the government would ever recover this last minute investment of taxpayer funds. In their view, this practice showed the government's willingness to continue to use taxpayer funds to enrich members of the country's political elite. The purpose of the government's expansion of credit to the SOEs was to make these companies as valuable as possible for their new owners. If the government could be induced to absorb some of the costs of rehabilitating the SOEs while it was still the owner, passing the improvement costs on to the Tanzanian taxpayer, prospective purchasers could profit handsomely by purchasing the divested companies at a small fraction of their newly appreciated worth.

The two outcomes of divestiture suggest that both sides have complied with the terms of the grand bargain set in place by the Advisors Group. Tanzanians have agreed to proceed in a timely manner with economic reforms that would transform the national economy from state ownership and control to private ownership and market forces. The donors have reconciled themselves to the government's determination to pursue this change in a manner that benefited and entrenched the country's political-economic oligarchy.

Conclusion: Contemporary Tanzania

Tanzania has attained its post-reform equilibrium. During five decades of independence, it has morphed from a failed experiment in socialist egalitarianism to a dystopian realm in which economic and political inequalities have taken on every appearance of permanence. The principal political characteristics of contemporary Tanzania are dominance by a political-economic oligarchy embedded within the CCM hierarchy, the propensity of many members of this oligarchy to use corruption as a means of consolidating and maintaining their dominance, and a pattern of economic growth that benefits those at the top of the society. Although not all the members of the Tanzanian oligarchy are among the *mafisadi* (corrupt ones), many engage in the practice, and the visibility of high profile corruption scandals has tainted the CCM leadership cadre as a whole. The generosity of the donor community strengthens this equilibrium. Tanzania now receives nearly $3 billion annually in foreign direct assistance, almost 13 percent of gross national income (GNI), and is the world's third largest recipient of nonmilitary development assistance behind only Iraq and Afghanistan.[1] China is now joining Western donors in ways that further reinforce the dominance of the CCM oligarchy.

The Tanzanian state also derives stability from democratic legitimation: the CCM has managed decisive, though variable, victories in all four of the country's multiparty elections. Although there have been allegations of electoral irregularities—including doubts about the neutrality of electoral monitors, the CCM's use of *takrima* (gifts) to obtain votes, poor management of election ballots, and physical harassment of opposition parties and their supporters—these do not yet add to wholesale electoral theft. It seems incontrovertible that the Tanzanian electoral process is imperfect, damaged by the fact that the CCM leadership has used all these tactics to maintain a winning share of the vote. Despite these concerns and the obvious need for major improvements in the country's electoral process, no one has yet suggested that the outcome of these elections would have been significantly different had the election taken place under a more perfect set of election procedures. Nor has any electoral observer organization chosen to describe Tanzania's election results as other than broadly free and fair.[2] Tanzania does not receive an honors grade in democracy, but it does not receive a failing grade either.

The majority of Tanzanians including supporters of opposition parties appear to accept that their country's election results are, overall, an accurate reflection of their political preferences. As a result, Tanzania has not experienced the sort of post-election violence that has taken place in several other African countries. Tanzania stands out from its regional neighbors based on what has not taken place there in the last twenty-five years. It has not experienced genocidal events (Rwanda, Sudan). It has not experienced ethnic cleansing or ethnically based electoral violence (Kenya); it has not had to navigate the distance between military rule and an elected presidency (Uganda); it has not experienced violently repressive dictatorship (Zimbabwe); and it has not experienced the utter political breakdown sometimes described as a "failed state" (Somalia). Tanzanians are aware that Tanzania is the non-Somalia, the non-Sudan, the non-Rwanda, and even the non-Kenya of Eastern Africa. Despite seemingly intractable problems of electoral irregularities, pervasive corruption, persistent poverty, and widening socioeconomic inequality, they appreciate their country's tradition of civil peace.

Tanzania's economic achievement was its peaceful liberalization of the economy. In the decade from 1985 to 1995, the CCM transformed the country from a single-party socialist regime to a multiparty democracy presiding over a market-based economic system. The restructuring of the economy, which had the technical and financial support of IMF agreements, World Bank structural adjustment programs, and financial aid from bilateral donors and NGOs, did not provoke major episodes of political turbulence. Although it was an imperfect process, it did not launch urban riots or other mass protests among affected segments of its population. Tanzania has not experienced a version of the Arab Spring or even the Occupy Movement. Indeed, the country's economic changes appear to enjoy the broad support of the Tanzanian people.

Tanzania accomplished this transformation while allowing the country's economic elite to consolidate control over the state. That outcome was the subtext of the grand bargain with the donors that resolved the 1994–1995 aid crisis. The journalistic term for Tanzania's current system of governance is "crony capitalism," an expression that, though coarser than the softer academic notion of political-economic oligarchy, is identical in conveying a state of affairs in which political power and economic wealth are inextricably intertwined. The Tanzanian 1 percent consists of the country's highest-ranking political leaders and administrative officials, their families, and their associates in the business community. For members of this privileged group, political power and economic wealth reinforce each other. It is unimportant to consider the direction of causality, whether wealth is a source of political power or power is the gateway to wealth. Both are true. In a crony capitalist system, the most lucrative business opportunities find their way into the hands of the family members, friends, and close associates of the highest-ranking members of the political elite. The wealthiest business entrepreneurs, many of whom attained this status through their political connections, use their economic resources to help that elite remain in power. The challenging question is not how the system operates from day to day but, rather, how to assess its potential for longer-term stability.

Growth and Poverty

An important determinant of future stability will be the extent to which this oligarchy is prepared to share the benefits of economic growth. Close observers of the Tanzanian polity base their assessment of stability in part on the view that Tanzania's economy has been growing steadily during the era of economic reform. Tables 2 and 3, which draw on data provided by the World Bank and the African Development Bank, show Tanzania's GDP growth and GDP per capita growth for the thirty-year period from 1981 to 2010. These tables suggest that Tanzania has done well since the early 1980s. An IMF economist has described Tanzania's economic performance as a "remarkable turnaround." He stated "Twenty years later (1985–2005), Tanzania looks radically different. Inflation has declined to single digits. . . . Economic growth is buoyant, averaging 7 percent a year since 2000. Real per capita income has risen by 50 percent. Poverty, while still widespread, is heading downward."[3] The UNDP has joined in offering a buoyant assessment. Although it ranks Tanzania as 152nd of 1986 countries on its human development index, its most recent report (2013) indicates that Tanzania attained an average HDI index improvement of 2.15 percent per year between 2000 and 2012.[4] If these estimates are accurate, Tanzania has attained an impressive growth rate and a pattern of economic growth that, while uneven, has spread across a variety of sectors. The image that these figures seek to convey portrays an economic success story where the transition to market-based policies has begun to bring about real improvements in the quality of life.

Firsthand observers anticipate a continued improvement in Tanzania's economic trajectory. The Economist Intelligence Unit, for example, anticipates that Tanzania's economic growth will continue to average about 7 percent. It further suggests that there will be a gradual lowering of inflation as government efforts to improve revenue collection lower the fiscal deficit relative to GDP.[5] Although donor representatives continue to express concern about Tanzania's corruption problem and its corrosive effects on the country's political and economic life, the recriminatory aid relationship of the mid-1990s is past history. The donor community provides financial support in the form of direct budgetary assistance and project lending; Tanzania accepts it.

Table 2. GDP Growth (Annual %) 5-Year Average, 1981–2010

	1981–1985	1986–1990	1991–1995	1996–2000	2001–2005	2005–2010
Tanzania	0.97	5.71	1.80	4.31	7.05	6.88
Ghana	−0.25	4.81	4.28	4.34	5.09	6.61
Kenya	2.97	5.64	1.60	2.08	3.78	4.61
Malawi	2.18	2.33	2.92	4.39	2.26	7.22
Senegal	2.92	2.38	2.09	4.12	4.68	3.45
Uganda	2.13	5.09	7.04	7.53	7.56	7.17

Sources: World Bank, *World Development Indicators*, www.worldbank.org; African Development Bank, *Data Portal*. www.afdb.org. Table prepared by Dr. Julia Kim.

Table 3. GDP Per Capita Growth (Annual %) 5-Year Average, 1981–2010

	1981–1985	1986–1990	1991–1995	1996–2000	2001–2005	2005–2010
Tanzania	−2.10	2.56	−1.38	1.63	4.50	3.89
Ghana	−3.43	1.97	1.47	1.89	2.59	4.11
Kenya	−0.78	2.03	−1.48	−0.53	1.13	1.98
Malawi	−0.85	−2.63	1.84	1.80	−0.39	4.10
Senegal	0.11	−0.60	−0.78	1.54	1.94	0.74
Uganda	−0.95	1.46	3.67	4.39	4.21	3.81

Sources: World Bank, *World Development Indicators*, www.worldbank.org; African Development Bank, *Data Portal*. www.afdb.org. Table prepared by Dr. Julia Kim.

The economic challenges that Tanzania faces are the normal questions that face any developing country. Will a downturn in the global economy affect demand for Tanzanian exports? Will global commodity prices for Tanzania's major exports remain high enough to sustain a continued improvement in export-generated revenues? Will the cost of vital imports such as fuel remain sufficiently stable to keep inflation low? Although these are serious matters, most official observers believe that Tanzania has improved its ability to address these challenges.

Since both government and donors accept the Bank's optimistic economic picture, the figures on economic growth have given rise to a friendly disagreement over who can claim credit for Tanzania's new reality. Tanzanian officials assert that the impressive growth figures are a result of the many challenging reforms they enacted during the 1990s. In their view, its donors should have expected their reforms to take effect slowly and should have been prepared to wait more patiently for the results of their efforts. Some donor representatives insist the reform efforts might not have gone forward at all without the intense pressure they brought to bear before and during the aid crisis. Both sides claim credit for the apparent improvements in Tanzania's economic growth; if the economic figures are anything close to correct, both should share in the congratulatory atmosphere.

The buoyant economic numbers call for a measure of caution, however. One source of concern has to do with the accuracy of Tanzania's growth figures. As early as 1982, the International Labor Organization (ILO), long considered one of the more sympathetic and supportive of the international organizations participating in Tanzanian development, had observed, "all is not well with Tanzanian statistics."[6] Donor community doubts about the accuracy of Tanzania data have continued and were a contributing factor to the 1994-1995 aid crisis. The section on "data deficiencies" in the joint World Bank/IMF 1993 report on structural adjustment, for example, raises additional concerns about the accuracy of Tanzania's economic statistics. It directs attention, for example, to "the flawed compilation of the national accounts data."[7]

Tanzania's data problems are both systemic and political. Much of the economic data that provides the basis for World Bank and IMF figures on growth originates in the various statistical offices of the Tanzanian government including the Central Bureau of Statistics. The problem of Tanzanian economic statistics begins with poorly trained personnel working under difficult conditions with minimal resources, struggling to compile quantitative data for poorly understood and vaguely framed analytic categories. It includes a poor system of communications between the Central Bureau and the satellite offices that collect the primary data. The data difficulties further include the daunting challenge of collecting accurate information about a population that is overwhelmingly rural, widespread, and still extensively engaged in forms of agricultural production that combine subsistence farming with variable levels of participation in the monetary economy. Perhaps most important, much of Tanzania's rural population has inherited the climate of mistrust that arose during decades of excessive taxation and regimentation and that, to this day, continues to be wary of official information-gathering efforts. In addition, some of the most important statistical information that goes into the GDP figures requires estimates of data categories that are impossibly difficult to measure accurately, such as the changing value of the subsistence portion of household consumption among rural families or the changing composition of the basket of goods consumed by urban households.[8]

Political factors also raise doubts about the accuracy of the statistical data. Tanzania's political leaders have long been aware that the continued flow of foreign assistance on which their country is so dependent rests on their ability to show positive economic results. Besides the funds the aid organizations bring into the country for budgetary support and countless development projects, their mere presence in the country is economically vital. In addition to the numerous bilateral aid and diplomatic missions, Tanzania's aid community includes numerous agencies of the United Nations, including the UNDP, the United Nations Children's Educational Fund (UNICEF), and the Food and Agricultural Organization (FAO). The Tanzanian aid community also includes over one thousand registered NGOs. Practically all these organizations maintain offices in Dar es Salaam. The official aid organizations and the NGO representatives who reside in Tanzania are an important economic presence. They not only contribute to the total ensemble of Tanzania's development efforts, they are a source of demand for housing and office space as well as a host of other locally provided services. The members of the aid community are customers at local stores; they send their children to local private schools; they purchase and service their vehicles at local automotive dealerships; they dine at local restaurants; and they avail themselves of local travel services when they visit Tanzania's scenic locations. They are also a source of well-paid employment for thousands of Tanzanian staff members whose salaries inject a purchasing power stimulus into the economy. The economic importance of the donor community is so great that Tanzania has always used economic data to present a favorable image to those who provide it with development assistance.

This problem grew more acute during the 1990s aid crisis, when donor representatives became more insistent on firm evidence that their investment of funds was producing tangible results. Tanzanians had always felt some pressure to generate statistical data that demonstrated positive development outcomes but this pressure increased when several large donors stopped aid disbursements and others threatened to end their aid efforts and leave the country. It would be unfair and inaccurate to blame the Tanzanians alone for seeking to present a rosy picture of their economy. The donor organizations, which are under political pressures of their own to demonstrate positive results for their expenditures, were partners in this process. No one in the aid community would go as far as to say that aid representatives have asked for selective data that would enable them to make the most positive case to their home authorities. However, mutual need locks the Tanzanian government and the donor agencies into a symbiotic relationship. Tanzania has a multidimensional need for the donor presence and donor agencies have an institutional interest in maximizing the appearance of benevolent outcomes. When there is a choice about which data to omit or understate and which data to present for official display, the tendency on both sides is to select the most favorable. All these circumstances, taken together, call for caution in reading Tanzania's economic statistics. In the end, the figures showing such a high growth trajectory provide at best a crude approximation of the country's evolving economic reality.

Even if the economic data are close to correct, however, they do not convey the extent to which Tanzania's positive economic performance remains dependent upon continued financial support from the donor community. Foreign aid now contributes about 5 percent of Tanzania's gross domestic product (GDP) of about $60 billion and about $65 per capita, or almost 5 percent of Tanzania's per capita income. In practical terms, these figures mean that little has changed with respect to Tanzania's aid dependency. Virtually every major sector of Tanzanian society, including the day-to-day functioning of the government itself, depends to some degree on foreign aid or on the involvement of well-funded NGOs. There is nothing hypothetical about what might happen to the Tanzanian economy if the donors withdrew or reduced their assistance. This would diminish such vital government services as education and health. It would curtail or end numerous efforts to improve the country's physical and communications infrastructure. It would end numerous agricultural improvement projects. Moreover, it would impair the operation of the private economy by lowering the demand for goods and services that support numerous local businesses. Given the cordial working relationship that now exists between Tanzania and its donors, there is no imminent likelihood of that happening. The purpose of stating those outcomes is to make clear that Tanzania's economic growth has yet to become self-sustaining. It remains dependent on donor assistance.

A more troublesome question concerns the relationship between economic growth and social inequality. Economists believe that a certain amount of inequality may be essential for economic growth anywhere: it provides an opportunity for upward mobility and thereby affords indispensable incentives for entrepreneurship and risk taking. Extreme inequality, on the other hand, may be a deterrent to robust and sustainable economic growth since rising social discontents can create a climate of instability that deters investment and causes capital flight. Extreme inequality may also mean insufficient growth in demand for goods and services. Where this is the case, economic growth may be anemic and short-lived.[9] The relationship between inequality and growth, then, lends itself to the "goldilocks" principle: when it comes to inequality, the best recipe for economic development calls for not too much, not too little, just the right amount.

The relationship between economic growth and social inequality is an intensely contested topic in the field of development studies. The development economists shared a conviction that growth figures based on primary exports did not indicate social or economic improvements for the broader society. Prominent economists outside the development economics tradition have long cautioned against any facile tendency to identify growth with development. Nearly fifty years ago, for example, Robert Clower showed that economic growth figures may reflect the performance of only one narrow sector of an economy and that gains in that sector may flow to a small stratum of a society, principally the members of its governing class. His study of Liberia showed that economic growth produced by rubber exports provided benefits to the owners of the rubber plantations and members of the political elite without providing spillover benefits to the majority of the population, comprising smallholder farmers outside the plantation economy that surrounded Monrovia.[10]

This explains why both scholars and policy practitioners of economic development attach such great importance to poverty reduction and why there is growing concern about the longer-term future among informed observers of contemporary Tanzania.[11] The World Bank's leading economists for the Africa region have recently stated that, for all the reported improvements in GDP and GDP per capita since the 1990s, Tanzania's many economic reforms have had almost no effect in reducing poverty.[12] The irreducible fact is that the improvements in Tanzania's GDP per capita are not a proxy for poverty alleviation, nor do they indicate a lessening of social inequality. Georgetown University economist Martin Ravallion, formerly director of the Development Research Group at the World Bank, has shown that, given a certain initial level of social inequality, economic growth may worsen rather than ameliorate poverty and inequality.[13] Tanzania fits his model.

Visual evidence alone confirms that Tanzania is experiencing economic growth at least in the capital city and other urban centers: the real estate boom, the proliferation of expensive shopping areas, the spread of affluent neighborhoods, the profusion of luxury housing, and the massive traffic congestion in Dar es Salaam—all these attest to the rising prosperity of some Tanzanians. Visual evidence also attests to a growing middle class of Tanzanians who work in managerial and clerical levels of banking, financial and information services, building trades, and other parts of the service sector, including medicine and law. Neither of these observations is inconsistent with the proposition that Tanzanian poor are increasing in absolute numbers and as a percent of the country's rapidly growing population. There is scant evidence that economic growth is producing material improvement in the social conditions of the overwhelming majority of Tanzanians, who continue to be rural, agricultural, and desperately poor.

The figures that convey such impressive rates of economic growth fail to convey the fact that a small political-economic oligarchy, largely resident in Dar es Salaam, has captured a large share of the benefits of economic growth. The exact profile of social inequality in Tanzania will remain a matter of conjecture until more trustworthy data on income distribution over time become available. It will also remain a matter of conjecture as to whether the inequality between the governing elite and the mass of the population is greater than it was during the period of socialism, when the country's political leaders took pains to conceal the large gaps between wealth and poverty. What is not a matter of conjecture is the fact that economic liberalization has made great wealth available to some Tanzanians and that the Tanzanian wealthy no longer feel the need to refrain from conspicuous displays of that wealth. There is an even more troublesome aspect of the newly acquired wealth of the wealthiest Tanzanians: many Tanzanians have come to believe it is the result of corruption and political connections rather than the legitimate reward for entrepreneurial or professional skill.

The government's image of Tanzania as a society where economic growth is reducing poverty does not accurately convey the way in which life is lived in much of the Tanzanian countryside. The conditions of life for Tanzanian small farmers, who still comprise about 75 percent of the Tanzanian population, have barely changed, if at all, during the past twenty years. Most continue to live in the perilous margin between bare survival and the near-famine conditions caused by periodic crop failures. For overwhelming numbers of rural Tanzanians, weather instability—not government policy—remains the single most important determinant of income fluctuations. The adverse effects of global climate change combined with population increase that has caused overcrowding in some of the best agricultural regions have more greatly impacted the lives of Tanzanian farmers than policy factors that have produced such positive numbers in the tables on economic growth. Episodic outbreaks of violence between pastoral and agricultural communities attest to growing land scarcity and impoverished conditions in some of the more marginal areas. The tendency for both agricultural and pastoral communities to encroach onto land that did not previously provide economic sustenance is additional evidence of impoverishment at the bottom of Tanzania's economic scale.[14] Other violent phenomena such as attacks on albinos, a rash of "witch killings" in certain areas of the country, the spread of vigilante (*sungusungu*) groups as a means of dealing with petty crime, and the heightened incidence of robberies also hint at social stresses just beneath the surface.[15]

The portentous feature of social inequality in Tanzania as in so many other developing countries is not simply that it has expanded the visible gap between wealth and poverty, but the extent to which it changed the social expectations of different classes. The basic reasons are no different in Tanzania from anywhere else. Tanzania's affluent families can afford better education for their children from the primary through the university level; they can also afford the accoutrements necessary to enhance their children's educational attainment, including better schools, private tutoring, and a supportive study environment. When children of wealthy families complete their early education, family connections provide better chances for higher education and, beyond that, for lucrative employment. The young people who grow up in an environment of wealth and privilege also inhabit a cultural universe in which professional careers and profitable investment opportunities are the ordinary subject matter of dinner table conversation. The people of power and privilege who can help them bring these ambitions to fruition are regular dinner guests. Children of poor families, especially the rural poor, inhabit a different cultural milieu, one in which the psychological horizon of personal opportunity is more constricted. Wealth and poverty reproduce themselves in Tanzania just as they do everywhere else.

Poverty alleviation programs everywhere have the greatest difficulty addressing this cluster of factors, and Tanzania is no different. Its approach to poverty reduction bears a close resemblance to its approach to corruption. Politicians address themselves regularly to the problem in order to create the image of a government vigorously addressing its socioeconomic disparities, with a vast outpouring of poverty alleviation strategies. These derive from a host of official reports, consulting studies, and investigative assessments by both the government of Tanzania[16] and the World Bank.[17] Much research has been devoted to establishing the criteria of poverty, locating it in physical space, and measuring it quantitatively. Much effort has also been devoted to determining whether the level of poverty has worsened or improved as economic reforms have taken place. In addition, the government and donors have allocated modest resources for experimental poverty alleviation programs such as cash for work.

The basic outcome of all this effort can be summarized as follows:[18]

- Somewhere between 35 and 40 percent of the Tanzanian population, at an absolute minimum, live in poverty.[19] The overwhelming majority of the Tanzanian poor are small-scale farmers whose economic lifestyle combines subsistence production with modest participation in the cash economy. Most of these farmers have limited access to land, insufficient cash income to acquire purchased inputs and limited or no opportunities for education beyond the primary level. For lack of education and other reasons, these farmers do not have economic alternatives. Tanzania's poorest farmers have seen little or no improvement in their quality of life during the past twenty-five years; for many, conditions may have worsened.
- Depending on where the poverty line is drawn, the percentage of Tanzanians who live in poverty may be much higher. If the poverty line is drawn at an income level of $1/day, nearly 60 percent of Tanzanians could be said to live in poverty. The overwhelming majority would be small-scale farmers but this figure would also include a substantial

number of urban dwellers. The poverty of Tanzanian small farmers varies greatly over time: subsistence-oriented farmers typically exhaust their own-produced food staples within six to eight months after harvest. After that, they must enter the marketplace for food items, that is, at a time when scarcity is causing food prices to rise.

- Poverty also varies by region and location. Most but not all this poverty is concentrated in the rural regions, in areas that are difficult to reach. Some evidence, albeit fragmentary, points to modest reductions in urban poverty. Figures on income improvements in urban centers call for utmost caution: urban incomes for the poor, though improving, have often failed to keep pace with price inflation for necessities such as rent, transportation and foodstuffs.

- Statistics about improvements in the level of poverty also require careful interpretation. Poverty in Dar es Salaam may have declined in the statistical sense that the percentage of Dar es Salaam residents who live in poverty may be decreasing. This does not suggest a narrowing of the income gap between wealthy and poor residents of Dar es Salaam nor a decrease in the number of poor people. Since the population of Dar es Salaam and other urban centers is increasing rapidly, the number of people living in extreme poverty is also increasing. The living circumstances of the poorest of the poor—a heterogeneous group that includes AIDs orphans, widows and divorced women without property rights, underemployed and undereducated urban youth, subsistence-oriented agriculturists in marginal regions, and many categories of manual workers—remain abysmal. Even the most optimistic observers cited by Devarajan and Fengler do not claim an improvement in the economic conditions of the poorest social strata.

- Figures on changes over time for poverty are so small as to be within the margin of statistical error. Because poverty trends vary greatly by region and specific location, it is not possible to identify a single national trend. In sum, there is no discernible relationship between economic growth and the reduction of poverty or inequality.

The broad picture that emerges is globally familiar. Although Tanzania has enjoyed a certain amount of economic growth because of the policy reforms that began in the 1980s, a narrow stratum at the top of the society has benefitted the most. Although there has been some trickle down, such as to Tanzanians who attain higher education, conditions for the majority of poor

Tanzanians have changed very little. Given the unproven connection between growth and poverty alleviation and the extent and persistence of poverty, it is difficult to accept the Tanzanian government's view that "the key to significant poverty reduction in Tanzania is accelerated growth."[20]

Many of the poverty studies contain elaborate strategic and policy recommendations that address the challenge of poverty reduction and these, in turn, range from employment-generating public works projects to straightforward cash transfers to the poorest of the poor. Although the government and the Bank have implemented a few of these projects, including an experimental work for cash program, these are mostly pilot projects of limited scale. Despite the rhetoric of democratic empowerment, the poorest Tanzanians do not feel empowered, nor do they feel that democratic institutions enable them to hold their government accountable. Most rural Tanzanians experience their government as an unhelpful presence in their struggle to cope with poverty. Frank Ellis and Ntengua Mdoe capture this reality as follows: "Qualitative research suggests that the institutional environment facing rural citizens in Tanzania does not actively foster the flourishing of diverse activities that is required for rapid poverty reduction. The legacy of the past in the form of generally obstructive public agency responses to business, trade and exchange lingers on into the present for most rural citizens."[21] Despite all the official attention poverty receives, then, it remains, like corruption, an enduring and pervasive reality.

Tanzanian leaders have responded publicly to the persistence, spread, and visibility of poverty. In addition to the well-publicized flow of official studies and the high visibility of Tanzania's National Strategy for Growth and the Reduction of Poverty (NSGRP), there has a been continuous media coverage of the government's efforts to address poverty. Political leaders regularly seek and obtain news coverage for their appearances at rural and urban development projects. This affords high profile political leaders an opportunity call attention to their awareness of the problem and their determination to use the powers and the resources of government to reduce it.

Does Democracy Help?

The need for political leaders to address poverty provides a basis for optimism among those who view democratization as a remedy for Africa's chronic problems of poverty and inequality.[22] The results of Tanzanian democratization are not encouraging. Tanzania has had four multiparty national elections since 1995. The one unquestionable generalization that emerges from all these elections is that the CCM enjoys a firm grasp on the presidency and on the National Assembly. Unlike countries such as Ghana and Kenya that have evenly balanced party systems, Tanzania does not. In all Tanzania's multiparty elections, the CCM has won both the presidency and a large majority of seats in the National Assembly.

Table 4 shows the percentages won by the CCM presidential candidate and the next most popular candidate in the four multiparty presidential elections.[23] The CCM has also won large majorities in the Tanzanian National Assembly. Table 5 shows the CCM share of the popular vote, the number of single-member seats it won and the percentage of seats it gained in each of the four multiparty elections. Table 5 shows that the CCM's ability to carry out well-organized election campaigns has consistently enabled it to win between 80 and 88 percent of the single member seats in the National Assembly with the exception of the most recent election, when its percentage of these seats fell slightly, to 77.8. [24]

The CCM deserves credit for carrying out these elections in a manner that is, overall, peaceful and fair. Contrary to the hopes of the democratic optimists such as Radelet, cited above, the great tragedy for much of modern Africa is that the return to multiparty politics, which began in the early 1990s, has often brought about an increase in social turbulence. Multiparty politics has sometimes evoked violent protests by groups who believe that the governing party has rigged the process against them. This violence has sometimes had an ethnic dimension.

Fear that ethnic factors might come to dominate the political process was the reason why a majority of Tanzanians were skeptical of multi-democracy in the first place. In the early 1990s, an overwhelming majority of Tanzanians were opposed to the transition to multipartyism. The Nyalali Commission reports that almost four-fifths of Tanzanians preferred that the CCM continue as a single party. It states, "The data shows that 77.2% of the Tanzanians preferred to continue with the single party system, while 21.5% favoured the adoption of multiparty system. In regard to the Mainland 79.7% supported the single party system and in Zanzibar 56.4%. Those who supported the adoption of multiparty system form 19.0% in the Mainland and 43.0% in Zanzibar."[25] The Nyalali Report and a wealth of follow-up research about this topic make it clear that democratization in Tanzania was a top-down process, brought about by a governing elite that was responding to changing interna-

Table 4. CCM Percent of Popular Vote in Four Multiparty Presidential Elections, 1995–2010

	1995	2000	2005	2010
CCM candidate	Mkapa	Mkapa	Kikwete	Kikwete
CCM	61.8	71.7	80.3	63
2nd party	27.7	16.3	11.7	27
2nd party candidate	Mrema/NCCR	Lipumba/CUF	Lipumba/CUF	Slaa /(Chadema)

Compiled from various sources including reports of the National Electoral Commission of Tanzania for 1997, 2001, 2006, elections archive of the Electoral Institute for Sustainable Democracy in Africa (EISA), International Foundation for Electoral Systems of USAID (IFES) and data provided through the National Electoral Commission of Tanzania.

Table 5. Parliamentary Election Results in Single-Member District Seats, 1995–2010

	1995		2000		2005		2010	
	No. of seats	% seats	No. of seats	% seats	No. of seats	% seats	No. of seats	% seats
CCM	186	80	202	87.4	206	88.8	186	77.8
All others	46	20	30	12.6	26	11.2	55	22.2

Compiled from various sources including reports of the National Electoral Commission of Tanzania for 1997, 2001, 2006, elections archive of the Electoral Institute for Sustainable Democracy in Africa (EISA), International Foundation for Electoral Systems of USAID (IFES) and data provided through the National Electoral Commission of Tanzania.

tional norms and expectations more than to popular pressures from below.[26] The Nyalali report does not speculate explicitly as to the reason for this reluctance but a desire to avoid ethnically based politics is not difficult to discern. Despite Tanzanians' reservations about the period of single party CCM rule, and the seemingly universal wish to have greater freedom of political choice, the distaste for ethnically based politics was even greater. Most Tanzanians preferred a continuation of CCM rule with all its shortcomings to the emergence of a multiparty system that might arouse the kinds of ethnic divisions that have disturbed the social peace elsewhere.[27]

Certain of Tanzania's opposition parties have sought to exploit religious or ethnic discontents, but they have been conspicuously unsuccessful in doing so. In 2000, the political attention of the Tanzanian public became preoccupied with the politicized discontent of Tanzania's Muslim majority. The possibility that Tanzanian Muslims may have participated in the U.S. Embassy bombing of August 1998 drew dramatic attention to Muslim discontent both globally and within Tanzania. The bombing and other violent incidents seemed to suggest the transient character of the culture of religious peace or, in the view of some Muslim leaders, the extent to which Tanzania's leaders had used that norm to paper over the legitimate grievances of their community. [28] Among Tanzania's Muslims, who may well constitute 50 percent or more of the mainland population, there was—among some, there remains—a sense of having been excluded from opportunities available to other Tanzanians.[29] With the imminent advent of multiparty politics in the early 1990s and the greater atmosphere of political freedom, long latent feelings about this matter gave rise to an opposition party named the CUF, which presented itself as the preferred organization of Muslim identity.

The salience of religious strain was, paradoxically, a boon to the CCM's electoral success because it enabled the CCM to display itself as the party of national unity. The 2000 general election was a kind of referendum on Tanzania's tradition of ethnic and religious peace: a vote for the CCM was a vote for this tradition; a vote against the CCM was not. By posing voter choices in these terms, the CCM ensured that the election would be fought out on an issue on which it retained a reservoir of public good will, namely, its commitment to a society in which religion and ethnicity would not become the bases of political divisions. The CCM's ability to define the election on its own terms produced a major triumph. CUF received only about 16 percent of the presidential vote. Outside Zanzibar and certain portions of Dar es Salaam, its showing was even poorer.

What distinguishes contemporary Tanzania, then, is a pattern of self-censoring whereby parties seeking to exploit racial, religious, or ethnic feelings have great difficulty generating electoral support. The best example of this phenomenon may be Tanzania's Democratic Party. An evangelical Christian minister, the Reverend Christopher Mtikila, founded this party during the 1990s. During its early years the DP was best known for its outspoken anti-Asian and anti-Muslim views, characteristics that initially prevented it from becoming a legally registered party under the Political Parties Act of 1992, a law proscribing parties that appeal on the basis of ethnic or religious divisions.[30] Having finally modified its public persona sufficiently to become registered, the DP contested the presidential election of 2005, but gained only 0.27 percent of the popular vote. The DP did not win any seats for the National Assembly. Nor has the Reverend Mtikila's relentless legal quest for the legalization of individual candidacies, which is widely perceived as the opening wedge for ethnically based candidates, elicited widespread support among Tanzanians. When asked to comment on why Tanzanians had so overwhelmingly rejected a political party that seemed intent on taking advantage of a racial divide between Asian Tanzanians and Tanzanians of indigenous descent, one informant said simply, "it isn't Tanzanian."

Otherwise, the political dominance of the CCM in an era of multiparty competition remains the great puzzle of Tanzanian politics and scholars of the Tanzanian political experience will undoubtedly grapple with this issue for many years to come.[31] Here, after all, was the political party whose policies resulted in twenty years of economic decline. Here, too, was a party that had politically maintained itself through a host of repressive measures, such as the constitutional declaration of a one-party state and the use of oppressive laws to enforce its rule. Here was a party that had sought to implement a widely hated system of collective villages that uprooted millions of Tanzanians from ancestral homes and villages, used coercion to relocate them in unfamiliar surroundings, and caused famine conditions that drove many rural families to become homeless urban refugees. Many Tanzanians also hold their governing party responsible for the widespread corruption that has enabled members of the political and administrative elite to enrich themselves beyond the dreams of ordinary Tanzanians.

The CCM's ability to engineer successive electoral victories in the face of this daunting set of circumstances cries out for explanation. The most obvious factor is the CCM's unique legacy as the party of Tanzanian nationalism: the CCM may forever enjoy some level of affection from Tanzanians as the party that won the country's freedom from colonial rule. Another factor is the advantage of incumbency. The CCM no longer monopolizes the Tanzanian media as it once did, but the organizational resources it derives from political power enable it to present itself far more prominently and favorably than any political rival does. The greatest electoral advantage of the CCM may well be its vast and omnipresent organizational structure. Since its formation in the mid-1950s, the CCM has had almost six decades to construct an unmatched network of local branches and supportive organizations such as women's organizations and youth groups that mobilize the votes of their members.

These efforts had been underway for almost forty years before any of today's opposition parties could even register. Because of these efforts, the CCM can claim to be a genuinely national political party. Visit a village in almost any remote region of Tanzania and there will be a local branch of the CCM displaying the CCM flag, with its image of crossed agricultural implements on a solid green background, directly alongside the Tanzanian national flag, with its diagonal green, gold, black, and blue stripes. The party's symbolism is unmistakable: the CCM is Tanzania and Tanzania is the CCM. A majority of Tanzanians continue to cast their votes accordingly. At each of the CCM's rural branches, there will also be a CCM leader who is personally familiar with the party's local network of members and supporters, and who can point out what CCM rule has brought to the village, whether a primary school, a clinic, a water supply, or a trunk road. It is beyond doubt that the CCM candidate's campaign address will remind Tanzanians of their good fortune in being citizens of such a peaceful country and credit the continuity of CCM leadership for having made that possible.

The CCM's electoral popularity also rests on voter appreciation of its positive achievements, the most obvious of which is that it has navigated Tanzania's economic and political transitions in ways that have produced both a stronger economy and a freer political environment. Tanzania is not a perfectly free society, but it is freer by far than was previously the case. After decades with only two newspapers, the *Daily News* and the *Daily Standard*, both pro-government, Tanzanians can now choose among a whole array of newspapers, several of which are critical and outspoken. They can use the internet freely to access the news of the world and their own country. They can choose between multiple political parties and can associate freely with a vast array of independent civil society associations. Tanzanians also define their freedom in the manner of Franklin Roosevelt, as the absence of the fears that afflict the citizens of neighbor states such as fear of ethnic and religious persecution, victimization by criminal gangs, or predations of regional warlords.

Central to most explanations of the CCM's electoral success is the party's uncanny ability to reinvent its political identity, transforming its public persona from the party of economic ruin and autocratic rule to the party of economic reform and political openness. Once the party of socialist regimentation, which governed through a monopoly of political power and a legal framework that suppressed opposition, the CCM now presents itself as the champion of political competitiveness and an open marketplace. Even while transforming itself in these ways, the CCM has kept alive its identification with the memory of the founder-president, Julius Nyerere. His image as a social idealist softens the party's harsher image as a corrupt organization.

Some of this imagery is invented memory, but invented memories can influence electoral preferences as much as real ones. Explanations of the CCM's successive election victories also direct attention to the divisions among Tanzania's opposition parties, which have been unable to unite with one another and which seem prone to their own organizational and leadership difficulties. One common weakness is that many have been personal creations that rise and fall with the popularity of their individual leaders. Although each of the opposition parties has undergone a registration process that requires a nationwide organizational presence, most remain regional or even highly personal in character.

The CCM's principal vulnerability is its reputation for corruption. The salience, magnitude, and sheer hubris of elite corruption have captured the attention of Tanzanians to such a degree that this matter has a large bearing on how well or how poorly the CCM performs at the ballot box. When the CCM can present a credible commitment to reform, it can do well. It succeeded in doing so in the election of 2005; it failed to do so in the election of 2010. For the 2005 election, the CCM gained an electoral advantage in the public persona of its new presidential candidate, Jakaya Kikwete, who presented himself as the personal embodiment of all that was best in the CCM tradition. Kikwete's early image was a mixture of idealism in the Nyerere tradition and economic pragmatism regarding the reforms needed to bring about greater reliance on market forces.[32] Most Tanzanians wanted a candidate who could combine their long-standing comfort factor with the CCM with their hope for a president strong enough to reform the party from within. Kikwete made it appear likely that he would be able to do so. Unlike other high-ranking members of the party, he came from a military background, not a political one, having risen to the rank of lieutenant colonel in the Tanzanian Army before entering politics.[33] The voters flocked to Kikwete's support: he gained over 80 percent of the popular vote.[34]

By the election of 2010, Kikwete and the CCM had forfeited their ability to project an image of reform from within. High visibility corruption scandals have given the CCM an indelible image for corruption among the party's highest-ranking leaders. The first is the Richmond Energy Scandal, which took place in 2006, the first year of the new Kikwete administration. The story in brief is that Tanzania was suffering from a drought during this period. Since hydroelectric generators supply much of Tanzania's electricity, the drought caused shortages and brownouts. To address this difficulty, the government signed an emergency $115 million contract with a U.S.-based company known as Richmond Energy. The contract called for Richmond Energy to install diesel generators with enough capacity to provide emergency power. The generators failed to arrive on time, and when they did arrive they performed poorly. According to the terms of the contract, however, the Tanzanian government was obliged to pay Richmond Energy a large daily fee regardless how its generators performed. By the time the government was able to terminate the contract, the cost of the failed energy project amounted to approximately $150 million. Much of this went toward the commissions paid to private sector Tanzanians who had acted as intermediaries between the Tanzanian government and Richmond Energy.

The flagrantly disadvantageous terms of the Richmond contract led to demands for a parliamentary inquiry. The Tanzanian press gave extensive coverage to the scandal, calling attention to the fact that Richmond had performed badly under a previous contract with the Tanzanian government. Press coverage also exposed the fact that Richmond might not even exist as a legally registered company but, rather, was a kind of sham operation that subcontracted with other companies for their services. The publicity caused the resignation of three high-ranking officials, including Prime Minister Edward Lowassa, who had lobbied for the contract.[35]

Tanzania is especially vulnerable to corruption in the energy sector, and scandals there follow an almost standard template. Hydroelectric facilities generate almost 80 percent of Tanzania's energy. The Kidatu dam, in the Rufiji River Basin south of the town of Morogoro, provides almost 40 percent of this energy, nearly one-third of the country's total electrical supply. When drought affects central Tanzania, a frequent occurrence, the river level falls and this lowers the electricity output from the dam. During shortages, the government takes advantage of the unmet demand for electricity by signing costly emergency contracts with foreign companies to provide electricity by alternate generating methods such as diesel or natural gas. Because emergency electricity generation is a complex matter and Tanzania does not have an independent regulatory authority, these contracts are almost impossible to evaluate or monitor. They have become a continuing source of high-level official corruption.[36] This occurred in 1994, for example, when the government signed a costly energy contract with a Malaysian company named Mechmar Corporation. It occurred again on several occasions during the latter part of the 1990s.

The second of the Kikwete-era corruption scandals involved a $40 million contract with a British defense contractor, British Aerospace Engineering

(BAE). The contract called for BAE to provide Tanzania with a military air traffic control system. As the Tanzanian Air Force largely consists of a small number of obsolete aircraft that barely operate due to training and maintenance difficulties, the BAE contract provided a radar capability far in excess of the country's present or future operational needs. Indeed, the contract would have provided a vast overcapacity even if Tanzania used the radar system for civilian purposes. The terms were so egregious that it became the subject of one of the largest investigations ever conducted by the British Serious Fraud Office.[37] The British government made the results of the inquiry public in early 2007. One of the principal disclosures was that one-third of the contract, about $13 million, went to offshore bank accounts as commissions to various intermediaries.[38]

The third scandal involved the Bank of Tanzania. A corruption investigation showed that the governor of the Bank, Daudi Ballili, had used his position to defraud the Tanzanian government of several hundred million dollars. By some estimates, Ballali's embezzlements were so great as to have accounted for a significant portion of Tanzania's foreign exchange shortage and exerted pressure on the exchange rate. The allegations against Ballali, which were widely covered in the Tanzanian press, suggested that he had embezzled more than $100 million from the Central Bank External Payments Account (EPA). According to a BBC report, Ballali, acting in collusion with local business leaders, had set up nearly two dozen ghost companies to receive payments.[39] Although Ballali was dismissed from his position as governor of the Central Bank in January 2008 and died soon thereafter of medical conditions, the magnitude of the financial losses and the fact that these went on for a number of years have added to the ongoing taint of corruption that has enveloped the CCM.[40]

These incidents and countless others are the subject of almost daily reporting in the Tanzanian media. Since Tanzanians enjoy high-speed Internet access, they can access the global news outlets that also report on their country's corruption difficulties, visit websites such as the Tanzania Corruption Tracker System,[41] download reports prepared by FACEIT,[42] or analyze the data gathered by global anti-corruption organizations such as Global Integrity or Transparency International.[43] Perhaps the greatest difference between the new and old Tanzania is that the governing oligarchy can no longer hide its corruption from view. By the 2010 election, many Tanzanians had come to believe the Kikwete administration was so corrupt it could not weed out the party's most corrupt elements. Some voters blamed the president personally for the growing socioeconomic inequality, which stems directly from the vast fortunes corrupt officials were acquiring. From having once personified the party's capacity for youthful renewal, Kikwete had acquired an image as simply one more member of the corrupt CCM establishment.

The diplomatic community shared this perception. A July 24, 2007 cable from the U.S. Embassy seemed to confirm in fact what many Tanzanians had already come to believe about their president's weak commitment to the country's anti-corruption efforts: "He [director of the Prevention of Corruption Bureau Edward Hoseah] noted that President Kikwete does not appear comfortable letting the law handle corruption cases which might implicate top level officials. According to Hoseah, President Kikwete is hesitant to pursue cases which may implicate former President Benjamin Mkapa: 'Kikwete is soft on Mkapa. He does not want to set a precedent by going after his predecessor'."[44] On the eve of Tanzania's 2010 election, the Tanzanian *Guardian* estimated that Tanzania was losing as much as a third of its annual $9 billion revenues to corruption.[45]

The leading opposition candidate was Dr. Willibrod Slaa, who led a party called the Chadema. Slaa's clerical background, as a former Catholic priest[46] with a doctorate in law, and his lively anti-corruption campaign made him especially appealing to young people. As an outspoken opposition member of the National Assembly for fifteen years, he had created a powerful image as an anti-corruption crusader as early as 2007 by publishing a famous "list of shame" that named a number of high-ranking officials who had engaged in corruption. Slaa's list encouraged the individuals he had named to sue him: none did. The CCM's poor showing in 2010 showed the extent to which corruption could shift a substantial segment of the popular vote. In the presidential election, Kikwete's share of the popular vote fell abruptly, dropping by about 17 percent, to about 63 percent. Chadema gained about 27 percent of the vote. The CCM also lost 55 of the single member districts, more than twice as many as in 2005. Chadema leaders believe that the abrupt fall in the CCM share of the presidential vote was a sign that the CCM's inability to control its corruption problem has placed its command of the government at risk. Some press reports agree and interpret the drop in the CCM share of the 2010 presidential vote as an indication that the CCM will experience greater difficulties in the next election, which will take place in 2015.[47] Speculation about future elections is premature. If there is any single lesson from the past 50 years of Tanzanian political history, it is the political resiliency of the CCM and the determination of CCM leaders to remain in power.

The thorny question is whether the CCM will continue to allow free and fair elections. Some Chadema leaders insist that the CCM has been willing to allow relatively fair elections only so long as it seemed assured of victory. If the CCM's electoral position should become insecure, they believe it will use more blatant voter suppression tactics to remain in power. Chadema supporters point out that many repressive tactics were already in place in the 2010 election, including inflation of the electoral rolls with "ghost" voters who presumably cast their their votes for CCM candidates. They further allege that there were irregularities in the counting of votes by the National Election Commission. They also claim that Chadema candidates for the National Assembly would have done even better if it were not for the harassment of voters perceived to be pro-Chadema and efforts to intimidate voluntary organizations thought to be critical of the government. Chadema leaders also interpret low voter turnout, about 43 percent of eligible voters, as the outcome of CCM efforts to frighten away potential opposition voters.

As of this writing (spring 2013), there is no compelling reason to dissent from the Economist Intelligence Unit observation that CCM dominance is sufficiently entrenched to prevent imminent threats to its stability.

> Tanzania is unlikely to face any significant threats to its political stability during the forecast period owing to the dominance of the President, Jakaya Kikwete, and the ruling party, Chama Cha Mapinduzi. However, since the start of 2011 it has become increasingly clear that there will be a background rumble of discontent as the Chama Cha Demokrasia na Maendeleo (Chadema), which emerged as the main opposition party at the 2010 elections, seeks to establish a more high-profile political role.[48]

The CCM continues to enjoy huge electoral advantages. It has had more than fifty years to develop a nationwide organization and during this period has accumulated vast experience dealing with political opponents. Since it is the preferred party of the country's business elite, the CCM can tap into considerable resources for financing expensive nationwide campaigns, including the cash payments parties give to their supporters. In addition, CCM leaders point to their beneficial working relationship with the donor organizations that provide Tanzania with generous financial support.

For some observers, the most serious threat to CCM dominance is the possibility of a factional fracture within the CCM itself. This is unlikely.

Corruption and wealth are powerful bonding agents and they require a firm grasp on political power. Anticipating that the CCM's reputation as a corrupt organization might widen the window of opportunity for opposition parties, President Kikwete has attempted to create a more favorable image for the party by calling on leaders with a reputation for corruption to relinquish their senior positions in the party hierarchy.[49] Since this would place their access to important governmental positions at risk, his appeal has had limited effect.

Although CCM factional politics are intense, the possibility that prominent leaders might leave the CCM to join other parties or form new parties of their own is small. Most CCM leaders are apprehensive about forming opposition groups. They may be aware that the CCM is unlikely to allow an opposition party to prevail in an election. They may also be aware of the element of economic risk. The all-important variable of lateral mobility is still lacking in Tanzanian society. Although the economy has become more complex and diversified during the era of economic reform, the inseparable connection between political power and wealth remains intact. High-ranking political leaders could not exit the party and still expect to have an assured pathway to wealth and social status. For even the most prominent party leaders, the gains derived from a leadership position in a party that maintains its grip on power are too great to put at risk through factional or personal differences.

Trade with China

The economic variable with the greatest potential to affect Tanzania's future is its growing trade relationship with China. China has been a significant economic presence in Tanzania since the construction of the TAZARA Railroad in the early 1970s.[50] Although it was among the first African countries where China began to develop a major economic presence, Tanzania's contemporary relationship with China has been slower to develop than that of many other African countries, principally because it has not had exportable quantities of oil, natural gas, or metal ores. Since the full dimensions of China's economic relationship with Tanzania are only beginning to unfold, there is a large speculative element in any effort to assess the future significance of this connection. However, Tanzania is among the many African countries where the scale of Chinese economic activity has the potential to transform the economy.

The broad contours of China's economic relationships with African nations are familiar and its evolving relationship with Tanzania follows a similar pattern.[51] To provide for its expanding industrial economy, China needs vast amounts of energy and raw materials. To obtain these, China enters into long-term trade agreements with numerous countries around the world, many of which are in sub-Saharan Africa. These trade agreements follow a standard template: they call for the host country to supply China on a long-term basis with primary commodities such as oil or coal, metal ores, and timber or agricultural commodities such as cotton. As part of the agreement, China commits itself to invest, sometimes heavily, in the development or rehabilitation of the productive capacity for these goods and the infrastructure improvements necessary to export them. To redirect some of China's funds back to China, the African country agrees to import Chinese manufactured goods.

This trade pattern gives rise to concerns about the meaningfulness of the recent figures that show such high GDP growth for Tanzania and other African countries. By enabling a large increase in commodity exports, trade with China can add greatly to a country's GDP and, therefore to its per capita GDP. Primary commodity exports, however, may not contribute to diversification of the national economy or to in long-term employment opportunities. At its core, China's economic relationship with countries such as Tanzania is neocolonial: African countries export primary commodities and use some portion of their export earnings to purchase Chinese manufactured goods. Several African countries including Nigeria and South Africa have already begun to vocalize their concern that the economic relationship with China is causing deindustrialization.[52] In economies such as Tanzania, where the manufacturing sector was small to begin with and only in the first stages of recovery from the failures of the ISI era, the import of large volumes of manufactured goods could have a similar effect in crowding out domestic industrial growth.

Tanzania's trade policy has moved steadily away from the protectionism of the ISI era in the direction of greater openness to trade. It is among the many African countries that have adopted an export-led growth strategy. In doing so, Tanzania has set aside the warnings of the development economists, who cautioned that primary commodity exports might not confer sustainable or widely distributed benefits. They should perhaps have been more cautious. China does not match Tanzania's openness to trade with reciprocal openness of its own. It pursues a policy of managed trade. It undervalues its exchange rate, for example, to make imports expensive while lowering the prices of the manufactured goods it exports.

An asymmetry in power relationships reinforces the asymmetry in trade policy. Many African countries have become more financially dependent on their exports to China than China is on its trade with them. For some African countries, exports to China already constitute a large fraction of total exports whereas China's imports from any single African country are a small percentage of total imports even by commodity. This asymmetry in power relationships gives China a great advantage in its ability to negotiate over matters such as Chinese immigration to Africa and the opportunities Chinese immigrants will enjoy to become permanent residents and purchase businesses and farms. China's economic importance also gives it great bargaining power over such questions as the percentage of Chinese workers to be employed and the labor and environmental practices in its various projects.

Although Africa's trade relationship with China has neocolonial features, this concept does not capture the full complexity of what is taking place. Some observers point out that Chinese project loans do not have the strict conditions that accompany Western assistance, and that there are long periods before a country must begin repayments. In addition, China offers low interest rates and often forgives loans to make it possible for African governments to invest elsewhere in their economies. The Chinese have also been willing to invest in the kinds of costly, challenging, and controversial long-term projects that other donors now avoid, such as hydroelectric dams, railroads, pipelines, and port facilities.[53] Chinese leaders point out their many goodwill projects in Africa such as soccer stadiums, presidential residences, parliamentary and government office buildings, and hospitals, and that they offer many educational scholarships for African teachers, technicians, and doctors. They further point to the many Chinese-owned businesses in Africa, such as factories, farms, and retail enterprises, which generate employment opportunity for African workers. Perhaps most important, they call attention to the fact that their investments in mining, forestry, and oil and gas extraction and large-scale agricultural ventures such as cotton and sisal farming generate employment opportunities for Africans.

Tanzania's relationship with China is expanding at a rapid pace. The World Bank carefully monitors the growing economic relationship between China and African countries and it has documented contracts for about a dozen public works projects totaling nearly $220 million in the last three years.[54] In addition to the projects on the Bank list, China has agreed to construct a high capacity port at the town of Bagamoyo, about 90 miles north of Dar es Salaam. The new port will require new railroad lines to connect it to the existing railroad infrastructure. A bottleneck at the harbor entrance causes congestion at the port of Dar es Salaam, and the new port will give Tanzania an improved capacity to handle exports from Malawi, Zambia, and the Democratic Republic of Congo (DRC) as well as increase the volume of its own exports.

Tanzania's economic relationship with China carries great possibilities and great risks. It could contribute to the development of the country by enabling Tanzanians to take advantage of hitherto unutilized or underutilized resources; it could facilitate a transfer of beneficial skills such as those needed for road building, railroad and harbor construction, and gas-fueled electricity generation. China's many development projects could also provide thousands of Tanzanian workers and technicians with incomes far in excess of those available to semi-subsistence smallholder farmers. They could help Tanzania expand the size of its middle class of accountants, managers, engineers, and technical personnel. Furthermore, they could generate substantial revenues for the Tanzanian government, enabling it to reduce its dependence on Western donor organizations. If managed in a sustainable manner, China's projects could yield these benefits for decades to come, during which time Tanzania would have a flow of economic resources for a variety of public benefits including health and education and projects for the rural poor.

The challenge in assessing these possibilities lies in determining how much weight to attach to Tanzania's endemic problem of elite corruption. Chinese spokespersons insist that they do not take advantage of Africa's economic dependency by attaching burdensome economic and political conditions to their assistance. They claim that by construing their economic activities as purely business rather than aid, they place their relationships with Africans on a peer-to-peer basis, rather than the more paternal tone inherent in Western conditions. Chinese claims are not entirely true, since China's trade agreements and development projects call for mutual understandings about the need to import Chinese consumer goods, accept Chinese immigrants, and allow Chinese laborers and technicians to participate in constructing the projects. China's concept of nonconditionality refers narrowly to the fact that it does not insist on strict financial accounting, nor does it come with the democratic, environmental, and human rights conditions that often accompany Western aid.

China's insistence that it does not attach financial or democratic conditions to its projects is an implicit assurance that China will look the other way if issues of fiscal probity should arise in connection with Tanzania's use of its funds—an open invitation to corruption. Much of this book has concerned the tendency for corruption to transform well-intended plans into bad outcomes. The great danger in Tanzania's relationship with China is that this will happen again, on an even larger scale. Since political corruption has had profound influences on Tanzania's development trajectory, it seems inevitable that a portion of China's funds will find their way into the private hands of the governing elite. There is little doubt that China's involvement in Tanzania will make it a wealthier country. The unanswered question is where and to whom this wealth will flow, whether it will benefit the majority of Tanzanians or the political-economic oligarchy that governs the country. The one certainty in all this is that the increased wealth afforded by China's development involvement will raise the stakes of the political process and increase the incentive for the CCM to cling to political power. In Tanzania, those in the winner's circle will stand to gain greater rewards than ever before; those outside it will lose out. Owing to China's economic involvement, control over the political system has become a prize of even greater value.

China's involvement with Tanzania is unlikely to change the country's power structure. It is more likely to accentuate the dominant features of the present system. The scholars of the aid process who have criticized Western donors for enabling corrupt and repressive regimes may soon have occasion to level those same charges at China, which does not condition its assistance on democratic reforms. The CCM has already shown that it is prepared to use undemocratic methods to prevent the political opposition from challenging its position. The wealth that emerges from the China trade could also cause Tanzania's corruption problem to grow. This would further cloud the country's future by eroding popular support for the CCM but not to the point of fatally weakening its hold on political power. The political system will continue to be presided over by an entrenched political-economic oligarchy whose members' political power and economic wealth are inextricably interconnected. For members of the Tanzanian political elite, private wealth will continue to be the by-product of a powerful position; and political preeminence will continue to rest on ability to mobilize the political networks that only extensive private resources can make available.

Tanzania has traveled a great distance from Nyerere's vision of social democracy in the direction of becoming a bourgeois democracy, with some of the virtues and many of the flaws inherent in that form of governance. Whether Tanzanians prefer this outcome, against the background of the presidential vision that accompanied their struggle for independence, is a matter for them to decide.

Chapter 1. Introduction: A Tanzanian Overview

1. United Republic of Tanzania, *Report of the Presidential Commission on the Establishment of a Democratic One-Party State.*

2. For a collection of essays, see Nyerere, *Freedom and Socialism.*

3. Peter, *Constitution-Making in Tanzania.*

4. Killian, "Pluralist Democracy and the Transformation of Democratic Attitudes."

5. Chirot, "Introduction," 3.

6. Throughout this volume, the term rent seeking is used to describe the behavior of public officials who increase their incomes by using their government positions to extract bribes.

7. Hydén, "Top-Down Democratization in Tanzania."

8. Rothchild, *Racial Bargaining in Independent Kenya.* The concept of hegemonial rule by an ethnic group is developed in this book.

9. Kaiser, "Structural Adjustment and the Fragile Nation."

10. In East African terminology, the term "Asian" refers to persons of South-Asian descent, that is, persons whose family backgrounds can be traced to India, Pakistan, or Bangladesh.

11. For example, see Ludwig, "Is Religious Revivalism a Threat to Tanzania's Stability?"

12. For an excellent appraisal of these matters, see Tripp, "The Political Mediation of Ethnic and Religious Diversity in Tanzania."

13. Kauzeni et al., "Land Use Planning and Resource Assessment in Tanzania," Sec. 2.3.1.

14. Bryceson, " 'Harbour of Peace' in East Africa."

15. Austen, *Northwest Tanzania Under German and British Rule*; and Iliffe, *Tanganyika Under German Rule, 1905–1912.* These are the best books on German colonial administration in Tanganyika.

16. Tripp, "Political Mediation," 38–39.

17. Chidzero, *Tanganyika and International Trusteeship.* This argument is indebted to Chidzero's book.

18. See principally Furnivall, *Colonial Policy and Practice*.

19. For the best example, see Kuper andSmith, eds., *Pluralism in Africa*.

20. See Aminzade, "The Politics of Race and Nation"; Aminzade, "From Race to Citizenship"; and Aminzade, "Nation-Building in Post-Colonial States." The indigenization debate and the political cleavages it produced have been the subject of a series of important articles by sociologist Ronald Aminzade.

21. Bates, *Markets and States in Tropical Africa*, 3.

22. World Bank, *Accelerated Development in Sub-Saharan Africa*.

23. Barker, "The Paradox of Development."

24. Tripp, *Changing the Rules*. The emergence, magnitude, and dependence of ordinary Tanzanians on this economy form the subject matter of Tripp's important book.

25. United Republic of Tanzania, Prevention and Combating of Corruption Bureau, *National Governance and Corruption Survey*, vol. 3.

26. U.S. Department of State, Bureau of Democracy, Human Rights, and Labor, *2010 Human Rights Report: Tanzania*.

Chapter 2. Economic Decline and Authoritarian Rule

1. Krueger, "The Political Economy of the Rent-Seeking Society."

2. Nyerere, *Freedom and Socialism*.

3. World Bank. *Tanzania at the Turn of the Century*

4. Berg, "Socialism and Economic Development in Tropical Africa."

5. Wood, *The Groundnut Affair*.

6. World Bank, *Accelerated Development in Sub-Saharan Africa*, 26.

7. World Bank, *Tanzania at the Turn of the Century*, 193–94.

8. Acquisition of Buildings Act, 1971, no. 13/71, Parliament of the United Republic of Tanzania.

9. An Act to Amend the Economic Sabotage (Special Provisions) Act, 1983, no. 10/83, Parliament of the United Republic of Tanzania.

10. Nagar, "The South Asian Diaspora in Tanzania," 72.

11. Mutahaba, "Pay Reform and Corruption in Tanzania's Public Service," 3.

12. Transparency International, *Country Study Report: Tanzania 2003*, 12.

13. Armah, *The Beautyful Ones Are Not Yet Born*.

14. Widner, *Building the Rule of Law*.

15. Hoseah, *Corruption in Tanzania*.

16. Hoseah, *Corruption in Tanzania*, 33.

17. Commonwealth Human Rights Initiative, *The Police, The People, The Politics*.

18. United Republic of Tanzania, *Presidential Commission of Inquiry Against Corruption*, 1: 46.

19. Transparency International ranked Tanzania at about 126 of about 180 countries listed in 2009, suggesting that its corruption had grown worse in recent years.

20. United Republic of Tanzania, Prevention and Combating Corruption Bureau, *National Anti-Corruption Strategy and Action Plan Phase II*.

21. A taxi in Dar es Salaam might be required to show as many as seven different government certificates, including a fire safety certificate, a certificate from the Tanzanian Revenue Authority, a license to carry passengers, a motor vehicle license, a certificate from the Commissioner of Insurance, a road service license, and a permit to discourage over-speeding.

22. Krueger, "Rent-Seeking Society," 291–303.

23. Kagashe, "Tanzania: Over 30 Percent of Budget Eaten by Corrupt Officials, Says President."

24. Transparency International, U4 Anti-Corruption Resource Centre, CHR, Michelsen Institute, *Overview of Corruption in Tanzania*.

25. World Bank, *Tanzania at the Turn of the Century*, 145. By the 1990s, Tanzania had no less than four separate government agencies responsible for combating corruption: the Prevention of Corruption Bureau, the Permanent Commission of Enquiry (later renamed the Commission of Human Rights and Administrative Justice), the Ethics Secretariat (for high-ranking political and administrative leaders), and the Inspectorate of Ethics (for lesser-ranking civil servants).

26. "The Secret Behind Dar's Posh Homes."

27. United Republic of Tanzania, Prevention and Combating of Corruption Bureau, *Analysis of Main Findings, Conclusions and Recommendations*, vol. 1, *Governance and Corruption Survey*.

28. Domasa, "Survey: Police, Judiciary, Lands, TRA Most Corrupt."

29. Transparency International UK, Defense and Security Programme, *Government Defence Anti-Corruption Index 2013*.

30. "Corruption at Dar es Salaam Port."

31. "Tanzanian Transporters Pay $13,000 in Bribes per Month—A New Report Reveals."

32. Cooksey and Kelsall, *The Political Economy of the Investment Climate in Tanzania*, 87.

33. Ostrom, *Governing the Commons*.

34. Nyalali Commission, *Report and Recommendation of the Commission on the Democratic System in Tanzania*, vol. 1, sec. 2, 166ff.

35. National Security Act, 1970, no. 3/70, Parliament of the United Republic of Tanzania.

36. Regions and Regional Commissioners Act, 1962, no. 2/62, Parliament of Tanganyika.

37. Maguire, *Toward "Uhuru" in Tanzania*.

38. United Republic of Tanzania, *Democratic One-Party State*.

39. Bates, "Agricultural Policy and the Study of Politics in Post-Independence Africa."

40. Ndulu, "The Evolution of Global Development Paradigms."

41. Prebisch, *The Economic Development of Latin America and Its Principal Problems*.

42. See Wacker, "The Impact of Foreign Direct Investment on Developing Countries' Terms of Trade," 1; Gatsios, "Terms of Trade Shocks and Domestic Prices Under Tariffs and Quotas."

43. Lewis, "Economic Development with Unlimited Supplies of Labour."

44. Ndulu et al., *Political Economy of Economic Growth in Africa*, 1: 320.

45. The list of the most prominent development economists would include W. W. Rostow, Albert Hischman, W. Arthur Lewis (later Sir Arthur Lewis), Ragnar Nurkse, Gunnar Myrdal, Barbara Ward (later, Lady Jackson), Hans Singer, Henry Bruton, Dudley Seers, and Raul Prebisch.

46. Shao, "Politics and the Food Production Crisis in Tanzania," 97–98.

Chapter 3. The Failure of Central Planning

1. Riggs, *Administration in Developing Countries*; Burke, *Tanganyika: Preplanning*.

2. Ndulu, *Political Economy*, 449–50.

3. National Union of Tanganyika Workers (Establishment) Act, 1964, no. 18/64, Parliament of Republic of Tanzania.

4. Jennings, "Oxfam and the RDA in the 1960s."

5. Coulson, *Tanzania: A Political Economy*.

6. United Republic of Tanganyika and Zanzibar, *Tanganyika Five-Year Plan*.

7. Segal, *East Africa: Strategy for Economic Cooperation*.

8. Tanganyika and Zanzibar, *Tanganyika Five-Year Plan*, 1: 96–98.

9. United Republic of Tanzania, *Tanzania: Second Five-Year Plan*, vol. 1, *General Analysis*, ix, 208ff.

10. United Republic of Tanzania, Ministry of Economic Affairs and Development Planning, *A Mid-Term Appraisal of the Achievements Under the Five Year Plan*, 16.

11. Ibid.

12. Keegan, *Negotiations for a Gin Distillery*.

13. Burke, *Local Governance and Nation Building in East Africa*.

14. This term indicates the change in prices farmers received for the goods they produced relative to the prices of the goods they needed to purchase.

15. Ellis, "Agricultural Price Policy in Tanzania," tables 1, 5, 6.

16. For clarity, a currency is considered overvalued when the exchange rate per U.S. dollar is too low, that is, when it requires too few units of local currency to purchase a U.S. dollar.

17. National Milling Corporation Act, 1968, no. 19/68, Parliament of the United Republic of Tanzania.

18. Green, "Developing State Trading in a Peripheral Economy," 27.

19. Ellis, "Agricultural Price Policy," 276.

20. NMC bookkeeping was so poor that no one has ever been able to determine whether it represented a net gain in generating finance for industries or simply one more costly burden on the country's farming population. World Bank economists became convinced that it was a large net drag on the economy.

21. Putterman, "Economic Reform and Smallholder Agriculture in Tanzania," 314.

22. Regulation of Prices Act, 1973, no. 19/73, Parliament of the United Republic of Tanzania.

23. Rugumisa and Semboja, "Price Control in the Management of an Economic Crisis."

24. Mtatifikolo, "Tanzania's Incomes Policy."

25. For a comprehensive study, see McHenry, *Tanzania's Ujamaa Villages*.

26. For an excellent discussion, see Ergas, "Why Did the Ujamaa Village Policy Fail?"

27. Thiele, "The Tanzanian Villagisation Programme."

28. von Freyhold, "Individualism and Communalism Among Peasants."

29. Fortmann, *Peasants, Officials and Participation in Rural Tanzania*, 77–78.

30. To read the classic theoretical critique, see Lal, *The Poverty of "Development Economics."*

31. For one such effort, see World Bank, *The East Asian Miracle*.

32. The list of "favorable" conditions is usually said to include large population, hence large market size, the existence of a sizable middle class, and large number of university graduates with degrees in business management, accounting, and engineering.

33. World Bank, *Tanzania at the Turn of the Century*, 306.

34. Stolper and Samuelson, "Protection and Real Wages." Economists will immediately recognize the Stolper-Samuelson theorem concerning factor endowments.

35. Perkins, "Technology, Choice, Industrialization and Development Experiences in Tanzania."

36. Lewis, "Economic Development."

37. Krueger, "Comparative Advantage and Development Policy Twenty Years Later." This analysis closely follows Krueger's use of the term *indivisibility*. To the extent that capital costs of an industry are an irreducible fixed amount, small economies that cannot sustain large production runs will have a greater tendency toward inefficiency than larger economies.

38. McHenry, *Limited Choices*, 140.

39. In all fairness, Tanzanian spokespersons insist that this war was not their policy choice but was forced on the country by Uganda's unilateral seizure of such a large and important land area.

40. Nguyuru, "Policy Reforms for Economic Development in Tanzania," 58.

Chapter 4. The Path to Economic Reform I: The Aid Debate

1. Follow-up agreements with the IMF were signed in 1987, 1988, and 1990. There had been agreements in the early 1980s that the government of Tanzania did not comply with.

2. Among those accused of treason were former minister of labor Michael Kamaliza and former leader of the women's wing of the governing party Bibi Titi Mohamed. The

government claimed they were under the influence of a former minister of defense, already in exile, Oscar Kambona.

3. Verhagen, "Changes in Tanzanian Rural Development and Change 1975–1978."

4. The Villages and Ujamaa Villages (Registration, Designation and Administration Act), 1975, Parliament of the United Republic of Tanzania.

5. Maghimbi, *Cooperatives in Tanzania Mainland*, 5.

6. Co-operative Societies Act, 1991, no. 15/91, Parliament of the United Republic of Tanzania. This Act reestablished the principle of free and voluntary cooperative organizations.

7. For a complete study of the 1976–1977 coffee boom and how the proceeds from this boom were treated in Tanzania and Kenya, see Bevan, Collier, and Gunning, *Peasants and Governments*.

8. One example was a company to produce steel tools fabricated from rolls of steel supplied by a Swedish firm.

9. Nord et al., "Structural Adjustment, Economic Performance, and Aid Dependency in Tanzania," 4.

10. Ibid., figs. 2 and 4b.

11. Jackson and Rosberg, "Why Africa's Weak States Persist."

12. Moyo, *Dead Aid*.

13. Easterly, "Foreign Aid for Scoundrels"; Easterly, *The White Man's Burden*.

14. Pender, "Country Ownership: The Evasion of Donor Accountability," 112. Some authors believe this should be described as a real loss of a nation's sovereignty.

15. United Republic of Tanzania, Ministry of Planning and Financial Affairs, National Economic Survival Programme.

16. The Advisory Group consisted of three independent persons, chaired by Swedish ambassador to Tanzania Ernst Michanek, former head of the Swedish International Development Agency. The others were University of Toronto professors Gerald Helleiner and Cranford Pratt.

17. Loxley, "The Devaluation Debate in Tanzania."

18. Ibid.; Sarris and van den Brink, *Economic Policy and Household Welfare During Crisis and Adjustment in Tanzania*, 41–43; Bigsten and Danielson, *Tanzania: Is the Ugly Duckling Finally Growing Up?*

19. The principal Tanzanian spokesperson was Dr. Kighoma Malima, who as a graduate student in the United States studied under two of the leading development economists, receiving a master's degree in economics at Yale University under Dr. Albert Hirschman and a Ph.D. at Princeton University under W. Arthur Lewis ("The Economics of Cotton Production in Tanzania: An Examination of Some of the Factors That Influence Agricultural Development").

20. Pinto, "Black Market Premia, Exchange Rate Unification, and Inflation in Sub-Saharan Africa."

21. Wangwe, "Economic Reforms and Poverty Alleviation in Tanzania," 3. Wangwe's

numerous articles and monographs are indispensable reading for the student of economic reform in Tanzania.

22. Svendsen, "The Creation of Macroeconomic Imbalances and a Structural Crisis," 72–73.

23. Malima continued to be a highly influential figure in Tanzanian politics. He rose to minister of finance again in the early 1990s and was considered by some to be among those responsible for the aid crisis of 1994–1995. He was among the rivals for the CCM presidential nomination in 1995. After the nomination was awarded to Benjamin Mkapa, he resigned and joined the opposition party, the National Reconstruction Alliance.

24. This was a clear signal to the ILIs, already identifying the NMC as an early target for reform.

25. Havnevik, *Tanzania: The Limits to Development from Above*, 290.

26. Krueger, *Liberalization Attempts and Consequences*.

27. Leith, *Ghana*.

28. Ibid., 163.

29. It would only be fair to add that some economists had always dissented from the development economics paradigm and tried to show the greater benefits of a free market based approach; cf. Berg, "Socialism and Economic Development."

30. Krueger became director of research for the World Bank in 1982 and remained with the Bank until 1986.

31. Edwards, "Is Tanzania a Success Story?" 12.

32. See Tsikata, "Owning Economic Reforms: A Comparative Study of Ghana and Tanzania.".

33. Milosz, *The Captive Mind*.

34. Cooperative Societies Act, 1991, no. 15/91, Parliament of the United Republic of Tanzania.

35. Regulation of Prices Act, 1973, no. 19/73, Parliament of the United Republic of Tanzania.

36. Foreign Exchange Act, 1992, no. 1/92, Parliament of the United Republic of Tanzania.

37. Finance Bill, 1992, no. 14/92, Parliament of the United Republic of Tanzania.

38. Loans and Advances Realization Trust [Act], 1991, no. 6/91, Parliament of the United Republic of Tanzania.

39. Public Corporations Act, 1992, no. 2/92, Parliament of the United Republic of Tanzania

40. Political Parties Act, 1992, no. 5/92, United Republic of Tanzania.

41. Organization of Tanzania Trade Unions Act, 1991, no. 20/91, Parliament of the United Republic of Tanzania.

42. Banking and Financial Institution Act, 1991, no. 12/91, United Republic of Tanzania.

43. Capital Markets and Securities Act, 1994, no. 5/94, Parliament of the United Republic of Tanzania, April 10, 1994.

44. Muganda, *Tanzania's Economic Reforms*, 4.

45. Ibid., 5.

46. Courtnadge and Theisohn, *Moving Beyond the "Munchhausen Approach."*

47. Other members were Tony Killick, Benno Ndulu, Nguyuru Lipumba, and Knud Erik Svendsen.

48. Helleiner et al., "Development Cooperation Issues Between Tanzania and Its Aid Donors."

49. Wangwe, *NEPAD at the Country Level*, 4.

50. See Kelsall, "Shop Windows and Smoke-Filled Rooms," 599. This article cites James Wolfensohn's speech.

51. Therkildsen, "Public Sector Reform in a Poor, Aid-Dependent Country" 62.

52. Ibid., 4.

53. Helleiner et al., "Development Cooperation Issues," 46, table 3.

54. World Bank, World Development Indicators online, "Debt outstanding and disbursed, Public and publicly guaranteed (PPG) long-term debt (DOD, current US$) Public and publicly guaranteed debt comprises long-term external obligations of public debtors, including the national government, political subdivisions (or an agency of either), and autonomous public bodies, and external obligations of private debtors that are guaranteed for repayment by a public entity. Data in current U.S. dollars; percent GDP calculated by author; some data on GDP for Tanzania from Global Finance Data online

55. See "New Prime Minister and Cabinet Following Revelations of Massive Tax Avoidance."

56. Malima met an untimely end. He resigned from the government shortly thereafter and joined an opposition party, the National Reconstruction Alliance, with the idea of becoming its presidential candidate in the 1995 election. He suffered a stroke on a trip to London in August 1995 and passed away the following month.

57. The constitutional change to a multiparty system can be dated from the Political Parties Act of 1992, but the first multiparty election did not take place until 1995.

Chapter 5. The Path to Economic Reform II: Internal Alignments

1. Goodman, "Trade Unions and Political Parties: The Case of East Africa."

2. Trade Unions Ordinance (Amendment) Act, 1962, no. 51/62.

3. Trade Dispute (Settlement) Act, 1962, no. 43/62, Parliament of Tanganyika.

4. An Act to Amend the Laws Relating to Membership of Trade Unions and to Participation in Strikes, 1964, no. 64/64, Parliament of the United Republic of Tanzania.

5. National Union of Tanganyika Workers (Establishment) Act, 1964, no. 18/64, Parliament of Republic of Tanzania.

6. Rosenberg, "The 'Labor Aristocracy' in Interpretation of the African Working Classes."

7. Several informants pointed out that pilferage of gasoline and automobile parts or office stationery became limited forms of rent-seeking.

8. In the early 1980s, the CCM had approximately 1.5 million members, about one-quarter of the eligible electorate.

9. Bienen, "The Party and the No Party State."

10. The *Report of the Presidential Commission on the Establishment of a Democratic One Party State* became the basis for the interim constitution of 1965, which formally legalized the single-party system.

11. Tsikata, "Owning Economic Reforms."

12. Nyerere continued to exercise influence in the party even after that: he is thought to have vetoed the choice of a reformist candidate for president in the 1995 election.

13. Mans, "Tanzania: Resolution Action," 285.

14. United Republic of Tanzania, Ministry of Agriculture, *The Tanzania National Agricultural Policy*.

15. Manji, "Gender and the Politics of the Land Reform Process in Tanzania."

16. Ibid., 108.

17. Barzel, *Economic Analysis of Property Rights*; North, *Institutions, Institutional Change and Economic Performance*; Alchian and Demsetz, "The Property Right Paradigm."

18. Bruce and Migot-Adholla, eds., *Searching for Land Tenure Security in Africa*.

19. United Republic of Tanzania, Ministry of Lands, Housing, and Urban Development, *Report of the Presidential Commission of Inquiry into Land Matters*, vol. 1, *Land Policy and Land Tenure Structure*.

20. Land Act, 1999, no. 4/99; Village Land Act, 1999, no. 5/99, Parliament of the United Republic of Tanzania.

21. Haki Ardhi continues to be a powerful voice in Tanzania to this day. Those interested in land issues in Tanzania would be rewarded by a visit to its website, http://www.hakiardhi.org/.

22. Shivji, *Not Yet Democracy*.

23. Funke, "Timing and Sequencing of Reforms"; Martinelli and Tommasi, *Economic Reforms and Political Constraints*.

24. Barker, "Paradox of Development."

25. Rutasitara, "Exchange Rate Regimes and Inflation in Tanzania," 1.

26. Tripp, *Changing the Rules*.

27. Bagachwa and Naho, "Estimating the Second Economy in Tanzania," 1388.

28. Sarris and Brink, *Economic Policy*, 52, table 15.

29. Bagachwa and Naho, "Estimating the Second Economy," 1387–99.

30. Ibid., 1393.

31. Economic and Social Research Foundation and Tanzania Business Centre, "The Parallel Economy in Tanzania," 9, 59.

32. Skof, "The Informal Economy."

33. Tripp, *Changing the Rules*.

34. A popular Swahili joke in Dar es Salaam referred to Nyerere as "Moses." The joke depended on the double entendre that he was not Moses the lawgiver and philosopher but Moses who led his people into the desert for 40 years.

35. Masoko, *Preliminary Report on the Parallel Market for Grains in Tanzania*, 17.

Chapter 6. Cases in Economic Reform

1. Foreign Exchange Act, Parliament of the United Republic of Tanzania.

2. World Bank, *Accelerated Development in Sub-Saharan Africa*, 224–26.

3. Bank of Tanzania Act, 1966, no. 12/96, Parliament of the United Republic of Tanzania.

4. Private individuals were not permitted to hold East African shillings after fall 1967. The shilling remained in existence for interbank transfers through 1969.

5. During spring 1967, parallel markets in Nairobi were demanding TShs 10 to 12 per U.S. dollar or for 7 East Africa shillings.

6. Kaufman and O'Connell, "The Macroeconomics of Delayed Exchange-Rate Unification."

7. Mshomba, *Africa in the Global Economy*, 33–34.

8. Mshomba, "The Magnitude of Coffee Arabica Smuggled from Northern Tanzania into Kenya."

9. Nord et al., *Tanzania: The Story of an African Transition*, 11; see fig. 4

10. Mtei, *From Goatherd to Governor*, chap. 17, "Events Leading to My Resignation."

11. Julius Nyerere, "No to IMF Meddling," 7.

12. Kaufman and O'Connell, "Exchange Rate Unification," 3.

13. Nord et al., *Tanzania: The Story of an African Transition*, 10.

14. Foreign Exchange Act, Parliament of the United Republic of Tanzania.

15. The actual calculation is performed by discounting the numerical changes in the exchange rate by domestic and international inflation. An increase in the RER (changes in the numerical exchange rate outpacing inflation) is a powerful indicator that devaluation is real. If changes in the numerical exchange rate do not outpace inflation, the RER will fall, indicating that the scenes currency manipulation is responding to domestic political pressures to continue overvaluation.

16. Mans, "Tanzania: Resolute Action," 369.

17. For clarity it may be helpful to state exactly what this meant: in 1996, a Tanzanian who could acquire the basket of goods at the official exchange rate would be able to obtain them for only about three-fifths of the U.S. price.

18. Kayizzi-Mugerwa, *Reforming Africa's Institutions*.

19. Kravis, "Trade as a Handmaiden of Growth."

20. Krueger, "The Political Economy of the Rent-Seeking Society."

21. Bhagwati, "Directly Unproductive, Profit-Seeking (DUP) Activities."

22. O'Connell, "Short and Long-Run Effects of an Own-Funds Scheme."

23. See Kaufman and O'Connell, "Exchange Rate Unification," 3, fig. 1.

24. Nash and Foroutan, *Trade Policy and Exchange Rate Reform in Sub-Saharan Africa*, 79.

25. DeRosa, "Protection and the Own-Funds Window in Tanzania."

26. Nord et al., "Structural Adjustment," 6–7.

27. Yeats, "On the Accuracy of Economic Observations" Under-invoicing exports as a means of sequestering hard currency earnings in overseas accounts is a continent-wide problem.

28. Mans, "Tanzania: Resolute Action," 372.

29. One informant described the customs long room, where importers receive final clearance for their containers, as the "Abu Ghraib" of the Tanzanian trade process.

30. United Republic of Tanzania, Ministry of Industry and Trade, *National Trade Policy: Trade Policy for a Competitive Era and Export-Led Growth*.

31. Walkenhorst, "Trade Policy Developments in Tanzania."

32. See, for example, Stiglitz and Charlton, *Fair Trade for All*; and Krugman, *Development, Geography and Economic Theory*.

33. Gerschenkron, *Economic Backwardness in Historical Perspective*.

34. Chang, *Kicking Away the Ladder*.

35. Loans and Advances Realization Trust [Act], 1991, 6/91, Parliament of the United Republic of Tanzania.

36. Public Corporations Act, 1992, 2/92, Parliament of the United Republic of Tanzania.

37. Capital Markets and Securities Act, 1994, 5/94, Parliament of the United Republic of Tanzania.

38. Organization of Tanzania Trade Unions Act, 1991, 20/91, Parliament of the United Republic of Tanzania.

39. The author is indebted to his former colleague Professor Jack Hirschleifer for these observations.

40. IMF, *Tanzania: Selected Issues and Statistical Appendix*, 94.

Chapter 7. Conclusion: Contemporary Tanzania

1. Citizen Reporter, "Why Is TZ Top 'Beggar' After Iraq Afghanistan."

2. See, for example, Tanzania Election Monitoring Committee, *An Interim Report on Performance of Tanzania's 2010 General Elections in Tanzania*.

3. Nord et al., *Tanzania: The Story of an African Transition*, 1.

4. UNDP, *Human Development Index Trends, 1980–2012*.

5. Economist Intelligence Unit, *Country Report: Tanzania*.

6. International Labour Organisation and Jobs and Skills Programme for Africa, *Basic Needs in Danger*, 251.

7. Nord et al., "Structural Adjustment," 8.

8. It is almost impossible to determine how much of a family's increased expenditure on rent purchases improved housing as opposed to the portion that is simply an adjustment for the inflationary increase in urban rents, especially in Dar es Salaam.

9. For one review of the economic literature, see Aghion, Caroli, and García-Peñalosa, "Inequality and Economic Growth."

10. Clower et al., *Growth Without Development*.

11. For an excellent discussion, see Cooksey and Kelsall, *The Political Economy of the Investment Climate*.

12. Devarajan and Fengler, "Africa's Economic Boom," 69.

13. See Ravallion, "Growth and Poverty"; "Can High Inequality Countries Escape Absolute Poverty?"; and "Growth, Inequality and Poverty."

14. Odgaard, "Scrambling for Land in Tanzania."

15. Paciotti and Mulder, "Sungusungu."

16. See, for example, United Republic of Tanzania, *Poverty and Human Development Report 2005*; United Republic of Tanzania, Vice President's Office, *National Strategy for Growth and Reduction of Poverty*; and United Republic of Tanzania, Ministry of Finance and Economic Affairs, *National Strategy for Growth and Reduction of Poverty II*.

17. See, for example, Ferreira, "Poverty and Inequality During Structural Adjustment in Rural Tanzania."

18. For an excellent summary, see Hoogeveen, "The Challenge of Reducing Poverty."

19. World Bank, *Tanzania: Poverty, Growth and Public Transfers*, 6, table 1.

20. "Poverty," Tanzania National Web Site, http://www.tanzania.go.tz/poverty.html.

21. Ellis and Mdoe, "Livelihoods and Rural Poverty Reduction in Tanzania."

22. Radelet, *Emerging Africa*.

23. More complete and detailed presentations of the results of all Tanzania's general elections can easily be found online under "Tanzanian elections."

24. Tanzania has a double electoral system. Thirty percent of the seats in the National Assembly are reserved for women. The women candidates for each party are elected by proportional representation according to that party's percentage share of the total parliamentary vote.

25. Nyalali Commission, *Report and Recommendation of the Commission on the Democratic System in Tanzania*, vol. 1, *The Presidential Commission on Single Party or Multiparty System in Tanzania*, 8.

26. Hydén, "Top-Down Democratization in Tanzania." Hydén, the most authoritative political scientist writing on modern Tanzania, has suggested that this may be true even of Tanzania, describing its transition to democratic politics as "top-down democracy" to suggest a strategy that qualifies democratic freedoms in the interest of political peace.

27. Killian, "Pluralist Democracy."

28. See, for example, Said, "Islamic Movement and Christian Hegemony."

29. Becker, "Rural Islamism During the 'War on Terror.'"

30. Mtikila's candidacy for president was the subject of one of Tanzania's most famous constitutional cases, *Rev. Christopher Mtikila v. the Attorney General*, case no. 5 of 1993, High Court of Tanzania. In this case, Mtikila contested the constitutionality of the sub-provision of Article 39 requiring that presidential candidates be nominees of registered political parties. This judgment upholding the provision can be found online at

http://www.elaw.org/node/1298. The Tanzanian Constitution can be found online at http://www.kituochakatiba.co.ug/TanzaniaConstitution.pdf. See esp. secs. 39, 39 (c).

31. For an extensive discussion of Tanzania's first multiparty general election, that of 1995, see Cranenburgh, "Tanzania's 1995 Multi-Party Elections."

32. Kiwete even made much of the fact that his initials, J. K., are the same as the first two initials of Nyerere's name, Julius K. Nyerere.

33. He had also distinguished himself as an energetically reformist minister of finance in the final years of the Mwinyi administration (1994–1995) and as an effective minister of foreign affairs under Mkapa.

34. Nyang'oro, *The 2005 General Elections in Tanzania.*

35. Two other cabinet ministers also resigned: minister for energy and minerals Nazir Karamagi and minister for East African cooperation Ibrahim Msabaha.

36. Gratwick, Ghanadan, and Eberhard, "Generating Power and Controversy."

37. For the final judgment of the British court, see "*R-v-BAE Systems PLC*-Sentencing Remarks."

38. One very high-ranking Tanzanian politician, Andrew Chenge, minister of infrastructure development in 2006-2008, was forced to resign in 2008 after SFO investigators discovered he had more than $750,000 in a Jersey bank account. He denied the money had come from BAE.

39. "Tanzania in Bank Scandal Sacking."

40. See Kabendera, "Balalli Surfaces on Twitter." Memories of the scandal were reignited recently when someone claiming to be Balalli surfaced on Twitter and threatened to expose wider circles of involvement in the Bank's losses.

41. *Tanzania Corruption Tracker,* http://www.corruptiontracker.or.tz/dev/.

42. Fjeldstad, Ngalewa, and Katera, "Citizens Demand Tougher Action on Corruption in Tanzania."

43. See *Global Integrity,* http://www.globalintegrity.org/; and *Transparency International,* http://www.transparency.org/.

44. The full diplomatic cable was made available through the Wikileaks website, http://wikileaks.ch.nyud.net/cable/2007/07/07DARESSALAAM1037.html.

45. "Can Fragile Opposition Defeat CCM?"

46. He is named after Saint Willibrod who lived in the seventh and eighth centuries.

47. Gaitho, "Tanzania: Election Results a Wake-Up Call for Ruling CCM Party."

48. Economist Intelligence Unit, *Country Report: Tanzania,* 4.

49. Ng'wanakilala, "Tanzania Ruling Party Plans Anti-Corruption Purge."

50. See Monson, *Africa's Freedom Railway.*

51. For the most comprehensive treatment of this topic, see Shinn and Eisenmann, *China and Africa.*

52. One was a 2006 statement by Thabo Mbeki, president of South Africa; see "Mbeki Warns on China-Africa Ties."

53. Brautigam, *The Dragon's Gift.*

54. World Bank Group, "World Bank Group Finances."

Bibliography

Acquisition of Buildings Act, 1971. 13/71. Parliament of the United Republic of Tanzania (April 22, 1971). POLiS. http://polis.parliament.go.tz/PAMS/docs/13-1971.pdf.

An Act to Amend the Economic Sabotage (Special Provisions) Act, 1983. 10/83. Parliament of the United Republic of Tanzania (July 2, 1983). POLiS. http://polis.parliament.go.tz/PAMS/docs/10-1983.pdf.

An Act to Amend the Laws Relating to Membership of Trade Unions and to Participation in Strikes, 1964. 64/64. Parliament of the United Republic of Tanzania (December 10, 1964). SAFLII. www.saflii.org/tz/legis/num_act/tuatdpa1964595.pdf.

Aghion, Philippe, Eve Caroli, and Cecilia García-Peñalosa. "Inequality and Economic Growth: The Perspective of New Growth Theories." *Journal of Economic Literature* 37, 4 (December 1999): 1615–69.

Alchian, Armen, and Harold Demsetz, "The Property Right Paradigm." *Journal of Economic History* 33, 1 (March 1973): 16–27.

Aminzade, Ronald. "From Race to Citizenship: The Indigenization Debate in Post-Socialist Tanzania." *Studies in Comparative International Development* 38, 1 (Spring 2003): 43–63.

———. "Nation-Building in Post-Colonial States: The Cases of Tanzania and Fiji." *International Social Science Journal* 59 (2008): 169–82.

———. "The Politics of Race and Nation: Citizenship and Africanization in Tanganyika." *Political Power and Social Theory* 14 (2000): 53–90.

Armah, Ayi Kwei. *The Beautyful Ones Are Not Yet Born.* Oxford: Heinemann, 1989.

Austen, Ralph. *Northwest Tanzania Under German and British Rule: Colonial Policy and Tribal Politics, 1889 to 1939.* New Haven, Conn.: Yale University Press, 1968.

Bagachwa, Mboya S.D., and Alex Naho. "Estimating the Second Economy in Tanzania." *World Development* 23, 8 (August 1995): 1387–99.

Bank of Tanzania Act, 1966. 12/96. Parliament of the United Republic of Tanzania (January 6, 1966). POLiS. http://polis.parliament.go.tz/PAMS/docs/12-1966.pdf.

Banking and Financial Institution Act, 1991. 12/91. United Republic of Tanzania (May 8, 1991). POLiS. http://polis.parliament.go.tz/PAMS/docs/12-1991.pdf.

Barker, Jonathan S. "The Paradox of Development: Reflections on a Study of Local-Central Political Relations in Senegal." Chap. 3 in *The State of the Nations:*

Constraints on Development in Independent Africa, ed. Michael F. Lofchie. Berkeley: University of California Press, 1971.

Barzel, Yoram. *Economic Analysis of Property Rights*. Cambridge: Cambridge University Press, 1989.

Bates, Robert H. "Agricultural Policy and the Study of Politics in Post-Independence Africa." In *Africa 30 Years On*, ed. Douglas Rimmer, 115–29. London: James Currey with Royal African Society, 1991.

———. *Markets and States in Tropical Africa: The Political Basis of Agricultural Policies*. Berkeley: University of California Press, 1981.

Becker, Felicitas. "Rural Islamism During the 'War on Terror': A Tanzanian Case Study." *African Affairs* 105, 421 (2006): 583–603.

Berg, Elliot J. "Socialism and Economic Development in Tropical Africa." *Quarterly Journal of Economics* 78, 4 (November 1964): 549–73.

Bevan, David, Paul Collier, and Jan Willem Gunning. *Peasants and Government: An Economic Analysis*. Oxford: Clarendon, 1989.

Bhagwati, Jagdish. "Directly Unproductive, Profit-Seeking (DUP) Activities." *Journal of Political Economy* 90, 5 (October 1982): 988–1002.

Bienen, Henry. "The Party and the No Party State: Tanganyika and the Soviet Union." *Transition* 13 (March–April 1964): 25–32.

Bigsten, Arne, and Anders Danielson. *Tanzania: Is the Ugly Duckling Finally Growing Up?* Uppsala: Nordic Africa Institute, 2001.

Brautigam, Deborah. *The Dragon's Gift: The Real Story of China in Africa*. Oxford: Oxford University Press, 2009.

Bruce, John W., and Shem E. Migot-Adholla, eds. *Searching for Land Tenure Security in Africa*. Washington, D.C.: World Bank, 1994.

Bryceson, Deborah Fahy. "'Harbour of Peace' in East Africa: Tracing the Role of Creolized Urban Ethnicity in Nation-State Formation." UNU-WIDER Working Paper WP2010/19. Helsinki, 2010. http://hdl.handle.net/10419/53988.

Burke, Fred G. *Local Governance and Nation Building in East Africa: A Functional Analysis*. Syracuse, N.Y.: Maxwell Graduate School of Citizenship and Public Affairs, 1961.

———. *Tanganyika: Preplanning*. Syracuse, N.Y.: Syracuse University Press, 1964.

Campbell, Bonnie, and John Loxley, eds. *Structural Adjustment in Africa*. Hampshire: Macmillan, 1989.

"Can Fragile Opposition Defeat CCM?" *Guardian* (Dar Es Salaam). August 15, 2010.

Capital Markets and Securities Act, 1994. 5/94. Parliament of the United Republic of Tanzania (April 10, 1994). IMoLIN. http://www.imolin.org/doc/amlid/Tanzania_Capital%20Markets%20and%20Securities%20Act%201994.pdf.

Chang, Ha-Joon. *Kicking Away the Ladder: Development Strategy in Historical Perspective*. London: Anthem Press, 2002.

Chenery, Hollis B. "Comparative Advantage and Development Policy." *American Economic Review* 51, 1 (March 1961): 18–51.

Chidzero, Bernard T. G. *Tanganyika and International Trusteeship*. London: Oxford University Press, 1961.

Chirot, Daniel. "Introduction." In *Ethnopolitical Warfare: Causes, Consequences, and Possible Solutions*, ed. Daniel Chirot and Martin E. P. Seligman. Washington, D.C.: American Psychological Association, 2001.

Citizen Reporter. "Why TZ Is Top 'Beggar' After Iraq Afghanistan." *The Citizen*, December 3, 2011.

Clower, Robert W., George Dalton, Mitchell Harwitz, and A. A. Walters. *Growth Without Development: An Economic Survey of Liberia*. Evanston, Ill.: Northwestern University Press, 1966.

Commonwealth Human Rights Initiative. *The Police, the People, the Politics: Police Accountability in Tanzania*. London: Commonwealth Human Rights Initiative, 2006.

Cooksey, Brian, and Tim Kelsall. *The Political Economy of the Investment Climate in Tanzania*. London: Overseas Development Institute, 2011.

Cooperative Societies Act, 1991. 15/91. Parliament of the United Republic of Tanzania (May 8, 1991). POLiS. http://polis.parliament.go.tz/PAMS/docs/15-1991.pdf.

"Corruption at Dar es Salaam Port: Containers Losses and Illicit Cargo Smuggle Is an Insider Job, Says Minister." *Tanzania Corruption Tracker System*, April 18, 2013.

Coulson, Andrew. *Tanzania: A Political Economy*. Oxford: Clarendon, 1982.

Courtnadge, Philip, and Thomas Theisohn. *Moving Beyond the "Munchhausen Approach": Honest Brokering and Independent Monitoring in Development Partnerships*. Hamburg: German Institute of Global and Area Studies, 2005.

Cranenburgh, Odavan. "Tanzania's 1995 Multi-Party Elections: The Emerging Party System." *Party Politics* 2, 4 (1995): 535–47.

DeRosa, Dean A. "Protection and the Own-Funds Window in Tanzania: An Analytical Framework and Estimates of the Effects of Trade Liberalization." *Journal of African Economics* 2, 1 (1993): 24–48.

Devarajan, Shantayanan, and Wolfgang Fengler. "Africa's Economic Boom: Why the Pessimists and the Optimists Are Both Right." *Foreign Affairs* (May/June 2013).

Domasa, Sylvester. "Survey: Police, Judiciary, Lands, TRA Most Corrupt." *The Guardian* (Dar es Salaam), November 19, 2011. Cited in IPP Media, http://www.ippmedia.com/frontend/?l=35538.

Easterly, William. "Foreign Aid for Scoundrels." *New York Review of Books*, November 10, 2010.

———. *The White Man's Burden: Why the West's Efforts to Aid the Rest Have Done So Much Ill and So Little Good*. Oxford: Oxford University Press, 2006.

Economic and Social Research Foundation and Tanzania Business Centre. "The Parallel Economy in Tanzania: Magnitude, Causes, and Policy Implications." ESRF Discussion Paper 11, ESRF, Dar es Salaam, 1996.

Economist Intelligence Unit. *Country Report: Tanzania*, London: The Economist, 2011.

Edwards, Sebastian. "Is Tanzania a Success Story? A Long Term Analysis." Working Paper 17764, NBER, New York, January 2012.

Ellis, Frank. "Agricultural Price Policy in Tanzania." *World Development* 10, 4 (1982): 263–83.

Ellis, Frank, and Ntengua Mdoe."Livelihoods and Rural Poverty Reduction in Tanzania." *World Development* 31, 8 (August 2003): 1367–84.

Ergas, Zaki. "Why Did the Ujamaa Village Policy Fail?: Towards a Global Analysis." *Journal of Modern African Studies* 18, 3 (September 1980): 387–410.

Ferreira, Luis M. "Poverty and Inequality During Structural Adjustment in Rural Tanzania." Policy Research Working Paper 1641. World Bank, Washington, D.C., 1996.

The Finance Bill, 1992. 14/92. Parliament of the United Republic of Tanzania, May 1, 1992. POLiS. http://bunge.parliament.go.tz/PAMS/docs/14-1992.pdf.

Fjeldstad, Odd-Helge, Erasto Ngalewa, and Lucas Katera, "Citizens Demand Tougher Action on Corruption in Tanzania." Brief 11, Research on Poverty Alleviation, Dar es Salaam, April 2008. http://www.cmi.no/publications/file/3035-citizens-demand-tougher-action-on-corruption.pdf.

Foreign Exchange Act, 1992. 1/92. Parliament of the United Republic of Tanzania (February 17, 1992). POLiS. http://bunge.parliament.go.tz/PAMS/docs/1-1992.pdf.

Fortmann, Louise. *Officials and Participation in Rural Tanzania: Experience with Villagization and Decentralization*. Ithaca, N.Y.: Rural Development Committee, Cornell University, 1980.

Freyhold, Michaela von. *Ujamaa Villages in Tanzania: Analysis of a Social Experiment*. New York: Monthly Review Press, 1979.

Funke, Norbert. "Timing and Sequencing of Reforms: Competing Views." *Kyklos* 46, 3 (August 1993): 337–62.

Furnivall, J. S. *Colonial Policy and Practice: A Comparative Study of Burma and Netherlands India*. New York: New York University Press, 1956.

Gaitho, Macharia. "Tanzania: Election Results a Wake-Up Call for Ruling CCM Party," *All Africa*, November 8, 2010.

Gerschenkron, Alexander. *Economic Backwardness in Historical Perspective: A Book of Essays*. Cambridge, Mass.: Harvard University Press, 1962.

Goodman, Stephen H. "Trade Unions and Political Parties: The Case of East Africa." *Economic Development and Cultural Change* 17, 3 (April 1969): 342–44.

Gratwick, Katherine, Rebecca Ghanadan, and Anton Eberhard. "Generating Power and Controversy: Understanding Tanzania's Independent Power Projects." *Journal of Energy in Southern Africa* 17, 4 (November 2006): 39–56.

Green, Reginald Herbold. "Developing State Trading in a Peripheral Economy: Reflections on Tanzanian Experience and Its Implications." IDS Discussion Paper, University of Sussex, July 1980.

Harries, Lyndon. "Language Policy in Tanzania." *Africa: Journal of the International African Institute* 39, 3 (July 1969): 275–80.

Havnevik, Kjell J. *Tanzania: The Limits to Development from Above*. Motala, Sweden: Motala Grafiska AB, 1993.

Hoogeveen, Johannes. "The Challenge of Reduction Poverty." Chap 2 in *Sustaining and*

Sharing Economic Growth in Tanzania, ed. Robert J. Utz. Washington, D.C.: World Bank, 2008.

Hoseah, Edward. *Corruption in Tanzania: The Case for Circumstantial Evidence*. Amherst, N.Y.: Cambria Press, 2008.

Hydén, Göran. "Top-Down Democratization in Tanzania." *Journal of Democracy* 10, 4 (October 1999): 142–55.

Iliffe, John. *Tanganyika Under German Rule, 1905–1912*. London: Cambridge University Press, 1969.

International Labour Office and Jobs and Skills Programme for Africa. *Basic Needs in Danger: A Basic Needs Oriented Development Strategy for Tanzania: Report to the Government of Tanzania*. Addis Ababa: International Labour Office, Jobs and Skills Programme for Africa, 1982.

International Monetary Fund. *Tanzania: Selected Issues and Statistical Appendix*. IMF Staff Country Report. Washington, D.C.: IMF, 2003.

Jackson, Robert H., and Carl Gustav Rosberg. "Why Africa's Weak States Persist: The Empirical and the Juridical in Statehood." *World Politics* 35, 1 (October 1982): 1–24.

Jennings, Michael. *Surrogates of the State: NGOs, Development and Ujamaa in Tanzania*. Bloomfield, Conn.: Kumarian Press, 2008.

Kabendera, Eric. "Balalli Surfaces on Twitter." *The Guardian* (Dar es Salaam), February 26, 2012.

Kagashe, Beatus. "Tanzania: Over 30 Percent of Budget Eaten by Corrupt Officials, Says President." *The Citizen*, July 10, 2009.

Kaiser, Paul J. "Structural Adjustment and the Fragile Nation: The Demise of Social Unity in Tanzania." *Journal of Modern African Studies* 34, 2 (June 1996): 227–37.

Kaufman, Daniel, and Stephen A. O'Connell. "The Macroeconomics of Delayed Exchange-Rate Unification: Theory and Evidence from Tanzania." Policy Research Working Paper 1, World Bank Development Research Group, Economic Development Institute, Regulatory Reform and Private Enterprise Division, Washington, D.C., 1999.

Kauzeni, A. S., I. S. Kikula, S. A. Mohamed, J. G. Lyimo, and D. B. Dalal-Clayton. "Land Use Planning and Resource Assessment in Tanzania: A Case Study." IIED Environmental Planning Issue 3, IRA Research Paper 35, London, December 1993.

Kayizzi-Mugerwa, Steve. *Reforming Africa's Institutions: Onwership, Incentives and Capabilities*. New York: UN University Press, 2003.

Kelsall, Tim. "Shop Windows and Smoke-Filled Rooms: Governance and the Re-Politicization of Tanzania." *Journal of Modern African Studies* 40, 4 (December 2002): 597–619.

Keegan, Warren J. *Negotiations for a Gin Distillery: A Case Study Project Appraisal and Negotiation in an African Country*. Dar es Salaam: University College, 1964.

Killian, Bernadeta. "Pluralist Democracy and the Transformation of Democratic Attitudes in Tanzania." Ph.D. dissertation, University of California, Los Angeles, 2001.

Kravis, Irving B. "Trade as a Handmaiden of Growth: Similarities Between the

Nineteenth and Twentieth Centuries." *Economic Journal* 80, 323 (December 1970): 850–72.

Krueger, Anne O. "Comparative Advantage and Development Policy Twenty Years Later." In *Economic Structure and Performance: Essays in Honor of Hollis B. Chenery*, ed. Moshe Syrquin, Lance Taylor, and Larry E. Westphal. Orlando, Fla.: Academic Press, 1984.

———. *Liberalization Attempts and Consequences.* Vol. 10 of *Foreign Trade Regimes and Economic Development.* New York: NBER and University of Columbia Press, 1978.

———. "The Political Economy of the Rent-Seeking Society." *American Economic Review* 64, 3 (June 1974): 291–303.

Krugman, Paul. *Development, Geography and Economic Theory.* Cambridge, Mass.: MIT Press, 1998.

Kuper, Leo, and M. G. Smith, eds. *Pluralism in Africa.* Berkeley: University of California Press, 1969.

Lal, Deepak. *The Poverty of "Development Economics."* Cambridge, Mass.: Harvard University Press, 1985.

Land Act, 1999. 4/99. Parliament of the United Republic of Tanzania (May 15, 1999). POLiS. http://bunge.parliament.go.tz/PAMS/docs/4-1999.pdf.

Leith, J. Clark. *Ghana.* Vol. 2 of *Foreign Trade Regimes and Economic Development.* New York: NBER and Columbia University Press, 1974.

Lewis, W. Arthur. "Economic Development with Unlimited Supplies of Labour." *Manchester School of Economic and Social Studies* 22, 2 (May 1954): 139–91.

Loans and Advances Realization Trust [Act], 1991. 6/91. Parliament of the United Republic of Tanzania (June 30, 1991). POLiS. http://bunge.parliament.go.tz/PAMS/docs/6-1991.pdf.

Loxley, John. "The Devaluation Debate in Tanzania." Chap. 1 in *Structural Adjustment in Africa*, ed. Bonnie Campbell and John Loxley. Hampshire: Macmillan, 1989.

Ludwig, Frieder. "After Ujamaa: Is Religious Revivalism a Threat to Tanzania's Stability?" In *Questioning the Secular State: The Worldwide Resurgence of Religion in Politics*, ed. David Westerlund, 216–36. London: Hurst, 1996.

Maghimbi, Sam. *Cooperatives in Tanzania Mainland: Revival and Growth.* Dar es Salaam: ILO Country Office for United Republic of Tanzania, Kenya, Rwanda, and Uganda, 2010.

Maguire, Gene Andrew. *Toward "Uhuru" in Tanzania: The Politics of Participation.* Cambridge: Cambridge University Press, 1969.

Manji, Ambreena. "Gender and the Politics of the Land Reform Process in Tanzania." *Journal of Modern African Studies* 36, 4 (December 1968): 645–67.

Mans, Darius. "Tanzania: Resolution Action." Chap. 8 in *Adjustment Africa: Lessons from Case Studies*, ed. Ishrat Husain and Rashid Faruqee. Washington, D.C.: World Bank, 1994.

Martinelli, Cesar and Mariano Tommasi. "Economic Reforms and Political Constraints:

On the Time Inconsistency of Gradual Sequencing." Working Paper 736, Department of Economics, University of California, Los Angeles, 1995.

Masoko, Sehemu ya Kuendeleza. *Preliminary Report on the Parallel Market for Grains in Tanzania*. Dar es Salaam: United Republic of Tanzania, Ministry of Agriculture, Marketing Development Bureau, 1983.

"Mbeki Warns on China-Africa Ties." *BBC*, December 14, 2006.

McHenry, Dean E., Jr. *Limited Choices: The Political Struggle for Socialism in Tanzania*. Boulder, Colo.: Lynn Rienner, 1994.

———. *Tanzania's Ujamaa Villages: The Implementation of a Rural Development Strategy*. Berkeley, Calif.: Institute of International Studies, 1979.

Milosz, Czeslaw. *The Captive Mind*. New York: Knopf, 1953.

Monson, Jamie. *Africa's Freedom Railway: How a Chinese Development Project Changed Lives and Livelihoods in Tanzania*. Bloomington: Indiana University Press, 2009.

Moyo, Dambisa. *Dead Aid: Why Aid Is Not Working and Why There Is a Better Way for Africa*. New York: Farrar, Straus, and Giroux, 2010.

Mshomba, Richard E. 2000. *Africa in the Global Economy*. Boulder, Colo.: Lynne Rienner, 2000.

———. "The Magnitude of Coffee Arabica Smuggled from Northern Tanzania into Kenya." *Eastern Africa Economic Review* 9, 1 (1993): 165–75.

Mtatifikolo, Fidelis P. "Tanzania's Incomes Policy: An Analysis of Trends with Proposals for the Future." *African Studies Review* 31, 1 (April 1988): 33–45.

Mtei, Edwin. *From Goatherd to Governor: The Autobiography of Edwin Mtei*. Dar es Salaam: Mkuki na Nyota, 2009.

Muganda, Anna. *Tanzania's Economic Reforms: And Lessons Learned*. Washington, D.C.: World Bank, 2004.

Mutahaba, Gelase. "Pay Reform and Corruption in Tanzania's Public Service." Paper presented at Seminar on Potential for Public Service Pay Reform to Eradicate Corruption Among Civil Servants in Tanzania, Economic and Social Research Conference Hall, Dar es Salaam, May 26, 2005. www.tzonline.org/pdf/payreformandcorruptionin tanzaniaspublic.pdf.

Nagar, Richa. "The South Asian Diaspora in Tanzania: A History Retold." *Comparative Studies of South Asia, Africa and the Middle East* 16, 2 (April 1996): 62–80.

Nash, John and Faezeh Foroutan. *Trade Policy and Exchange Rate Reform in Sub-Saharan Africa*. Canberra: National Center for Development Studies, 1997.

National Security Act, 1970. 3/70. Parliament of the United Republic of Tanzania (March 30, 1970). POLiS. http://tanzanet.org/downloads/laws/national_security_act_1970 _(3_1970).pdf.

National Union of Tanganyika Workers (Establishment) Act, 1964. 18/64. Parliament of Republic of Tanzania (February 24, 1964). POLiS. http://polis.parliament.go.tz/ PAMS/docs/18-1964.pdf.

Ndulu, Benno J., Stephen A. O'Connell, Robert H. Bates, Paul Collier, Chukwuma C. Soludo, Jean-Paul Azam, Augustin K. Fosu, and Jan Willem Gunning, eds. *The*

Political Economy of Economic Growth in Africa, 1960–2000. 2 vols. Cambridge: Cambridge University Press, 2007.

"New Prime Minister and Cabinet Following Revelations of Massive Tax Avoidance." *Tanzanian Affairs*, January 1, 1995.

Nguyuru, Lipumba. "Policy Reforms for Economic Development in Tanzania." Chap. 2 in *Africa's Development Challenges and the World Bank: Hard Questions, Costly Choices*, ed. Stephen K. Commins. Boulder, Colo.: Lynn Rienner, 1988.

Ng'wanakilala, Fumbuka. "Tanzania Ruling Party Plans Anti-Corruption Purge," *Reuters*, November 26, 2011.

Nord, Roger, Michael Mered, Nisha Agrawal, Zafar U. Ahmed. "Structural Adjustment, Economic Performance and Aid Dependency in Tanzania." IMF Working Paper WP/93/66, Washington, D.C.: IMF, 1993.

———. *Tanzania: The Story of an African Transition.* Washington, D.C.: IMF, 2009.

North, Douglass C. *Institutions, Institutional Change and Economic Performance.* Cambridge: Cambridge University Press, 1990.

Nyalali Commission. *Report and Recommendation of the Commission on the Democratic System in Tanzania.* Vol. 1, *The Presidential Commission on Single Party or Multiparty System in Tanzania.* Dar es Salaam: Nyalali Commission, 1991.

Nyang'oro, Julius. *The 2005 General Elections in Tanzania: Implications for Peace and Security in Southern Africa.* Paper 122. Pretoria: Institute for Security Studies, 2006.

Nyerere, Julius. *Freedom and Socialism: A Selection from Writings and Speeches, 1965–67.* Dar es Salaam: Oxford University Press, 1969.

———. "No to IMF Meddling." *Development Dialogue* 2 (1980): 7–9.

O'Connell, Stephen A. "Short and Long-Run Effects of an Own-Funds Scheme." *Journal of African Economies* 1, 1 (1992): 131–50.

Odgaard, Rie. "Scrambling for Land in Tanzania: Process of Formalisation and Legitimisation of Land Rights." In *Securing Land Rights in Africa*, ed. Tor A. Benjaminsen and Christian Lund, 71–88. Copenhagen: Centre for Development Research, 2003.

Organization of Tanzania Trade Unions Act, 1991. 20/91. Parliament of the United Republic of Tanzania (December 3, 1991). POLiS. http://polis.parliament.go.tz/PAMS/docs/20-1991.pdf.

Ostrom, Elinor. *Governing the Commons: The Evolution of Institutions for Collective Action.* New York: Cambridge University Press, 1990.

Paciotti, Brian, and Monique Borgerhoff Mulder. "Sungusungu: The Role of Preexisting and Evolving Social Institutions Among Tanzanian Vigilante Organizations." *Human Organization* 63, 1 (2004): 112–24.

Pender, John. "Country Ownership: The Evasion of Donor Accountability." In *Politics Without Sovereignty: A Critique of Contemporary International Relations*, ed. Christopher Bickerton, Philip Cunliffe, and Alexander Gourevitch, 112–30. Abingdon: University College London, 2007.

Perkins, F. C. "Technology, Choice, Industrialization and Development Experiences in Tanzania." *Journal of Development Studies* 19, 2 (1983): 213–43.

Peter, Chris Maina. *Constitution-Making in Tanzania: The Role of the People in the Process.* Dar es Salaam: University of Dar es Salaam, 2000.

Pinto, Brian. "Black Market Premia, Exchange Rate Unification, and Inflation in Sub-Saharan Africa." *World Bank Economic Review* 3, 3 (September 1989): 321–38.

Political Parties Act, 1992. 5/92. United Republic of Tanzania (July 1, 1992). Online Database, United Republic of Tanzania. http://www.tanzania.go.tz/pdf/Political%20 Parties%20Act%205.pdf.

"Poverty." Tanzania National Website, http://www.tanzania.go.tz/poverty.html.

Prebisch, Raul. *The Economic Development of Latin America and Its Principal Problems.* New York: UN, 1950.

Public Corporations Act, 1992. 2/92. Parliament of the United Republic of Tanzania (February 17, 1991). POLiS. http://bunge.parliament.go.tz/PAMS/docs/2-1992.pdf.

Putterman, Louis. "Economic Reform and Smallholder Agriculture in Tanzania: A Discussion of Recent Market Liberalization, Road Rehabilitation, and Technology Dissemination Efforts." *World Development* 23, 2 (February 1995): 311–26.

"*R-v-BAE Systems* PLC-Sentencing Remarks." Judicial Office of the United Kingdom. http://www.judiciary.gov.uk/media/judgments/2010/r-v-bae-systems-plc.

Radelet, Steven. *Emerging Africa.* Washington, D.C.: Center for Global Development, 2010.

Ravallion, Martin. "Can High Inequality Countries Escape Absolute Poverty?" *Economics Letters* 56 (1997): 51–57.

———. "Growth, Inequality and Poverty: Looking Beyond Averages." *World Development* 29 (2001): 1803–15.

———. "Growth and Poverty: Evidence for Developing Countries in the 1980s." *Economics Letters* 48 (1995): 411–17.

Regions and Regional Commissioners Act, 1962. 2/62. Parliament of Tanganyika (February 22, 1962). POLiS. http://polis.parliament.go.tz/PAMS/docs/2-1962.pdf.

Regulation of Prices Act, 1973. 19/73. Parliament of the United Republic of Tanzania (July 23, 1973). POLiS. http://polis.parliament.go.tz/PAMS/docs/19-1973.pdf.

Riggs, Fred W. *Administration in Developing Countries: The Theory of Prismatic Society.* Boston: Houghton Mifflin, 1964.

Rosenberg, David. "The 'Labour Aristocracy' in Interpretation of the African Working Classes." Working Paper 315, Institute for Developing Studies, University of Nairobi, Kenya, 1976. http://opendocs.ids.ac.uk/opendocs/bitstream/handle/1234567 89/1186/wp315-317743.pdf?sequence=1.

Rothchild, Donald S. *Racial Bargaining in Independent Kenya: A Study of Minorities and Decolonization.* London: Oxford University Press, 1973.

Rugumisa, S. M. H., and Joseph Semboja. "Price Control in the Management of an Economic Crisis: The National Price Commission in Tanzania." *African Studies Review* 31, 1 (April 1998): 47–65.

Rutasitara, Longinus. "Exchange Rate Regimes and Inflation in Tanzania." AERC Research Paper 138. African Economic Research Consortium, Nairobi, 2004.

Said, Mohamed. "Islamic Movement and Christian Hegemony: The Rise of Muslim Militancy in Tanzania." Manuscript, last modified September 25, 1998. www.zanzinet .org/files/msaid-islamic-move.doc.

Saidi Mwamwindi v. Criminal. Sess. 37-Iringa-72. *Tanzania High Court Digest* 6. Dar es Salaam: University of Dar es Salaam.

Sarris, Alexander H., and Rogier van den Brink. *Economic Policy and Household Welfare during Economic Crisis in Tanzania.* New York: New York University Press, 1993.

"The Secret Behind Dar's Posh Homes." *The Guardian* (Dar es Salaam), December 5, 2010.

Segal, Aaron. *East Africa: Strategy for Economic Cooperation.* Nairobi: East African Institute of Social and Cultural Affairs, 1965.

Shao, John. "Politics and the Food Production Crisis in Tanzania." Chap. 5 in *Africa's Agrarian Crisis: The Roots of Famine*, ed. Stephen K. Commins, Michael F. Lofchie, and Rhys Payne. Boulder, Colo.: Lynne Rienner, 1986.

Shinn, David H. and Joshua Eisenmann. *China and Africa: A Century of Engagement.* Philadelphia: University of Pennsylvania Press, 2012.

Shivji, Issa G. *Not Yet Democracy: Reforming Land Tenure in Tanzania.* Dar es Salaam: Haki Ardhi, 1998.

Skof, Annabella. "The Informal Economy." Chap. 8 in *Sustaining and Sharing Economic Growth in Tanzania*, ed. Robert J. Utz. Washington, D.C.: World Bank, 2008.

Stiglitz, Joseph and Andrew Charlton. *Fair Trade for All: How Trade Can Promote Development.* Oxford: Oxford University Press, 2005.

Stolper, Wolfgang F. and Paul A. Samuelson. "Protection and Real Wages." *Review of Economic Studies* 9, 1 (November 1941): 58–73.

Svendsen, Knud Erik. "The Creation of Macroeconomic Imbalances and a Structural Crisis." In *Tanzania: Crisis and Struggle for Survival*, ed. Jannik Boesen, Kjell J. Havnevik, Juhani Koponen, and Rie Odegaard. 59–78. Motala: Scandinavian Institute of African Studies, 1996.

Tanzania Constitution. http://www.kituochakatiba.co.ug/TanzaniaConstitution.pdf.

Tanzania Election Monitoring Committee. *An Interim Report on Performance of Tanzania's 2010 General Elections in Tanzania.* Dar es Salaam: Tanzania Election Monitoring Committee. http://www.tz.undp.org/ESP/docs/Observer_Reports/TEMCO_interim _report_UnionElections2010.pdf.

"Tanzania in Bank Scandal Sacking." *BBC*, January 10, 2008.

"Tanzanian Transporters Pay $13,000 in Bribes per Month—A New Report Reveals." *Tanzania Corruption Tracker System*, December 14, 2012.

Therkildsen, Ole. "Public Sector Reform in a Poor, Aid-Dependent Country, Tanzania." *Public Administration and Development* 20, 1 (February 2000): 61–71.

Thiele, Graham. "The Tanzanian Villagisation Programme: Its Impact on Household Productions in Dodoma." *Canadian Journal of African Studies/Revue Canadienne des Études Africaines* 20, 2 (1986): 243–58.

Trade Dispute (Settlement) Act, 1962. 43/62. Parliament of Tanganyika (July 18, 1962). POLiS. http://polis.parliament.go.tz/PAMS/docs/43-1962.pdf.

Trade Unions Ordinance (Amendment) Act, 1962. 51/62. Parliament of Tanganyika (July 18, 1962). POLiS. http://polis.parliament.go.tz/PAMS/docs/51-1962.pdf.

Transparency International. *Country Study Report: Tanzania 2003.* Berlin: Transparency International Secretariat, 2003.

———. U4 Anti-Corruption Resource Centre, CHR. Michelsen Institute. *Overview of Corruption in Tanzania.* Berlin: Transparency International, 2009. http://www .u4.no/publications/overview-of-corruption-in-tanzania/.

Transparency International UK, Defense and Security Programme. *Government Defence Anti-Corruption Index 2013.* http://government.defenceindex.org/sites/ default/files/documents/GI-main-report.pdf.

Tripp, Aili Mari. *Changing the Rules: The Politics of Liberalization and the Urban Informal Economy in Tanzania.* Berkeley: University of California Press, 1997.

———. "The Political Mediation of Ethnic and Religious Diversity in Tanzania." In *The Accommodation of Cultural Diversity,* ed. Crawford Young, 37–71. Houndmills: Macmillan, 1999.

Tsikata, Yvonne M. "Owning Economic Reforms: A Comparative Study of Ghana and Tanzania." UNU-WIDER Discussion Paper 2001/53, Helsinki, 2001. http://www .wider.unu.edu/ publications/working-papers/discussion-papers/2001/en_GB/dp2001 -53/.

United Nations Development Programme. *Human Development Index Trends, 1980– 2012.* Geneva: UNDP, 2013.

United Republic of Tanzania. *Poverty and Human Development Report 2005.* Dar es Salaam: Mkuki wa Nyota, 2005.

———. *Presidential Commission of Inquiry Against Corruption: Report of the Commission on Corruption.* Vol. 1. Dar es Salaam: United Republic of Tanzania, November 1996.

———. *Rev. Christopher Mtikila v. the Attorney General.* Civil Case 5 of 1993. High Court of Tanzania. http://www.elaw.org/node/1298.

———. *Report of the Presidential Commission on the Establishment of a Democratic One-Party State.* Dar es Salaam: United Republic of Tanzania, 1965.

———. *Tanzania: Second Five-Year Plan for Economic and Social Development 1st July 1969–June 30th 1974.* Vol. 1, *General Analysis.* Dar es Salaam: Government Printer, 1969.

———, Ministry of Agriculture of the Republic of Tanzania. *The Tanzania National Agricultural Policy (Final Report).* Dar es Salaam: Task Force on National Agricultural Policy, 1982.

———, Ministry of Economic Affairs and Development Planning. *A Mid-Term Appraisal of the Achievements Under the Five-Year Plan, July, 1964–June, 1969.* Dar es Salaam: Ministry of Economic Affairs and Development Planning 1967.

———, Ministry of Finance and Economic Affairs. *National Strategy for Growth and*

Reduction of Poverty (NSGRP) II. Dar es Salaam: Ministry of Finance and Economic Affairs, 2010.

———, Ministry of Industry and Trade. *National Trade Policy: Trade Policy for a Competitive Era and Export-Led Growth*. Dar es Salaam: Ministry of Industry and Trade, 2003.

———, Ministry of Lands, Housing, and Urban Development. *Report of the Presidential Commission of Inquiry into Land Matters*. Vol. 1 of *Land Policy and Land Tenure Structure*. Dar es Salaam: Nordiska Afrikainstitutet, 1994.

———, Ministry of Planning and Financial Affairs. *National Economic Survival Programme*. Dar es Salaam: United Republic of Tanzania, 1982.

———, Prevention and Combating Corruption Bureau. *National Anti-Corruption Strategy and Action Plan Phase II*. Dar es Salaam: United Republic of Tanzania, 2011.

———, Prevention and Combating Corruption Bureau. *National Governance and Corruption Survey*. 4 vols. Dar es Salaam: United Republic of Tanzania, 2009.

———. *National Strategy for Growth and Reduction of Poverty (NSGRP)*. Dar es Salaam: United Republic of Tanzania, Vice President's Office, 2005.

United Republic of Tanganyika and Zanzibar. *Tanganyika Five-Year Plan for Economic and Social Development 1st July 1964–30th June 1969*. 2 vols. Dar es Salaam: Government Printer, 1964.

U.S. Department of State, Bureau of Democracy, Human Rights, and Labor. *2010 Human Rights Report: Tanzania*. Washington, D.C.: Department of State, 1975.

Verhagen, Koenraad. "Changes in Tanzanian Rural Development and Change 1975–1978." *Development and Change* 11, 2 (April 1980): 285–95.

Village Land Act, 1999. 5/99. Parliament of the United Republic of Tanzania (May 15, 1999). POLiS. http://bunge.parliament.go.tz/PAMS/docs/5-1999.pdf.

The Villages and Ujamaa Villages (Registration, Designation and Administration Act), 1975. Parliament of the United Republic of Tanzania (August 12, 1975). POLiS. http://www.parliament.go.tz/Polis/PAMS/Docs/21-1975.pdf.

Wacker, Konstantin M. "The Impact of Foreign Direct Investment on Developing Countries' Terms of Trade." Working Paper 2011/06, UNU-WIDER, 2011. http://www.wider.unu.edu/publications/working-papers/2011/en_GB/wp2011-006/.

Walkenhorst, Peter. "Trade Policy Developments in Tanzania: The Challenge of Global and Regional Integration." Munich Personal RePEc Archive paper 23399, World Bank, 2005.

Wangwe, Samuel M. "Economic Reforms and Poverty Alleviation in Tanzania." Working Paper, International Labour Office, Employment and Training Department, Geneva, 1996.

———, ed. *NEPAD at the Country Level: Changing Aid Relationships in Tanzania*. Dar es Salaam: Mkuki na Nyota Publishers, 2002.

Widner, Jennifer A. *Building the Rule of Law: Francis Nyalali and the Road to Judicial Independence in Tanzania*. New York: Norton, 2001.

Wood, Alan. *The Groundnut Affair*. London: Bodley Head, 1950.

World Bank. *Accelerated Development in Sub-Saharan Africa: An Agenda for Action.* Washington, D.C.: World Bank, 1981.

———. *The East Asian Miracle: Economic Growth and Public Policy.* Oxford: Oxford University Press, 1993.

———. *Tanzania: Poverty, Growth and Public Transfers.* Washington, D.C.: World Bank, 2011.

———. *Tanzania at the Turn of the Century: Background Papers and Statistics,* ed. Benno J. Ndulu and Charles K. Mutalemwa. Washington, D.C.: World Bank, 2002.

Yeats, Alexander J. "On the Accuracy of Economic Observations: Do Sub-Saharan Trade and Statistics Mean Anything?" *World Bank Economic Review* 4, 2 (May 1990): 135–56.

Index

Acknowledgments

The helpful taxi driver is a fabled figure in African political studies, and this book owes more than most to such well-disposed individuals. The narrative that follows grows out of nearly fifty years of research on Tanzania, beginning with research on Zanzibar during 1962 and 1963 and continuing with visits to Tanzania almost every year since. It is squarely in the genre of scholarship that finds many of its most compelling sources of information in casual conversations with ordinary Tanzanians. In addition to taxi drivers, the author owes profound thanks to a somewhat broader circle that includes hotel staff, sales clerks, bank tellers, restaurant waiters, kiosk operators, street vendors, shopkeepers, bartenders, occasional passersby, and all those warmly supportive individuals who waited patiently together in lines at post offices, laundries, banks, gas stations, book stores, car rental agencies, the Office of the Government Printer, copy centers, exchange bureaus, internet cafes and airport formalities.

I am especially grateful to the many members of the Tanzanian academic community who were prepared to share their views, some on a not-for-attribution basis, over this long period. I owe thanks to the Tanzanian government officials, journalists, and students, both in Tanzania and abroad, who gave the benefit of their insights to a foreign scholar. Regrettably, the list of people whose reflections and experiences have helped to shape this book is so long that it is simply impossible to thank all of them by name, much less provide a reference for each conversation.

An incalculable debt of gratitude is owed to UCLA's James S. Coleman African Studies Center and to its founder-director, Jim Coleman, who afforded a beginning scholar a first-job arrangement that included an annual trip to Africa. Despite all-too familiar budget difficulties, the African Studies Center honored that arrangement for almost twenty-five years, providing the funds for the visits to Tanzania during which so many of the conversations that inform this volume took place. By the 1990s, when university-provided research funds had dwindled to an impractically low level, it became possible to observe the Tanzanian political process as a member of various USAID consulting projects. Dr. Anne Fleuret of USAID, amid her development assignments, conducted an informal multiyear seminar on Tanzanian society: innumerable graduate researchers, visiting academics, and consultants benefited from her knowledge and teaching skills. Although consulting research differs from scholarly research, and therefore does not often make its way into scholarly journals, it provides an opportunity for ongoing academic contact. I hope that these projects have afforded a special vantage point for this study.

Scholars of Tanzania stand on tall shoulders. We are especially fortunate that Tanzania's hospitable atmosphere for research has nurtured an extensive, rich, and highly variegated tradition of country studies. Tanzania may well be the best documented of African countries. It should go without saying—but will not—that this book is profoundly indebted to the work of many scholars including Göran Hydén, dean of Tanzanian social scientists, as well as Henry Bienen, Lionel Cliffe, William Tordoff, Reginald Green, Cranford Pratt, John Saul, Rwekaza Mukandala, Gelase Mutahaba, Aili Tripp, Benson Nindi, Louise Fortmann, Richard Mshomba, John Shao, Chris Maina Peter, Jennifer Widner, Issa Shivji, Dean McHenry, Jr., Sam Maghimbi, and Clyde Ingle. Scholars of contemporary Tanzania also owe a debt of gratitude to historians of colonial and postcolonial Tanzania including Ralph Austen, Bernard Chidzero, James Giblin, and James Brennan.

Any student of Tanzanian political economy is especially indebted to the work of several scholars whose pioneering studies provide the indispensable foundation for contemporary research on that subject. This book is especially indebted to the work of several individuals. Among economists of Tanzania, Frank Ellis stands out for early research that showed the extent to which post-independence agricultural policy was framed to impose high tax levels on agricultural producers; Louise Fortmann and Andrew Coulson offered convincing evidence of the dissonance between President Nyerere's vision of a communal society where local self-help initiatives would improve the condition of the rural poor and the reality of self-interested control by the country's centrally empowered and overbearing bureaucracy; Aili Tripp, writing in the 1990s, showed not only the magnitude, vitality, and complexity of Tanzania's parallel economy, but the extent to which the lives of ordinary Tanzanians had come to depend upon it; Gerald Helleiner for his uncanny ability always to provide observations that penetrate the surface of things and for his remarkable accounts of the early 1980s TAG experiment and the 1994–95 aid crisis. Conversations with Sebastian Edwards made it clear why he is a leading authority on exchange rates. This author also feels special indebtedness to the scholarship of Nguyuru Lipumba, Benno Ndulu, Samuel Wangwe, Paul Collier, and Brian van Arkadie, all of whom have added a note of sobriety into Tanzanian economic studies by focusing our attention on the country's troublesome policy choices. In no small sense, this book is a footnote to their research.

Several researchers have contributed greatly. I owe incalculable thanks to Dr. Janet Kaaya. Without her uncanny research skills, vast knowledge and profound affection for her country this book would not have come close to fruition. Deepest thanks, also, to Ms. Julia Kim, who led the discussions of the UCLA study group on exchange rates. Ms. Erica Solomon and Ms. Rujuta Gandhi took possession of an unruly manuscript and brought it to order.

The theoretical template of African area studies has undergone a tectonic shift in recent years. The earlier model of in-depth area knowledge gleaned from language study combined with historical and cultural familiarization, accompanied by extended visits to "the field" has given way gradually and sometimes grudgingly to a paradigm that places greater emphasis on statistical and quantitative methodologies. Each of these paradigms has its own method of attaining truthful insight, and this is not the place to rehearse the academic debate between the two. Suffice it to note that this book is the product of a deeply personal involvement with Tanzanian political studies and with the work of other scholars who share that interest.

The customary disclaimer therefore applies with special force: errors of fact, omission, and interpretation are solely the responsibility of the author.